LISTENING LEADERS™

THE TEN GOLDEN RULES
TO LISTEN, LEAD & SUCCEED

LISTENING LEADERS ™

The Ten Golden Rules
to Listen, Lead & Succeed

Dr. Lyman K. Steil &
Dr. Richard K. Bommelje

Foreword by Dr. Ralph G. Nichols, "Father of the Field of Listening"

Beaver's Pond Press, Inc.
Edina, Minnesota

ISBN: 1-59298-073-2

Library of Congress Catalog Number: 2004108347

Typesetting and design by Mori Studio
Cover photography by Jim Fuglestad at: *www.fuglestadphotography.com*

Printed in the United States of America

First Printing: June 2004

08 07 06 05 04   5 4 3 2 1

Beaver's Pond Press, Inc.   7104 Ohms Lane, Suite 216
Edina, MN 55439
(952) 829-8818
www.beaverspondpress.com

to order, visit *www.BookHouseFulfillment.com*
or call 1-800-901-3480. Reseller discounts available.

For more information: *www.listeningleaders.com*

Dedication

To my sweet bride, Dee, who has been a phenomenal "Listening Leader" for more than 40 years. Without her, life offers little to listen for. With her, life is a glorious symphony.

To our adult children and their spouses, Scott and Sarah, Sara and Sam, and Stacy, and to our grandchildren, Elliot, Josie, Benjamin, Joseph, and the new twins, Zachary and Sophia, always remember: "We lead at all ages and in many ways. More than anything, Leaders Listen to the: Opportunities of the Future, Voices of the Present, and Lessons of the Past." Thanks for being listening role models at every age.

—*Manny Steil*

To my loving wife, Quin, whose unconditional love has touched my listening soul with overflowing joy. Through her selfless actions, she consistently demonstrates listening leadership and has shown me how to…Make Today Count!

—*Rick Bommelje*

Contents

Foreword
vii

Acknowledgments
xi

Introduction
1

Golden Rule 1
"Listening Leaders Build Solid Foundations"
11

Golden Rule 2
"Listening Leaders Explore & Execute A-S-K"
39

Golden Rule 3
"Listening Leaders Develop Impactful Habits"
71

Golden Rule 4
"Listening Leaders Take Primary Responsibility"
105

Golden Rule 5
"Listening Leaders Find & Align Purpose"
139

Golden Rule 6
"Listening Leaders Apply SIER"
175

Golden Rule 7
"Listening Leaders Identify & Control Distractions"
217

Golden Rule 8
"Listening Leaders Identify & Use Structure"
247

Golden Rule 9
"Listening Leaders Identify & Control Emotions"
285

Golden Rule 10
"Listening Leaders Take Meaningful Action"
317

Epilogue
355

Appendix
"Golden Circle of Listening Leaders"
357

Resources
367

Foreword by
Dr. Ralph G. Nichols

"Father of the Field of Listening"
Member—ILA Listening Hall of Fame
Professor Emeritus—University of Minnesota

Time passes in the blink of an eye. More than half a century has passed since my 1948 ground-breaking research identified the differences between effective and ineffective listeners. Incredible as it may seem, in 1957, Leonard Stevens and I wrote the **very first book** devoted to *listening*, which is the oldest, most used, and most important communication activity. Our best-selling and pioneering book, *Are You Listening?*, was written for individuals engaged in management, industry, education, sales, and other fields in which effective communication is of primary significance. For more than 40 years, my field of study at the University of Minnesota focused primarily on understanding and advancing the art and science of listening. We were engaged in pioneering work, driven by the simple knowledge that human listening was: critical, yet neglected; elusive, yet measurable; often ineffective and consequently costly, yet improvable and potentially profitable.

In retrospect, it is clear that the core of my seminal research, educational programs, professional articles, popular books, and numerous speeches has helped a multitude of individuals and organizations become better listeners. Moreover, in the 97th year of my life, it is gratifying to know so many have followed my lead, and are continuing to advance the study and development of listening throughout the world. My longtime colleague and friend, Dr. Lyman K. (Manny) Steil, and Dr. Rick Bommelje have created a new benchmark, as they have taken the field of listening to a new level with their remarkable book, *Listening Leaders: The Ten Golden Rules to Listen, Lead, and Succeed.* Building on the "Minnesota Listening Model," they have broken new ground in the field of listening by making the vital connection between effective listening and leadership. Their 50 plus years of combined listening reseach, teaching, writing, consulting, and leadership coaching experience makes them a respected and unmatched team. They are the "Architects and Fathers of the Field of Listening Leadership."

This is the most significant book ever written on listening and leadership, and will profit leaders at all levels in all types of organizations and enterprises. It will help you to immediately apply life-changing "listening and leadership rules" in your professional, personal, and family life. Of special note, Dr. Steil and Dr. Bommelje have included special "golden nuggets of wisdom" drawn from personal interviews with more than 100 leaders throughout the world. Drawing on their extensive and exemplary leadership experiences, these "Golden Circle Listening Leaders" share their proven success strategies, methods, and tips to help you enhance your listening and leadership success. You will learn significant and practical methods for improving your listening leadership that have the potential of creating enormous rewards for you and those you lead.

From the beginning of time, the basic compelling needs of mankind have not changed. With unending conflict around the globe, the pressing need for listening and understanding is greater than ever. Yet, when it comes to developing listening, our educational systems and organizational training programs continue to operate upside down. Listening continues to be the activity that we practice the most often; yet the skill for which we provide the least amount of formal and focused education. With mankind's imperative to understand and be understood, listening leaders must take the lead. This insightful book offers a powerful and systematic three-stage approach to increase your listening and leadership attitudes, skills, and knowledge, and will enhance your success in all arenas of your life. As you listen, lead, and serve others, you will succeed. In turn, as those whom you listen to and lead, listen to and lead others, everyone will succeed.

Acknowledgments

"I gather the flowers by the wayside, by the brooks and in the meadows, and only the string with which I bind them together is my own."

—Montaigne

In the true spirit of Montaigne, let it be known that *Listening Leaders* was completed with the invaluable input and thoughtful support of many. To each, we extend our heartfelt appreciation and gratitude.

We were most fortunate to have many sources of encouragement and support along our creative journey. We are especially grateful to more than 100 Listening Leaders who shared their real world insights and wisdom regarding the direct link between listening and leadership. Our "Golden Circle of Listening Leaders" are listed in the Appendix. Without exception, their stories helped this book come alive with observations that hold special significance for all Listening Leaders.

As our combined experience represents more than five decades of listening and leadership research, teaching, writing, consulting, coaching, and speaking, we are indebted to the scores of thousands of leaders throughout the world who have helped us grow in courses, seminars, retreats, conventions, and coaching sessions. The best listeners and learners are clearly the best leaders and the best teachers.

We especially express our admiration and appreciation to our numerous International Listening Association friends and professional colleagues who are committed to the study, development, and teaching of listening throughout the world. In addition, we value the extended support of our past and present colleagues at Macalester College, Wayne State University, the University of Central Florida, the University of Minnesota, and Rollins College, who created environments for creativity and service. Of course, without the seminal work of Dr. Ralph "Nick" Nichols, the "Father of Listening," and the special friendship and support of Nick and his wonderful wife, Lucille "Colonel" Nichols, this book would not exist. Thank you, Nick and Colonel Nichols.

The journey of conception ultimately requires the blessing of delivery. We offer our special thanks to our partners at Beaver's Pond Press; Publisher Milt Adams, and his irreplaceable right hand, Judith. We were blessed by the editorial wizardry of Doug Benson, and the helpful proofreading of Sid Korpi, whose red pencils greatly enhanced this book. The indexing competencies of Ina Gravitz at I. Gravitz Indexing Services will aid every reader. In addition, Jack Carvela and Jay Monroe at Mori Studio, Inc. served as valuable professional guides and mentors as we traveled together through the arduous, but exciting, publication process. Everyone made the journey simple and pleasurable.

We also thank our expert transcribers, Laura Pfister, Nadine Speller, and Marge Raeder. Individually, they diligently and carefully typed over 1,000 pages of taped interviews. Additionally, our "wisdom readers," Karen Randall, Stacy Allred, and Sherri Kriesel-Bailey, have helped us to discover the gems imbedded in more than 100 Listening Leader interviews. Dr. Robert J. Walker and Carole Grau served as invaluable eagle-eyed content experts and constructive critics. We deeply appreciate everyone's significant contributions.

Finally, we thank our families and especially our wives, Dee and Quin. Their unending support and understanding of our mission and vision of this book provided us the time, space, and energy to pour our passion into this work. They are true "Listening Leaders" in every sense.

Introduction

Outstanding leaders are outstanding listeners! This is the simple premise of **Listening Leaders: The Ten Golden Rules to Listen, Lead, and Succeed.** Our purpose in writing this book is to help all leaders understand the importance of listening, and to provide proven strategies and activities for enhancing listening leadership effectiveness. As both effective listening and effective leadership are required for individual, organizational, and societal success, they are critical activities that fit together like hands in gloves. Our goal is to provide listening leaders the rules and tools necessary to thrive. Throughout history the effective employment of listening and leading skills has enabled individuals, organizations, and societies to succeed. On the other hand, in the absence of skilled and effective listening, leaders at all levels fail. And when leaders fail, individuals, families, organizations, governments, and societies suffer and fail.

From our combined 50 plus years of helping millions of individuals and countless organizations throughout the world improve their listening and leadership attitudes, skills, and knowledge, four key facts have emerged:

▶ 1. Effective listening and effective leadership are inseparable.

▶ 2. Effective listening is imperative for anyone who desires to lead cohesive, productive, and significant teams and organizations.

▶ Productive listening and leadership require the development of productive attitudes and values, specific behavioral skill sets, and a deep understanding of established knowledge.

▶ Listening and leadership can be measurably enhanced.

Based on our extensive study and international involvement with effective listening leaders, we have identified **Ten Golden Rules to Listen, Lead, and Succeed**. As you apply these **rules**, you will enhance your personal and professional performance, productivity, profitability, and pleasure. In addition, you will begin to transfer **The Ten Golden Rules** into building your "Listening Organization." When that transpires, everyone will win.

PIONEERING WORK

As **Rich DeVos**, co-founder of Amway Corp. (now Alticor), owner and Chairman of the Orlando Magic NBA franchise and a longtime listening leader told us, "What you are doing is pioneering work!" Rich DeVos astutely observed, "Listening provides the foundation of productive human relations, without which, society cannot function. If we do not listen to each other, we cannot learn from each other. Thus, we will never get along with each other. Listening is a vital skill. It is especially important in view of the enormous amount of information and misinformation that is exchanged in today's world."

As a highly successful listening leader, Rich DeVos reinforces the essence of this book. To be a successful leader, you must be an effective listener. We believe all roads to individual and organizational success flow from building supportive foundations of listening leadership.

This book is written for experienced and inexperienced leaders at all levels in all types of organizations. No matter what your public or private role, this book will help you become a more effective listening leader. Our goal is to provide answers to frequently asked questions that have taken us more than half a century and millions of miles of travel to answer:

▶ What is listening leadership?

▶ Why is listening the most important skill for leaders?

▶ What separates the outstanding listening leaders from their less-accomplished counterparts?

▶ What, specifically, do you need to do to become a better listening leader?

▶ Are there specific listening rules to help you and your associates succeed?

▶ What leadership benefits will you derive from improved listening?

▶ How can you build a Listening Organization?

In addition to devoting over 50 years of combined work to researching, developing, writing, consulting, teaching and training in the arenas of listening and leadership, we have interviewed more than 100 leaders around the globe. Embedded throughout the book, you will find golden nuggets of wisdom gained from their listening leadership experience. This group includes CEOs and front-line leaders, entrepreneurs and pastors, military officers, educators, pilots, celebrities, and homemakers, all of whom are known for their outstanding listening and leadership abilities.

We have developed a **Listening Leaders Pyramid** consisting of **Ten Golden Rules** that will help you achieve your listening and leadership objectives. Each rule has been time-tested and proven to be both practical and priceless. As gold is one of the world's most alluring and useful elements, it is our standard for listening leaders' performance. As you apply the **The Ten Golden Rules to Listen, Lead, and Succeed,** it is important to remember they are:

▶ **Learnable.** They are simple to understand and, with study and application, can be learned in a short period period of time.

▶ **Practical.** They can be applied anywhere, anytime, with anyone, and in any culture, both professionally and personally.

▶ **Invaluable.** They will give you an unquestionable "edge" in your leadership success. As you consistently apply them, you will reap amazing benefits.

▶ **Teachable.** They can be taught to everyone you lead, and in turn to everyone they lead, through successive generations.

Unfortunately, listening is frequently viewed as requiring nothing more than passive awareness and polite attention. Nothing could be further from the truth! Listening ranks among the most important and challenging of all human activities. It is multifaceted and complex. It is driven by innate, learned, and refined forces. It is the primary daily activity we utilize more than any other thing in our life, with the exception of breathing. Ironically, it also is the least developed.

In our experience, the majority of leaders throughout the world have not invested significant time or effort to fully assess and develop their own, and their organizations', listening leader attitudes, skills, or knowledge. **C. William Pollard**, the distinguished former CEO of ServiceMaster, Inc., concurred: "You're on to something because there isn't much focus on the subject of helping people become better listeners." Unfortunately, as a result of this significant benign neglect, many leaders have established negative listening behaviors and habits that have adversely affected their ability to communicate and lead as effectively as they might. Coupled with widespread individual neglect, few leaders have made listening development a central priority within their organizations. The negative consequences are costly and damaging, both individually and collectively. Consider the following example of an ineffective, nonlistening leader.

A SHOCKING CASE

A frustrated employee of a mid-sized company shared the following lament about her leader:

"You would think a CEO with a Yale education and extensive experience would have excellent listening skills. I certainly would expect him to be nothing less than a well-mannered communicator. What a joke we have! We don't have a large sales team. I handle the marketing for the entire company, another team member handles sales for the East Coast, and a third takes care of sales for the West Coast. Our CEO is also playing the role of acting Vice President of Sales until we can fill the position. On a weekly basis, we meet to discuss the status of the accounts we're working on. What amazes me is that, when we meet, the only one who can get in a word is our CEO. Whenever anyone else tries to speak, he cuts them off in mid-sentence and gives his own opinions. I could see it if his ideas were positive and helpful. But each time anyone else tries to contribute, they wind up feeling less of a person. He sits back in his chair with his arms crossed, his glasses at the edge of his nose, while he looks over them to see us. Every five minutes, he pushes himself away from the table and scoots over to his computer to read his e-mail. He answers every question with a question. If I, or anyone else in the room, feels a need to say something, he simply says our name over and over until we shut up and let him talk. Then what we were trying to say in the first place doesn't matter. I wonder if he realizes what an ineffective leader this makes him. Maybe he only acts this way with people who report to him. Regardless, he loses credibility every time he behaves this way. The most knowledgeable people in our company are the employees. When our leader won't let any of us finish a sentence, I wonder who he believes he is leading."

One might reasonably ask, "Why would anyone continue to work for such a person?" Surprisingly, many do. Consider for a moment the negative impact of this nonlistening leader on his immediate reports, on his organization, and on himself. Imagine his negative impact on the morale, productivity, and profitability of this organization. Imagine the negative impact of lost respect, unwillingness to follow, and the damage to teamwork. However, good news resides in the simple fact that any leader will profit from understanding and rigorously applying the **"Ten Golden Rules to Listen Lead, and Succeed,"** as illustrated in the following Listening Leader Pyramid.

LISTENING LEADERS™ GOLDEN RULES PYRAMID

The **Listening Leader Pyramid** is a complete and connected system involving stages A, B, and C. each stage includes three Golden Rules.

▶ **Stage A, Listening Leader Preparation**, is the crucial building block to position listening leaders in readiness. Chapters One, Two, and Three provide the necessary preparation points for ultimate listening and leadership success.

▶ **Stage B, Listening Leader Principles,** provides the core operational components for a thorough guideline for listening and leading. Chapters Four, Five, and Six establish the critical strategies for immediate application.

▶ **Stage C, Listening Leader Practices,** outlines specific activities and concrete methods to enhance all listening leaders' effectiveness and impact. Chapters Seven, Eight, and Nine provide the opportunity to assess and refine proven and practical behaviors.

Each of the stages includes Three Golden Rules, culminating in the tenth Golden Rule: **Listening Leaders Take Meaningful Action**. Chapter Ten outlines a variety of action steps and specific strategies and techniques used by representative listening leaders. As you journey through each progressive Golden Rule, we invite you to embrace the insights and experiences of our very successful **Golden Circle of Listening Leaders**. Their golden nuggets supplement and reinforce the lessons learned from millions of effective and productive listeners and leaders. In turn, as a listening leader, you will profit as you employ and share **The Ten Golden Rules to Listen, Lead, and Succeed** with those you are privileged to lead. Ultimately, the challenge for every listening leader lies in the development of other listening leaders and building a Listening Organization.

Golden Rule **1**

"Listening Leaders Build Solid Foundations"

"It is important to understand that the size of every foundation defines the size and height of the structure. Thus, if you listen to gain relevant information, knowledge, and wisdom, you'll make better decisions in all parts of your life. Building a solid foundation is the critical key in both listening and leading."

—*Joe Shuster*

Joe Shuster is an extraordinary entrepreneur who has founded and co-founded eight companies during his exceptional life. As a productive and profitable business professional, who has helped create hundreds of millions of dollars of market value and significant employment opportunities for thousands, Joe underscores the importance of **Golden Rule 1: "Listening Leaders Build Solid Foundations."** We consider "Building Solid Foundations" to be the number one Golden Rule for two basic reasons. First, it provides the basic springboard for the preparation of all listening leaders, as preparation sets the table for initial insight and growth. Second, with preparation, productive listening leaders build a rock-solid listening and leadership foundation that becomes the anchor for all of their personal and professional decisions and activities.

Like many leaders, Joe Shuster began to build his foundations early. When asked how listening has positively affected his leadership success, Joe shared a story that illustrated an early foundation and a major turning point for his adult life. Amazingly, a key experience for building a solid listening foundation occurred when he was a youngster in the fifth grade.

In 1943, I had a job for five dollars a week stocking shelves in a store. I did a good job because the job was important to me. I came from a background where you worked very hard for somebody who paid you. The owner of the store thought my workday extended into the evening, so I was working long hours. One day, a customer commented on how much he had to pay his caddy. I didn't know anything about golf or caddying, but I was listening, and my interest was aroused. So the next Saturday, I told my boss I would not be coming to work that day and headed out to find the Bunker Hill Golf Course the customer had mentioned. On my way I asked a lady for directions. She said it was a long trek and suggested I go to another course, called Tam O' Shanter. Well, I listened, and although it was also some distance away, I got there early and met a man by the name of Mr. Brooksbank. I will never forget him. It appeared that he wanted a caddy and I volunteered, saying, "Look, I've never caddied before." He replied, "Well, you can caddy for me, and I'll teach you." So while I caddied, I listened and learned. When I finished the morning round, the afternoon players were coming out, and I caddied another 18 holes. At the end of the day, I had made more money than I made in an entire week working in the grocery store. So listening at a very young age had a significant and very positive impact on my life.

In the process of listening, he gained information, knowledge, and wisdom that have served him and others well for 60 years. From a humble beginning, Joe has been enriched in many ways. Most importantly, by listening to and leading thousands, Joe has followed a productive entrepreneurial path, increased his understanding of the world of business, and helped enrich many. As Joe said:

Many of the Tam O' Shanter members were movers and shakers of the "Who's Who of Executives in Chicago" and, as I caddied, I listened with great attention to their chitchat. Over the years, I came to the simple conclusion that if these gentlemen could run companies, someday I could too. By listening to their conversations on the golf course, I often knew who, why, and when someone was going to get fired because these golfing executives always talked business.

For example, G. H. Kraft, a member of the founding family of the Kraft Food Company, and a number of his lieutenants were club members, so I usually knew who was, and who wasn't, in trouble at Kraft. The key is that one little bit of listening at a very young age, created a significant domino effect in my life. Eventually, I became an Evans Scholar, studied chemical engineering at the University of Minnesota, and consequently enjoyed numerous leadership opportunities in the entrepreneurial business world. I started young, but at every turn, listening provided a foundation for my leadership. I can say categorically that all the excellent leaders I have known were, in my view, excellent listeners.

> *"I started young, but at every turn, listening provided a foundation for my leadership. I can say categorically that all the really excellent leaders I have known were, in my view, excellent listeners."*
> —Joe Shuster

Golden Rule 1: "Listening Leaders Build Solid Foundations" focuses on the important questions: What is leadership? What is listening? What is listening leadership?

The first step in building your "listening leader's foundation" is to clarify your definition of leadership. In our research, we have found productive listening leaders are able to clearly define leadership in their own terms. Although numerous listening leaders express a variety of leadership definitions, we have identified a set of common themes. In one way or another, everyone describes leadership as involving: "a sense of movement and action towards meaningful goals; a positive influence on followers; a stepping-up and modeling of the way; a spirit of encouragement; and, serving as an instrument of noble purpose."

WHAT IS LEADERSHIP?

There are hundreds of definitions of leadership, ranging from the simple to the complex. As scholar **James MacGregor Burns** notes, "Leadership is the most observed and least understood phenomenon on earth." Burns concludes his penetrating investigation of leadership by observing that "the ultimate test of practical leadership is the realization of intended, real change that meets people's enduring needs." Stated another way, the *Leadership Manual* of the United States Army defines leadership with three words, "Be, Know, Do." **Dr. Peter Drucker**, the eminent management guru of the 20th Century, simply says, "A leader's job is not to provide energy, it is to release energy."

Hewlett-Packard's CEO, **Carly Fiorina,** expanded the definition of leadership during a commencement address at the Massachusetts Institute of Technology:

Leadership in this new landscape is not about controlling decision-making. We don't have time anymore to control decision-making. It's about creating the right environment. It's about enablement and empowerment. It is about setting guidelines and boundaries and parameters, and then setting people free. Leadership is not about hierarchy, title, or status. It is about having influence and mastering change. Leadership is not about bragging rights or battles, or even the accumulation of wealth. It is about connecting and engaging at multiple levels. It's about challenging minds and capturing hearts. Leader-

> "*Leadership in this new era is about empowering others to decide for themselves. Leadership is about empowering others to reach for their full potential.*"
> —*Carly Fiorina*

ship in this new era is about empowering others to decide for themselves. Leadership is about empowering others to reach their full potential. Leaders can no longer view strategy and execution as abstract concepts but must realize that both elements are ultimately about people.

In addition, consider some representative points of wisdom from some **Golden Circle Listening Leaders**. Immediately following the tragic terrorist activities of September 11, 2001, **Frances Hesselbein**, the former President of the Girl Scouts of the United States of America, and current Chairman of the Board of Governors of the Leader to Leader Institute (formerly the Drucker Foundation), observed, "As I look at these leaders, observe their actions, listen to their messages, almost everything has changed, but not my definition of leadership. Leadership is a matter of how to be, not how to do." Frances Hesselbein, was awarded the "Presidential Medal of Freedom," the United States of America's highest civilian honor in recognition of her outstanding leadership. Her view of leadership is worth emulating.

> *"Leadership is writing on a blank piece of paper. Leadership is going beyond the borders of where you are, and taking your organization to another and better place."*
> —Millard Fuller

Millard Fuller, the well-known founder of Habitat for Humanity International, simply defines leadership "as writing on a blank piece of paper." Understanding the force behind the extraordinary accomplishments and impact of Habitat for Humanity becomes clearer as you consider Millard Fuller's view that "leadership is going beyond the borders of where you are, and taking your organization and people to another and better place."

Likewise, **Ann Newhouse**, a productive leader wise beyond her years, is impacting Progress Energy Corporation and believes leadership, at its best, entails, "helping people go places they thought they would never be able to go, while enjoying the adventure and journey."

Reverend Patrick J. Caverly, V.G., has been a Pastor for 35 years and currently leads a 4,000-member congregation. He says, "My personal definition of leadership is to be a facilitator of the goodness and the talents of other people. And, obviously, before one can become a leader, one has to have first deeply internalized a goal or vision as to where one want's to lead the people."

Dr. John DiBiaggio, the deeply respected former President of Michigan State University, the University of Connecticut, and Tufts, advances a very simple definition, "Leadership is making a difference." Dr. DiBiaggio highlights the fact that "leaders influence change." Moreover, they significantly influence others by the way they behave, the kind of models they create, and their personality traits that inspire others.

Similarly, **Dr. John Guarneri**, a leading physician and recent recipient of the prestigious "Physician Humanitarian Award," believes leaders in the medical arena must lead by dealing with a patient's body, mind, and spirit. "Leaders must do more than talk the talk; they have to walk the walk. Influential leaders must demonstrate their model."

> *"Leaders must do more than talk the talk; they have to walk the walk. Influential leaders must demonstrate their model."*
> —Dr. John Guarneri

Meigs Glidewell, an author and consultant, simply believes that, "Leadership requires the ability and commitment to help people develop." Meigs believes leaders must serve as "Suggestion Boxes" as they create an organizational focus for collecting, integrating, and responding positively to enthusiastically accomplish meaningful individual and organizational goals.

Amanda Moraguez is a Supervisor in the Credit and Collections department of a public utilities company. She formerly was a Customer Service professional with US Airways, and believes, "Leadership is leading others for the good of the whole and not just for my own reasons. It is my duty to lead the Credit department to reduce the amount owed to us, and also to help and serve customers. We are committed to help those who are in financial need, without overextending our boundaries and weakening our company."

These various samples provide a sense of more than 100 of our **Golden Circle of Listening Leaders'** views of leadership. As you continue to build your leadership foundations, the following will help you refine your personal definition of leadership.

LEADERSHIP FOUNDATION FACTS

An important step in focusing on **Golden Rule 1: "Listening Leaders Build Solid Foundations"** begins with understanding, embracing, and advancing five important and universal leadership facts.

▶ **Leadership Fact 1: Leadership is relational and positional.** Although individuals are appointed to a supervisory, managerial, or leadership position, it does not mean they will automatically and effectively lead others. The key factor is the quality of the connected relationship between the leader and followers. Leadership can, and does, occur at any level of every organization, from the Janitor to the CEO. Smart leaders understand that some of the most effective leaders in their organization may not occupy "prime positions" on their organizational chart.

▶ **Leadership Fact 2: Leadership is about "being" not just knowing or doing.** Effective leaders are known as genuine as they "walk their talk." Over a period of time, it is impossible to fake your way to successful leadership. True leadership comes from an authentic desire to achieve by serving, helping, guiding, and teaching others. Leaders who effectively lead over a sustained period of time operate with a well-developed personal purpose and mission that is larger than self.

▶ **Leadership Fact 3: Leaders have committed followers.** One of the ultimate and true tests of effective leadership is whether people follow leaders because they choose to rather than because they have to. Some developing and aspiring leaders mistakenly believe they have followers when, in fact, all they have are compliant employees. The choice to follow defines true leadership.

4▶ **Leadership Fact 4: Leaders are learners.** Learning comes in many forms, and leaders optimize their ability and commitment to continuously engage the learning process. They stretch themselves and grow in the process. In doing so, they model the way for others. Leaders extend their learning by a constant commitment to teach others. As they learn, they teach, and as they teach, they learn. As they learn and teach, they lead.

5▶ **Leadership Fact 5: Leaders are listeners.** Effective leaders understand that all followers need to, expect to, and like to, be listened to. All followers are looking for the listening leaders of their dreams. Listening leaders recognize that listening and leadership are inseparable, as listening is the best way to learn about the true needs, expectations, and desires of their followers. Thus, they commit themselves to become lifelong students of, and excellent practitioners of, listening leadership.

These universal Leadership Facts are reinforced by all of our **Golden Circle Listening Leaders.** A listening leader with special insight is **Larry Spears**, President and CEO of The Robert K. Greenleaf Center for Servant-Leadership. Under Larry's dynamic leadership, The Greenleaf Center experienced tremendous growth and influence throughout the 1990s, and positively impacts leaders through international offices in Canada, Europe, the U.K., Australia, New Zealand, Korea, the Philippines, Singapore, Japan, and South Africa. As Larry clearly explains,

> *"I believe the most effective leadership is provided by those who see themselves first and foremost as servants to others."*
> —*Larry Spears*

"I believe the most effective leadership is provided by those who see themselves first and foremost as servants to others." Robert Greenleaf coined the term, "servant-leader" in his 1970 essay, *The Servant as Leader*. In the 30 plus years since then, the idea of servant-leadership has taken root with many people and in many organizations throughout the world.

Robert Greenleaf observed,

> Servant-leadership begins with the natural feeling that one wants to serve. Then conscious choice brings one to aspire to lead. The best test is, do those served grow as persons; do they, while being served, become healthier, wiser, freer, more autonomous, more likely themselves to become servants? What is the effect on the least privileged in society, and will they benefit?' I believe this understanding of servant leadership is founded upon the art of listening to others.

Don Williams is Executive Vice President and General Manager of Northstar International Trucking. The company generates approximately $50 million in sales each year and has a work force of more than 100 employees. Don is responsible for the daily operation of the total dealership and leasing company, and believes,

> A good leader is a person with compassion, empathy, and the desire to be a winner while teaching others to be winners. A good leader leads by example. I think that's very important in the business world. All leaders constantly operate under the magnifying glasses of their employees, customers, suppliers, and vendors. A good leader must be a good listener and have strong abilities to reason through problems and be fair. As a lis-

> "A good leader must be a good listener and have strong abilities to reason through problems and be fair."
> —Don Williams

tening leader over the years, I've tried to follow the timeless and simple, but powerful adage, "treat others as you would like to be treated yourself." Real leaders cannot be afraid of conflict and at times need to say "no." I strongly believe if someone asks a question, they deserve a thoughtful answer in a timely fashion; even if it isn't the answer they want to hear. As a former Marine, I listened and learned that combat training was designed to achieve critical objectives and return us home alive. Our leaders served us well. However, when I first entered the world of management many years ago, I earned a reputation of being a hothead.

I was a "slam my fist on the desk kind of guy," but I quickly discovered that does not work in the business world. It did not work well then, and it does not work well today. People worth leading will not tolerate harassing, intimidating, or dictatorial behavior from their leaders. Effective listening is critical if leaders desire to build and maintain the team and human spirit within every organization.

The facts of leadership impact all worlds. One of the most impressive listening leaders we discovered was **Anne Horne** who has served as a family leader on the home front for 52 years. In addition, she served as a pre-kindergarten and kindergarten teacher for 31 years. She is known by many as a highly inspirational leader who has had a positive impact on many people through her authentic listening. Her view of leadership provides a powerful model for defining leadership. Anne simply believes,

> To me, leadership encompasses many things. First of all, I think a true leader understands human nature and brings out the best in the people she leads. The true leader focuses on individuals' strengths and not on weaknesses. Leaders must listen and catch people doing something right and then affirm that behavior. Leader-

ship requires clear communication between family members. I have found it is important to not use too many words. Effective leaders use positive loving and encouraging words such as: "I can," "I will do it," "I want to," "I understand," "Hey, that is really interesting," "Tell me some more." The leader in the home must be non-judgmental, optimistic, but reality-oriented.

> *"Leadership in the home is not for the timid. It requires listening to family members, and confronting inappropriate and unacceptable behavior. That is, one has to love family members enough to confront them and then allow them to suffer the natural consequences of their actions."*
> *—Anne Horne*

As a quiet but powerful leader, Anne advances the clear position that:

Leadership in the home is not for the timid. It requires listening to family members and confronting inappropriate and unacceptable behavior. That is, one has to love family members enough to confront them and then allow them to suffer the natural consequences of their actions. Obviously, listening to, leading, and training children must begin when children are very young. Everyone must face choices at a very early age if we want them to learn their choices have consequences. This is the time when consequences for wrong choices are not so severe. By learning to make intelligent choices when they are young, our children and future leaders will be prepared to make significant choices as adults. Family leaders must instill these individual strengths if we hope to prepare future generations of leaders. Then when our children reach adulthood, they will have the confidence to take responsibility for making choices where the consequences are of much greater magnitude. This fits my view of leadership and is something that I have tried to improve through the years.

CREATING YOUR DEFINITION OF LEADERSHIP

The demand for effective leadership in our 21st Century is greater than ever. In a world of international terrorism; economic upheaval; corporate turmoil; world health challenges, and governmental, business, and educational uncertainty, the need for effective leadership is paramount. Thus, the initial step in building, advancing, or refining your foundation of leadership values and competencies begins with the development of your personal definition of leadership. We believe that if you cannot, or have not, defined leadership for yourself, you will be unable to see it, find it, do it, measure it, enhance it, teach it, live it and repeat it.

LEADERSHIP

See it	*Find it*	*Do it*
Measure it	*Enhance it*	*Teach it*
	Live it	*Repeat it*

So, with the foundation of five important leadership facts, we offer our definition of leadership to help you become a more productive captain of your listening leaders ship.

DEFINITION OF LEADERSHIP

Leadership is guiding yourself and others to positive results for the enhancement of all individuals, organizations, and society.

WHAT IS LISTENING?

The next step in preparing and building your Listening Leaders Foundation is to clarify your definition of listening. Over the years, we have posed the question, "How do you define listening?" to thousands of significantly positioned leaders and have continually found the clarity, completeness, and consistency of responses to be limited. However, as a number of our listening leaders responded to our explicit question, a variety of listening definitions were identified and a set of common themes begin to emerge.

Richard Anstruther, President of High Gain, leads a full-service training organization specializing in the development of listening. Perhaps out of professional frustration, Richard offers the position that endless hair-splitting about definitions of listening is interesting but ultimately does not matter. Richard believes listening centers around "how to pay attention, how to sense, hear, see, and feel what a person is really saying on all levels." Ultimately, listening involves, "qualifying exactly what was heard, and moving into the speaker's role."

Dr. Phan Quoc Viet, a dedicated educator and business professional in Vietnam, is raising the bar for listening leaders in Southeast Asia, and defines listening as:

> *"In Vietnamese, we have a saying that essentially summarizes listening. That is, one should hear the spoken meaning and understand the unspoken intentions. (nghe y, hieu tu.)"*
> —*Dr. Phan Quoc Viet*

The integration of hearing the spoken words while understanding the unstated meanings of the speaker. In Vietnamese, we have a saying that essentially summarizes listening. That is, one should hear the spoken meaning and understand the unspoken intentions. (nghe y, hieu tu.)

An ocean away, **Paul Skoutelas**, the highly effective CEO of the Port Authority of Allegheny County in Pittsburg, Pennsylvania, defines the activities of listening very literally. Paul believes listening requires an "exercise of restraint, so one is of a mind to not speak quickly, in order to fully listen to what others have to say." The great challenge is to "bring open-mindedness to the issues at hand." Skoutelas' definition of listening has grown out of his simple discovery as a working professional that he doesn't know all the answers. Rather, Paul listens and leads with the fundamental belief that he works with a lot of very bright people, and that he and the organization will be more successful when he brings the ideas and talents of others to the decision-making process. Thus, Paul's definition of the listening process is centered on "open mindedness and restraint," and leads to effective listening leadership behavior. As Paul noted, "When I maintain an open mind and restrain any tendency to automatically jump to the assumption that I am the boss, everyone profits."

In a similar vein, **Bill Kroll** is a dedicated and faithful District Sales Manager with Colgate Oral Pharmaceuticals, who sees "listening as the act of acknowledging the unique value of the thoughts and opinions of others."

> "Listening is the act of acknowledging the unique value of the thoughts and opinions of others."
>
> —Bill Kroll

Likewise, in her leadership role as a compassionate Human Resources Specialist with the American Automobile Association, **Nancy Darnall**, recognizes a common human flaw of many leaders. This flaw is, "our inward and self-centered tendencies to start formulating opinions, answers, and responses before people have completed their statements." As a result, Nancy defines the importance of developing listening with "practiced self-control" and a focus on "intake and interpretation," rather than premature evaluation and inappropriate response.

Chris Austin is the conscientious and highly skilled listening leader of Staffing, Employee Relations, and Work Force Development for the *Orlando Sentinel*. Chris defines listening as "staying in the present moment, hearing, understanding, and acknowledging what others are saying."

Dr. Jeff Carter, Director of the Oral Surgical Institute, views listening as a process of constant research.

> I've broken listening into two categories of external and internal. External listening is going out and undertaking research, and looking for new opportunities and new markets. Internal listening is basically trying to learn the strengths, weaknesses, and problems of the people that work with you. As a result, one discovers more about the internal challenges and opportunities within the organization. It can result from listening to what others say in meetings or around the lunch room or water cooler. It is listening and recording input. Over the years, listening has enabled me to understand where the opportunities reside. To me, listening is like a sonar guidance system. Listening helps you identify where the obstacles are. In turn, listening will clarify where the easy passages are. True listening is more of a focused action rather than a random movement.

> *"To me, Listening is like a sonar guidance system. Listening helps you identify where the obstacles are. In turn, listening will clarify where the easy passages are. True listening is more of a focused action rather than a random movement."*
> —Dr. Jeff Carter

As we have collectively gathered input around the globe about the definitions of listening for more than half a century, we have discovered a wide variety of perspectives. The foregoing samples provide a representative sense of our **Golden Circle of Listening Leaders'** views of listening. As you continue to prepare and develop your foundations, the following will help you define and refine your view of your listening.

LISTENING FOUNDATION FACTS

Peter Nulty, an inductee in *Fortune* magazines' **National Business Hall of Fame** aptly observed,

> Of all the skills of leadership, listening is the most valuable, and one of the least understood. Most captains of industry listen only sometimes, and they remain ordinary leaders. But a few, the great ones, never stop listening.

As you focus on the crucial **Golden Rule 1: "Listening Leaders Build Solid Foundations,"** it is important to begin by understanding, embracing, and advancing five important and universal Listening Facts. Facts about listening can be surprising. Many of them contradict conventional ideas about the listening process, but the following five facts are vital to establishing your personal foundation for practical application and listening growth.

▶ **Listening Fact 1: Listening is our primary communication activity.**

More than half a century of research in the field of listening proves beyond a doubt that we spend 80 percent of our waking hours communicating. At least 45 percent of that time is spent listening. For leaders, who average

> *"Of all the skills of leadership, listening is the most valuable, and one of the least understood. Most captains of industry listen only sometimes, and they remain ordinary leaders. But a few, the great ones, never stop listening."*
> —*Peter Nulty*

57 percent, the total time invested in listening is even higher. Numerous studies confirm that listening is identified as the most critical leadership success skill, and is consistently rated by employers as one of the top five skills they expect employees to have. More to the point, as leaders advance in their level of responsibility, the importance of listening increases dramatically. In short, listening is central to the personal and professional success of all leaders, at all levels, and in all endeavors.

Listening Fact 2: Listening is an innate, learned, and improvable behavior.

Listening activities are driven by a combination of instinctive, inherent, and innate forces, as well as a combination of learned skills and behaviors. Listening, in its full complexity, is a measurable, observable, testable, and improvable behavior. Tests clearly reveal most individuals do not listen well. Immediately after listening to a 10 minute presentation, the average listener has heard; correctly understood; properly evaluated; stored; and appropriately responded to approximately half of what was said. Within 48 hours, that drops to a final effectiveness level of 25 percent. However, there is overwhelming evidence that, with systematic, focused, and directed effort, listening effectiveness can be improved. This fact has been demonstrated in thousands of listening courses and seminars, workshops, and training programs throughout the world.

Like other innate and learned behavior, listening can be improved through an individual's conscious and planned effort. As a result of guided effort, hundreds of thousands of listening leaders have enhanced their awareness and attitude, increased their knowledge, and advanced their listening skills.

▶ Listening Fact 3: Poor listening is costly. Effective listening is rewarding.

Although listening is central to all leaders' success, few have been trained. The lack of training and attention results in the development of counterproductive and costly listening habits and ineffective behaviors. The costs of poor leadership listening are staggering. Specifically, ineffective and inefficient listening results in extraordinary loss of time, money, productivity, profitability, sales, customer service, self-esteem, reputations, opportunities, and more. On the other hand, effective, efficient, and productive listeners profit in a multitude of ways.

▶ Listening Fact 4: Responsible and active listeners are productive listeners.

Unfortunately, most leaders operate on the assumption that it's the speaker's responsibility to ensure successful communication. As leaders assume the primary responsibility of successful communication rests with the sender, they become passive listeners. Our experience clearly demonstrates that the irresponsible, inactive, passive listener is always a poor listener and an ineffective leader. Poor listeners are lazy, uninvolved, detached, and wait for the speaker to assume responsibility. In fact, they often blame the sender of message for any breakdown of communication. On the other hand, outstanding leaders assume responsibility for the success of all of their communication. When listening, these leaders display an attitude of responsibility, and exhibit concrete behaviors of productive and involved activity. The impact is always positive, profitable, and measurable.

▷ Listening Fact 5: Listening can be commanded only to the degree developed.

Many listeners deceive themselves with the inaccurate and harmful assumption that they can listen well whenever they really need to, want to, or have to. The misleading assumption that you can "turn good listening on at will," is both grossly wrong and counterproductive. First, nothing could be further from the truth. In reality, listeners can only "will" themselves to listen to the level they have developed. Second, the assumption that you can do more than you can actually do interferes with the investment necessary to focus, grow, and get better. Productive listeners clearly understand their strengths and limitations, and constantly strive to improve and achieve higher levels of performance.

CREATING YOUR DEFINITION OF LISTENING

Listening has been, is, and will continue to be central to your leadership success throughout your life.

Although this book advances a comprehensive, practical, proven, and operational definition of listening, we invite you to invest the necessary thought, time, and energy to create your own personal definition of listening.

Like the development of your personal definition of leadership, the next step in building, advancing, or refining your personal listening insights, values, and competencies lies in the development of your individual definition of listening. Our collective experience is clear. If you have not defined, or cannot define, listening for yourself, you will be unable to: see it, find it, do it, measure it, enhance it, teach it, or live it and repeat it.

LISTENING

See it	*Find it*	*Do it*
Measure it	*Enhance it*	*Teach it*
	Live it	*Repeat it*

With these five important Listening Facts as a foundation, we extend our definition of listening to help you become a more productive captain of your listening leaders ship.

DEFINITION OF LISTENING

Listening is the complex, innate and learned human process of sensing, interpreting, evaluating, storing, and responding to messages.

The final step in building your listening leaders foundation is to refine and apply your definition of listening leadership. To provide direction for your development, our definition of listening leadership is intended to be broad yet specific, inclusive and complete, pointed and practical, and useful in your daily listening leadership challenges.

Highly effective listening leaders clearly understand that listening and leading are inseparable. Moreover, highly effective listening leaders understand, value, and engage four levels of listening leadership.

> ## DEFINITION OF LISTENING LEADERSHIP
>
> *To guide yourself and others to positive results for the betterment of all by enhanced sensing, interpreting, evaluating, storing, and responding to messages.*

The four distinct levels of listening leadership that must be mastered and practiced include:

▶ Listening to and leading yourself.

▶ Listening to and leading others.

▶ Teaching and engaging other listening leaders.

▶ Teaching others how to teach and engage other listening leaders.

The powerful and proven connection of listening and leading, and the multiple opportunities and challenges of listening leaders, was captured by **Frances Hesselbein**, when she said,

> I believe it is the quality and character of a leader that determines performance and the results. As a leader, the success of your leadership depends upon how effectively you mobilize your people around your mission, values, and vision. If you are going to successfully lead the organization and your people, you have to listen very carefully to them. Just as you listen very carefully to all of your customers, we can never take for granted we know what they value. This requires very thoughtful listening. It means when a person is speaking, they must have your undivided attention. You must focus and listen

very carefully to the words that are spoken as well as unspoken. This means staying focused for every moment with every person. It indicates respect, it shows appreciation, and it requires anticipation. Listening is a very, very important part of leadership. Listening is one of the most effective ways to learn. We listen to all of the people within and beyond the walls of the organization because we have to know what they value. Through listening, we learn what they value. What does the person speaking to you value? As we understand and appreciate them, it brings us to a higher level of connection and service. This is very, very important.

> *"If you are going to successfully lead the organization and your people, you have to listen very carefully to them."*
> —Frances Hesselbein

Likewise, **Tom Moran**, President and Chief Executive Officer of Mutual of America, one of the most successful insurance companies in the United States, understands and values the connection of listening and leadership. Mutual of America is a $10 billion corporation with 1,100 employees in 34 offices around the U.S. Tom is proud of their company culture, wherein 97 percent of Mutual of America's employees participate in the company's community involvement programs.

We put a lot of emphasis on training, and I get a chance to meet with the new employees and our new managers. I always tell them I

> *"The only way you perfect an idea is to be able to adequately articulate the idea, enlist other people's reactions to the idea, get their feedback, and be willing to listen, adapt to changes, and make a decision. Listening and leadership are inseparable."*
> —Tom Moran

started working as a janitor at the high school when I was 13. Something that hasn't changed at all is that I hate bosses. I have never liked bosses. A boss, to me, is someone who is not a leader, but someone who yells out commands. I always tell new managers, if they think they're a boss, they are on the wrong side of me. As a new manager, their responsibility is to be a leader who can articulate an idea and recognize that in the early stages that idea is not yet perfected. The only way you can perfect an idea is to be able to adequately articulate the idea, enlist other people's reactions to the idea, get their feedback, be willing to listen, adapt to changes, and make a decision. Listening and leadership are inseparable.

Senator Feargal Quinn is a model listening leader and is considered to be an institution in Ireland. Feargal is the CEO of Superquinn, the market leader in retail grocery in greater Dublin, Ireland. His dynamic organization employs more than 4,500 employees and owns 19 large stores and nine shopping centers. Feargal is equally well known for his 10 year stint as Chairman of Ireland's National Postal Service. From 1979 to 1989, he led the transformation of a money-losing government institution into an innovative, profit-making semi-state enterprise. In 1993, he was elected as an independent member of the Irish Senate, the Upper House of the Irish Parliament. Nevertheless, as a listening leader, Quinn usually can be found in one of his stores, bagging groceries, talking to customers, checking in with employees, and straightening up displays. Feargal Quinn's view of listening leadership is simple:

> *"If we want to create a workplace where people can achieve things and realize their individual talents to the fullest, then we must find additional ways of listening to each other."*
>
> —Senator Feargal Quinn

I see leadership mainly as "setting the tone" in an organization. If management, in general, is "getting things done through other people," leadership is one of the ways you do that. It is certainly not about giving orders, especially not about the small details of how things get done. It's more about getting across to people that you have a very clear vision as to where you want to go and how you want to get there, and communicating that vision in a way that inspires and invites people to come along with you. Encouraging people to share your vision is really what it is about. The more we move to a knowledge society, the more important it becomes for people to work effectively in teams. The key is we must understand each other, and the best way to achieve that is by listening.

The old style of working treated people more as machines than as people. The old "command and control" model is actually very dehumanizing. If we want to create a workplace where people can achieve things and realize their individual talents to the fullest, then we must find additional ways of listening to each other.

THE POINT

As **Joe Shuster** so clearly observed after decades of hard work and enviable listening and leading success, "Building a solid foundation is the critical key in both listening and leading." Like the builders of lasting historical monuments, all exceptional leaders focus intensely on the value of building solid listening and leadership foundations. Build lasting foundations, and you will join the ranks of the world's outstanding and impactful Listening Leaders. The *preparation* is simple, practice **Golden Rule 1: "Listening Leaders Build Solid Foundations"** and you will Listen, Lead, and Succeed.

Golden Rule 1

"Listening Leaders Build Solid Foundations"

10 ACTION STEPS

1. Build your listening leadership foundations through daily study and disciplined practice.

2. Commit to enhance your listening relationships with those you lead.

3. Craft your personal listening and leadership vision and mission statement.

4. Create your personal and actionable definition of leadership.

5. Create your personal and actionable definition of listening.

6. Create your personal and actionable definition of listening leadership.

7. Assume a primary position of listening leader responsibility, actions, and results.

8. Foster the value and importance of listening throughout your organization.

9. Teach those you lead how to build solid foundations of listening leadership.

10. Make a commitment to build a "Listening Organization," and begin.

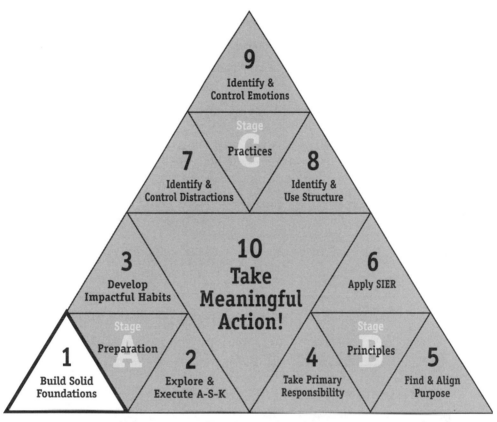

LISTENING LEADERS™ GOLDEN RULES PYRAMID

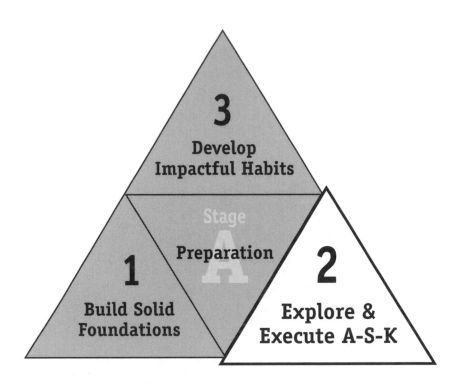

Golden Rule **2**

"Listening Leaders Explore & Execute A-S-K"

"Years ago, I was a K–12 Principal on a Sioux Indian reservation, and there was an old Sioux saying, 'If you listen for the whispers, you won't have to hear the screams.' I'm amazed at the leaders who get so caught up in their own ideas that they never hear their associates. They never hear their concerns. They never hear the suggestions of others because they are so intoxicated with their own voice."

—Dr. Al Argenziano

Dr. Al Argenziano is the dynamic Superintendent of Somerville Public Schools in Somerville, Massachusetts. As a long-time productive leader, he knows firsthand how important listening is to leadership success in the world of education. Dr. Argenziano's practical application of the powerful Sioux wisdom, "If you listen for the whispers, you won't have to hear the screams" illustrates the essence of **Golden Rule 2: "Listening Leaders Explore & Execute A-S-K."** For 30 years, A-S-K (the development of Attitudes, Skills, and Knowledge) has provided Dr. Argenziano with a set of useful listening leadership guidelines. As an outstanding listener, Al constantly reminds

"My strength as a listener is putting people at ease, while letting them know I care and will take appropriate action on what they want me to do. I won't just sit there."

—Dr. Al Argenziano

A-S-K

his colleagues that serving others begins and ends by refining listening attitudes, knowledge, and skills. Establishing positive and productive listening attitudes and constantly expanding your knowledge about listening and leadership provides the required foundation for developing and refining the basic under-pinning of specific listening skills and behaviors. As leaders in the educational arena work round the clock, Dr. Argenziano outlined some of his "listening to the whispers" strategies.

First of all, you have to make the people talking to you feel comfortable. You have to put them at ease. You have to make sure they know you care and that you hear and understand them. Ultimately, the most important part is doing something in response. If they want you to take action, then take it. That's the key. Everyone can listen, but if you don't do something in response, what is the sense of listening? You have to be action-driven.

When people come to you, you have to listen to what they offer you. Other people may ask for your thoughts about an idea or your help with a problem. You want to make sure you don't deflate them, especially if they want something that can't be done. My strength as a listener is putting people at ease, while letting them know that I care and will take appropriate action on what they want me to do. I won't just sit there.

Dr. Argenziano is clear about the impact others have had in his development of productive attitudes, skills, and knowledge as a listening leader.

Superintendent Mike Moran was one of my early lis-tening leader role models, and he taught me many sig-nificant things. First, and perhaps most important, he exhibited an attitude that invited open communication.

Second, he embodied the knowledge that listening was the key to effective leadership. Finally, he had the wonderful skill and ability to never diminish the value of the sender. When he disagreed with the practicality of ideas and proposals, he would simply say, "Al, philosophically you are right on the money, but the timing is wrong." Most important, he never left you hanging.

By incorporating the wisdom and insight of his environment, and the practiced behavior of role models, Dr. Al Argenziano illustrates the spirit and benefits of our **Golden Rule 2: "Listening Leaders Explore and Execute A-S-K."**

A-S-K is an acronym for **Attitudes, Skills,** and **Knowledge.** Listening is a complex activity that is affected by your attitudes, knowledge, *and* skills. Although the majority of leaders focus primarily on building listening skills, you will find great reward by also investing in developing your attitudes and knowledge. In fact, enhancing listening attitudes and knowledge provides the baseline foundation that supports enhanced listening skills. Action-oriented leaders understand that all three elements must be engaged for effective listening to take place.

The **A-S-K Model** highlights three basic elements that are crucial in all effective listening development programs. Any individual or organizational effort to improve listening and leadership must recognize and focus on the essence and importance of each element.

A=ATTITUDES

Attitudes underlie and permeate all behaviors. Listening leaders who establish and practice positive listening attitudes and values in all leadership situations thrive, whether at work, within their families, or in social settings. On the other hand, leaders who exhibit negative and counterproductive listening attitudes, and/or lack the requisite knowledge about listening, undermine their existing listening skills.

Positive listening attitudes begin with a bone-deep belief that listening is central to leadership success, and that the people you are privileged to lead and listen to deserve your total focus. **Dr. Jim Tunney,** a longtime educator, an outstanding author and a Hall of Fame professional speaker, is known as the "The Dean of NFL Referees" after refereeing for 31 years, including three NFL Super Bowls. Jim's experience in working with a multitude of leaders reinforces his belief that, "The keys to success are preparation and awareness, which affect attitude." Dr. Tunney reminds everyone of the ageless wisdom, "It's not our aptitude, but rather our attitude, that determines our altitude." Attitude is a critical component that requires constant attention from all serious listening leaders.

> *"I begin with an attitude that presumes all people are good at heart and have sound reasons for why they are saying what they are saying. I try to enter all communication with a positive attitude."*
>
> *—Gina Murphy*

Gina Murphy is the Director of Sales Training and Events for Tupperware, where she is in charge of inspiring 100,000 members.

When I am listening to somebody, I want to fully understand where they are coming from. I begin with an attitude that presumes all people are good at heart and have sound reasons for why they are saying what they are saying. I try to enter all communication with a positive attitude. My uncle, who was the Head Monsignor at Syracuse University for over 20 years, is a phenomenal listener and my role model. His ability to truly stay in the moment and to listen is a phenomenal gift. His caring attitude is worth emulating.

Jack Lowe Jr. is a second-generation committed listening leader. As President and CEO of TDIndustries, Jack, Jr. has followed the listening and leadership legacy of his father, Jack Lowe, Sr. Founded in 1946, TDIndustries is 100-percent employee owned and has grown into one of America's premier mechanical and electrical construction facilities management and services companies. TDIndustries has 1,460 partners, annually generates more than $217 million in business, and is consistently selected as "One of the 100 Best Companies to Work for in America" by *Fortune* magazine. In fact, TDIndustries has been ranked in the top 10 since 1998. Jack Lowe, Jr. continues to build a "Partnership of the Spirit" through the listening model of his father.

My dad was the founder of our company, and the best listener I have ever known. He always wanted to listen. When I came to TD and worked with him, I began to notice it even more. People constantly told me, "Your dad is a great listener." He was very focused on who he was listening to. He took notes and had an unbelievable interest in others and what they thought. His attitude and commitment to listen was obvious to all. On occasion, if he was busy and could not be interrupted,

> *"If you do not value the viewpoints of others, you will not value or understand the importance of listening. Positive attitudes are crucial."*
> —Jack Lowe, Jr.

he would let you know he wanted to listen by establishing a time to listen. He would say, "I can't give you my full attention right now. Let's set a date for another time. Let's find a time when I can listen to you." Although he did not say it, his message was, "I do not want to act like I am listening to you when I am not." I have seen a lot of people do just the opposite. They seem inclined to think, "Well, I can dispatch this listening experience quickly and move on." With this attitude, they do not really listen. If you do not value the viewpoints of others, you will not value or understand the importance of listening. Positive attitudes are crucial.

When you place value on listening to others, you will automatically be more successful. To emphasize how important attitudes are, I have discovered how critical it is to make time and not rush your listening. One technique I use when someone is pretty worked up or has a real passion about something is to take a lot of notes. It reinforces and expresses my attitude of caring and interest. This action lets the speaker know that, "I am interested and paying attention," and also helps me focus and pay full attention to their issues and problems. When I take notes, it helps me clarify the issues and not be distracted. It also slows the communication process down and encourages the other party to think more carefully about what they are saying because they want me to listen and make correct and meaningful notes. I find that others are more careful and thoughtful in their communications when I listen with a positive attitude and care enough to take notes.

John Caparella is the Senior Vice President and General Manager of the award-winning Gaylord Palms Hotel & Convention Center. John believes listening needs to be continually practiced. "You don't sit back and listen, you lean forward and

listen." The great tennis champion Arthur Ashe was a great listener and personal friend of John.

Arthur had the most amazing
gift of making everyone he talked
with feel important. He could be
in a large group of people and he
would give his total focus and
attention to the one he was with.

> *"Arthur had the most
> amazing gift of making
> everyone he talked with
> feel important."*
> —John Caparella

This was especially true with children. Arthur would
feel a tugging on his knee from an admiring child and he
would get down and talk to them. He would totally lock
in and really not know what was going on around him.

As John explained, several factors have helped him develop
his listening leadership attitudes and behaviors over the years.

I've been very blessed with great mentors and bosses
throughout my career. As I look back, it is astounding
that I had the incredible opportunity to work with the top
half-dozen senior leaders in the hospitality business. Also,
I grew up in a family where we sat around the table and
actually talked and listened to each other at dinner time.

Like all listening leaders, Jack Lowe Jr. and John Caparella emphasize how very special people in their lives exhibited positive listening
attitudes, became their listening leader role models, and encouraged
them to foster personal and professional listening leadership.

S=SKILLS

Skills center on a multitude of listening behaviors, competencies, techniques, and abilities necessary to thrive as a leader. First, as
just established, it is critically important to constantly have positive
listening attitudes. Second, combined with specialized listening

insights and depth of knowledge, it is imperative to translate your listening attitudes into specific skills that can create leadership value for yourself and others. There are many practical and productive skill sets in our Listening Leaders Pyramid that we will explore throughout this book. However, the skills only become operative and powerful when they are coupled with productive and positive attitudes and are grounded in solid knowledge. Consider and practice the numerous listening skills as discussed by members of our **Golden Circle of Listening Leaders**.

Dave Pontius is the former Senior Vice President of Operations for Hilton Resorts Corporation and is presently the President of RCI North America. Dave clearly understands the importance of building listening skills. Dave's team of 900 was responsible for leading the Hilton Grand Vacations Club product design, delivery and service area, as well as the resort property management, rental, retail and resale functions. As a vacation ownership industry veteran of 20 years, Dave Pontius has extensive experience in the disciplines of sales, marketing, product development, and finance. Moreover, he understands and values the importance of building listening skills.

> *"I think the key to developing effective listening skills comes from positive examples. Within our business, we have made it very clear that we must always take the high road in discussions with others and never wallow in the mud."*
> —Dave Pontius

I believe listening is the key to successful relationship selling. If you are going to sell anything to anybody, you have to understand where they are coming from. One of the most critical aspects of listening is that the sender perceives you as listening. You must make eye contact and put everything else aside so you can really focus on what the speaker is saying and how it relates to what his or her objectives are. Informally, I spend a lot of time with my team members trying to explain the psychology of sales and what makes a good salesperson. I end up putting my spin on it, emphasizing the importance of listening skills and abilities.

I think the key to developing effective listening skills comes from positive examples. Within our business, we have made it very clear that we must always take the high road in discussions with others and never wallow in the mud. To a great extent, that simply requires us to develop concrete listening skills that help us treat people with respect and treat them properly. The task is never-ending, as we consciously work hard to build a variety of listening skills to ensure we hear, understand, and fairly evaluate what others say. This attitude is imbedded in our organization and strengthens our listening and leading skills.

K=KNOWLEDGE

Knowledge about the degree, importance, costs, rewards, purposes, stages, process, strategies, and barriers of listening dramatically impacts both listening and leading attitudes and skills. What you don't know about listening will adversely color your attitudes and development of skills. On the other hand, heightened insight and understanding of specific facts about listening and leadership will provide meaningful substance to the "who, what, why, where, when, and how" as you listen and lead.

For example, just knowing eight simple, but powerful, benchmarks of listening can alter your focus on developing productive attitudes and important skills. Reinforced by the research of many, we understand that:

▶ Leaders are communicating beings. Communication is the primary activity of all effective leaders.

▶ Listening is the primary communication activity of all effective leaders.

▶ Listening is central to all leaders' success.

▶ Although listening is both an innate and a learned behavior, generally it is not overtly and systematically taught.

▶ Many leaders are generally ineffective and inefficient listeners.

▶ Poor listening results in extraordinary individual and organizational costs.

▶ With focused attention, all aspects of listening can be improved.

▶ When leaders grow as listeners, everyone wins.

Throughout *Listening Leaders:Ten Golden Rules to Listen, Lead, and Succeed*, you will discover an abundance of additional information designed to expand your knowledge of listening and leading. We believe it is important to recognize that the design of the A-S-K triangle positions the components of Attitude and Knowledge at the corners of the foundation level. Skills are located at the apex of the triangle and are supported by your Attitudes and Knowledge.

Obviously, for optimal listening and leadership impact, each of the three A-S-K components must be equally balanced and productively engaged. When combined, positive attitudes, refined skills, and greater knowledge feed, expand, and reinforce each other. Each component is strengthened or weakened by the existence or absence of the others. Your constant and ongoing challenge is to utilize the A-S-K model to advance your listening leadership attitudes, develop your listening leadership skills, and deepen your listening leadership knowledge.

For the past 14 years, **Karen Nelson** has been a leader at SPRINT. As an Access Service Provisioning Manager, she is currently responsible for listening to and leading an engineering team of 30 professionals. Karen's knowledge and insight about herself and others serves everyone well. As Karen observed,

> I am an upbeat and positive person and thus am drawn to those qualities in others. However, sometimes leaders are challenged because we have to listen to people complain, vent, and share their frustrations. So while I listen to the negative voices, I know I have to work at it because, generally, I just do not feel the same way. What someone else complains about, I may think is really great. So I have to work at understanding and listening to the negative voice. Without this insight, I would often not respond to the negative comments or complaints. Often, I would not agree but would simply not respond. Now, with newfound knowledge, I go out of my way to listen to the negative comments and simply draw them out by asking, "Why did you say that?" or, "Why do you think or feel that way?" As a result, I can better understand the other person's perspective. Any increased understanding is one of the numerous major benefits of listening carefully. Asking these kinds of additional questions, helps me understand better and therefore respond better. In addition, as a leader it helps

> *"Rather than avoiding complainers, or discounting complaints, I have made a greater effort to discover the reasons why people complain."*
> —Karen Nelson

me advance my team from negative complaints to positive resolutions. Rather than avoiding complainers, or discounting complaints, I have made a greater effort to discover the reasons why people complain. The resulting knowledge and insight actually helps everyone.

IT ALL BEGINS WITH AWARENESS

Throughout our professional careers of teaching, coaching, and developing listeners, we have observed that the leaders who are listening role models are aware of all the critical elements of the listening process. They have benchmarked and are aware of their attitudes, their knowledge, and their skills. They understand why a positive listening leadership attitude is imperative. In addition, they are committed to the importance of expanding their knowledge about listening. They are perpetual students of the listening and leading process. Moreover, they are constantly advancing their crucial listening skills and abilities. They understand that failure to be aware of, and to focus on, the state of their listening attitudes, skills, and knowledge will result in listening passivity.

To illustrate the importance of awareness, or lack thereof, consider the observation of **I. Warton Ong**, a professional business advisor in the Republic of Singapore. Warton, who has an engineering background and teaches at the Singapore Institute of Management, related his personal experience with a leader who exhibited a limited awareness of the importance of listening.

Many years ago, I went to one of my supervisors with a carefully thought-out business plan. Instead of listening carefully and saying, "This is a well-thought-out plan and here are some questions or suggestions," he simply said, "Here is what you might want to reconsider…" After leaving his office, I found myself in the position of having to rewrite the plan, which was now no longer "my plan." As a result, my commitment to the plan was diminished; I felt I no longer had full ownership. If this leader had simply taken a deep breath before he spoke and had carefully and thoroughly listened to my plan, I would have responded differently to his input. Since then, I recite a prayer every morning: "Lord, when I really care about others, help me to listen, observe, and take care of everyone's deepest needs." Awareness is the beginning key.

Mary Kay Ash, the entrepreneurial genius who created Mary Kay Cosmetics was well known for her sales savvy, pink Cadillacs, developing skilled and committed saleswomen, and her commitment to listening. In discussing the "art of listening," she believes that the first tenet of skilled listening and leading centers on providing undivided attention to others. Mary reminds us that most people will work out their own problems if they have a chance and a caring listener. She remembers a moment when one of her sales representatives was having marital problems and asked her whether she should divorce her husband. As Mary had never met the husband and knew nothing of the couple's situation, she knew she wasn't in a position to make any recommendations.

All I did was listen, nod my head, and ask, "What do you think you ought to do?" I asked her that several times, and each time she went on to tell me what she thought she should do. The next day, I received a beautiful bouquet of flowers and a lovely note thanking me for my terrific advice. Then about a year later, she wrote to tell me that her marriage was wonderful—and again my advice was credited!

Like all outstanding listening leaders, Mary Kay understood that most of the problems others face will best be solved by the person who owns the problem, provided someone cares and listens well enough.

Susan Adams Loyd, Vice President and General Manager of Clear Channel Television in Jacksonville, Florida, is another outstanding listening leader who knows that one of the many key elements of awareness is being mindful of your personal listening attitudes, skills, and knowledge.

> *"Some people are, by nature, better listeners, but even the best natural listener will benefit from focused, methodical, and systematic training in some form."*
> —*Susan Adams Loyd*

Susan developed a focused understanding of the importance of awareness by studying communication at both the undergraduate and graduate levels. In her ongoing development as a listening leader, she recognizes the critical factor of self-insight and awareness.

Maybe I am a little more sensitive to the components of communication, which include listening, than the average person. But that alone does not necessarily mean someone with academic training will automatically qualify as a good listener. I think outstanding listeners must refine their understanding and value of all the component parts of listening, and must take a constant and active role in developing their listening skills.

Based on her early academic and educational training, and her life-long commitment to continued learning, Susan has concluded that,

Like writing, reading and speaking, listening is a complex skill that is developed over time. Some people are, by nature, better listeners, but even the best natural listener will benefit from focused, methodical, and systematic training in some form. Listening skills will be enhanced by a deeper awareness of what listening requires, what attitudes and listening habits we hold, and how our listening skills, strengths, and limitations can be enhanced and developed over time. I believe an awareness of the complex listening process will help everyone be a better listener, and in turn, a better leader. In other words, being more sensitive to other perspectives, other lifestyles, other preferences, other learning methods, and other personal and professional experiences will help you become a better listener.

I realize now that I was not a natural-born listener. As I accepted management and leadership roles in both my professional and personal world, I became more aware of what an effective listener, and leader, contributes to an organization. In my listening development as a young leader, I learned from both good and bad examples. I was open to helpful feedback from people who felt I had talent but also felt I needed to work on my listening skills. The key starting point was my newfound awareness that a leader with bad listening skills can have a negative impact on everyone. Becoming aware of my need to improve my listening attitudes, skills, and knowledge enhanced my dedication to work harder. This is why I am so sensitive that listening is, and needs to be, a central and active part of everyone's life.

Susan Adams Loyd discovered a critically important reality of A-S-K. Listening leadership development begins with awareness of the interconnected elements of A-S-K. Awareness of the relevance of listening to leadership is a crucial beginning. Awareness of your listening habits, strengths, and limitations is a basic requirement. Awareness of the three stages of listening Preparation, Principles, and Practices, and the related **Ten Golden Rules to Listen, Lead, and Succeed** will point the way. Once you are aware of the opportunities for improvement, you are positioned to take action. Awareness leads to Readiness. Readiness leads to focused Aim. Aim leads to productive Action. Action leads to positive Habits. Habits result in automatic

Behavior. Over a period of time, repeated positive actions create a positive habit. Eventually, the power of repetitive and productive habits results in automatic and effective listening behavior.

Six Steps to A-S-K

1. Be Aware
2. Be Ready
3. Take Aim
4. Take Action
5. Build Positive Habits
6. Create Automatic Behavior

Six progressive listening steps will serve you well: Be Aware; Be Ready; Take Aim; Take Action; Build Positive Habits; Create Automatic Behaviors.

Ultimately, every leader is responsible for his or her individual listening and listening leadership development, and it all begins with awareness.

CONSCIOUS COMMITMENT TO LISTENING!

Beyond awareness and readiness, listening action requires the development of a conscious and ultimate commitment. **Frank Delle III**, a leader in the Creative Services and Promotions arena for Bright House Networks, clearly understands both the importance and impact of cultivating a conscious commitment to listening. Based on his successful experiences, Frank made a simple observation.

By being aware of the power of listening, I have changed my behavior by consciously committing myself to listen. This awareness has been beneficial to me and others, both professionally and personally, at work and in my home life. I know it shows others that I care about them, am committed to them, and I understand them. Because of my awareness of listening, I understand the negative impact when others do not listen when I speak. I am conscious of that.

I am aware when people take side trips while I am talking to them and trying to make a point. When that happens, I can make the necessary adjustments to bring them back, so they get and understand my point. In addition, when I become aware people are not listening, I can project how others probably feel when I do not listen to them. As I do not

> *"By having an awareness of the power of listening, I have changed my behavior by consciously committing myself to listen. This awareness has been beneficial to me and others, both professionally and personally, at work and in my home life."*
> —*Frank Delle III*

want people to be negative, my conscious commitment is to listen and stay focused.

Like all productive leaders, Frank Delle III clearly knows that knowledge and attitude pave the way to the practical and powerful development of listening skills.

THE GREAT MAGIC AND POWER OF WORDS

Listeners who experience significant leadership gains also know there are a multitude of skills represented in the Listening Leader Pyramid. These are the skills and actions that create value. One of those skills is allowing the speaker to hear the powerful sound of his or her own voice. The former CEO of Hearst Publishing Company, **Bob Danzig**, highlighted a major lesson a mentor taught him early in his career.

As a young classified advertising salesman, I was guided by a senior sales associate, Manny Krips, who took an interest in me. Manny gave me previews of his conduct and style as he called on clients who all seemed to treasure him. His key attribute was asking gentle questions

> "Manny taught me well, and I learned early on that there is great magic in letting people 'hear their own voice.'
> When it's accomplished, it completes the communication magic and lubricates the bonding relationship."
> —Bob Danzig

and listening, really listening, to customers. Because he listened so well, he remembered important personal items, special interests, family issues, and more. When he needed to, he could recall them to advance the client relationship. Manny taught me well, and I learned early on that there is great magic in letting people "hear their own voice." Allowing others to hear their own voice requires your skilled listening. When it's accomplished, it completes the communication magic and lubricates the bonding relationship. I found that attitude to be present whether selling two-line classified ads or, later on, as a CEO of a multibillion-dollar national company. I never forgot Manny, and I encouraged our local unit leaders to embrace listening—true and practiced listening—with their clients and colleagues.

Bob Danzig's wisdom and experience as a listening leader has even greater impact when you discover that Bob grew up in five foster homes, went to work at 16 as an Office Boy at the *Albany New York Times Union*, became Publisher 17 years later, advanced to the position of President and eventually served as the nationwide head of the multibillion dollar Hearst Newspaper chain. In his second career as a Professor, Speaker, and Author, Bob Danzig understands the power of words. Bob credits a Social Worker, Mae Morris, for repeatedly "tattooing his spirit" when he was 11 years old, with three words, "You are special." In addition, his first boss ignited his appetite for growth, with her simple, but powerful words, "I think you are full of promise."

A combination of 10 words, in Bob's perspective, "elevated and provided lubrication for my life."

Leaders who listen provide positive affirmations to others. Bob Danzig believes "leadership is all about tomorrow and being an instrument of noble purpose." His latest book, *Every Child Deserves a Champion*, is benefiting foster children everywhere because Bob reinforces the simple fact that everyone has an appetite to be celebrated. Listening leaders must celebrate the great magic and power of words. Celebration heightens awareness and leads to refinement of attitudes, growth of knowledge, and development of listening leader skills.

YOU CAN LEARN FROM EVERYONE

More than 50 years ago, **G.K. Chesterton** made the cogent observation; "There is no such thing as an uninteresting topic or issue, there are only uninterested people." The knowledge that you can learn something of value from anyone when you listen on purpose is clearly understood by **Dr. Sandy Shurgart**, President of Florida's Valencia Community College, the eighth largest community college in North America. As a vibrant and intelligent listening leader, Dr. Shurgart reinforces the relevance of the Knowledge component of A-S-K. "I can teach anybody to practice the listening techniques that will enable them to at least give the impression they have listened to

> *"There is no such thing as an uninteresting topic or issue; there are only uninterested people."*
> —G.K. Chesterton

the person they are engaged with, in just minutes. Unfortunately, that is counterproductive." In fact, it is much more important to help people understand the numerous facts about the listening and leadership process.

Specifically, President Shurgart concurs with the idea that we can learn important things from everyone.

Everyone has something to teach each of us, but it requires humility, and humility is about character, not about skill. Character is formed at a glacial rate. By comparison, skill is formed overnight. So, it is certainly helpful for everybody to be trained beyond the superficialities of listening. I believe it is critical that we begin by choosing leaders who are open to learn something from everybody.

> *"Everyone has something to teach each of us, but it requires humility, and humility is about character, not about skill."*
> —Dr. Sandy Shurgart

As Chesterton said, "...there are only uninterested people." You will profit by expanding your knowledge about listening. Explore the data that has been developed over decades of research by reputable and knowledgeable listening scholars. Discover as much information about listening as you can. Expand your knowledge by associating with well-versed listening experts and role models. Solicit as much feedback about your listening and leadership attitudes and behaviors as possible. Create time to review and evaluate your own personal listening experiences. Thoughtful review requires post-listening reflection regarding what you could have done differently or better. In addition, observe and learn from the poor listening and counterproductive leadership activities of others. As a wise man once said, "No one is completely worthless, for we can always learn from bad examples." Most important, if we listen, we can learn from anyone and everyone.

Paul Skoutelas, Chief Executive Officer of the Port Authority of Allegheny County underscores an important lesson he learned from his father, an outstanding listening leader. Paul recounts,

Perhaps this is a bit of an unusual story, but my dad is a businessman and, over many years, he worked in different businesses. When I was 10 or 12 years old, I remember riding with my dad between his work sites, and talking with him at his office when he had time. It is surprising, but he would talk to me about things he was thinking about and decisions he was going to make in his business. Even though I was very young, he would ask my opinion about business matters.

> *"My dad really spent time listening, and it molded my perspective. Having the opportunity to engage, to talk, and to express my youthful opinions and have my father actually listen really mattered... His positive role model made a distinct impression that drives me today."*
> —Paul Skoutelas

Although I don't know why he asked my opinion and listened to my young thoughts, it made a lasting impression about the true value of listening. My dad really spent time listening, and it molded my perspective. Having the opportunity to engage, to talk, and to express my youthful opinions and have my father actually listen really mattered. I knew that he valued me and my thoughts. His positive role model made a distinct impression that drives me today. Since then, I have discovered it does not necessarily matter how much formal education one might have, nor does it necessarily matter where you are positioned within the organization. Whether you are at the Senior VP level or two or three levels below, whether you are a producer or a consumer, whether you are young or old, everyone knows something you don't. No one knows everything and, when we listen, we bring different perspectives to each other. That is why I am so comfortable with the activity of listening.

PLACE VALUE ON LISTENING LEADERSHIP

Peter Blank has embraced **Golden Rule 2: "Explore and Execute A-S-K"** in a significant way, both professionally and personally. While serving as an instructor with Walt Disney World® Resort, Peter completed his Masters Degree in Human Resource Management. As part of his educational program, Peter became captivated with the relationship between listening and leadership, and immediately started to apply it in his personal and professional life. The driving force was his positive listening attitude. When asked to share three main points for developing listening leaders, Peter said,

First, you must place a value on listening leadership. This can be emotionally, relationally, professionally, financially, or some other kind of specific value that will raise your focus and activities of listening.

Second, stress the importance of flexibility in the listening leadership process. There are times when you need to guide excessive talkers. For example, if you have gotten the main point of the message and the person continues to ramble, you may need to say, "I have it. Let's move ahead."

> *"First you must place a value on listening leadership. This can be emotionally, relationally, professionally, financially, or some other kind of specific value that will raise your focus and activities of listening."*
> —Peter Blank

Third, it is never too early or too late to begin refining your listening leadership skills. I never consciously focused on the concept of listening until I was 31. Listening was never brought up in school. I never gave it much thought. Oh, every now and then, listening was mentioned in a couple of training classes.

Someone would say, "Now listen up," or, "Pay attention," or, "Hey, be a good listener!" However, in my early years, no one ever really placed a spotlight on the importance, the value, and the depth of listening.

The good news is, you can reap positive rewards by growing and advancing your listening competencies whenever and from wherever you are. It is largely a matter of desire and choice.

Dr. Craig McAllaster is the Dean and Professor of Management at the Roy E. Crummer Graduate School of Business at Rollins College in Winter Park, Florida. Dr. McAllaster has a rich perspective on listening and leadership as a result of working in the worlds of both industry and academia. Craig's many years in the consumer services and electronics industry in management, organizational, and executive development positions have helped him clarify the benefits of patient and persistent listening.

Listening has helped me solve significant problems and recognize numerous opportunities because, if you listen well, many times, the solutions are right in front of you. For example, people come in my door every day with problems. As I listen, they usually discover they have brought both the problem and the solution. Some leaders believe that if they are not talking, they are not really leading. I may not always like what is said, but if I fail to listen, I will never understand the various sides of the issue. Without full understanding, we will never know how to appropriately remedy, address, and resolve the issues, problems, opportunities, or concerns.

> *"Listening has helped me solve significant problems and recognize numerous opportunities because, if you listen well, many times, the solutions are right in front of you."*
> —Dr. Craig McAllaster

That is why listening is absolutely critical. On any given day, I listen to many people, including faculty members, staff, alumni, and business people. Their ideas are very important, as they provide vision and direction for this school. I do not believe most leaders are extraordinary visionaries. Rather, I think they are people who are highly skilled listeners and observers who discover the true potential of organizations.

THE COSTS OF INEFFECTIVE LISTENING

Listening leaders consistently add value to their own and others' lives. Unfortunately, ineffective listeners incur costs. Although costs come in many forms, they occur around the world. Two listening leaders who live half-way around the world from each other discussed specific costs of poor listening they have observed. Although the costs seem to differ in magnitude, each was severe within its respective culture.

Sumith Phantes is a teacher in Chieng Yun, Mahasarakan, Thailand. Sumith Phantes has an eclectic background, as he spent 10 years as a Buddhist Monk from age 11 to 21, and also worked with the United States Air Force prior to becoming a teacher. In discussing the costs of ineffective listening, he told us about a fellow teacher who paid a measurable price for not paying attention in a teachers' meeting.

> *"…He did not pay attention because he was talking to other teachers. The principal punished him by cutting his salary by five percent for three months."*
> —Sumith Phantes

My friend failed as a listener when he was a young teacher. During a teacher's meeting, when the Principal spoke, he did not pay attention because he was talking to other teachers.

The Principal punished him by cutting his salary by five percent for three months. This may seem like a small cost, but in Thailand, it was quite significant.

In Argentina, **Jorge del Aguila** is the General Manager of the Argentine Financial Executive Institute (IAEF), a professional nonprofit organization established in 1967 that brings together nearly 700 Chief Financial Officers from the most important companies in Argentina. Jorge heads a team of 10 very well-trained people, a part-time staff of three researchers, and 14 professors of different subjects. Jorge described a listening breakdown that occurred early in his career.

In 1981, I was appointed Operations Manager at the Argentine branch of Mary Kay Cosmetics in Buenos Aires. I was responsible for processing customer orders, for picking, packing, and shipping products, and for invoicing and collecting. We were a small team of four managers in charge of finance, marketing, manufacturing, and operations, led by an experienced CEO. We used to meet frequently to follow up on the progress of the marketing plans, budget control, and achievement of our goals. The CEO's main characteristic was that he did not like to listen to bad news. When a problem appeared during one of our presentations, he interrupted and lectured us about effective management and problem solving strategies. Invariably, these pieces of advice had nothing to do with the real problem. In a few months, our reports started to show the costs of ignoring the early signals and insisting on wrong strategies and tactics. The CEO continued lecturing about his experience and skills for managing difficult situations and complaining about our incompetence. Finally, in the first year of operations in Argentina, the company lost almost all of its equity. Three of the managers, including myself, were fired, and the company never recovered its market share.

THE CHALLENGE OF TIME

On another front, the attitude, skills, and knowledge one brings to the listening table are tested in the crucible of limited available time. **Ben Sachs** is a highly regarded entrepreneur and business turnaround specialist. Ben is brought into organizations that are in deep trouble, in situations where time is short and of the essence. Although the majority of life situations provide the opportunity to listen patiently, Ben's pressure-filled, turnaround role demands pinpoint and laser-focused listening. He uses the power of listening to quickly learn about the organization and assess where the key problem areas are.

When I come into a troubled company, my first objective is to stop the bleeding. So I come in asking questions. Obviously, the President who had run the company is going to tell me anything to protect himself. So, although I listen to him, his information is usually tainted. As his leadership has failed, we normally remove him immediately. Over the years, I have generally found the majority of the first-tier leadership team also focuses on protecting and covering themselves. So our usual practice is to invest our time and energy in listening to the second-tier leaders because they usually have great insight. In the majority of the 18 companies we have turned around, the second-tier leaders became first-tier leaders. They move up because they have nothing to lose and they tell the truth.

So, my task is to listen to people who are focused on solving the problems and are willing to try to do things in a new way. We need people who have eliminated the word "no" from their vocabulary. I pour my energy into listening to problem-solvers. I do not listen to people who are negative and say they can't do what is necessary. In our short time frame, there is no time or room to listen to excuses or negativity. I am inspired by listening to people who say, "Let's go." I cut off the people who say "no," because my experience has proven they will not make any significant contribution to the new organization. I stop listening to the people who say, "no" because they are negative thinkers, and in the turnaround business, negative thinkers do not survive. I want to know what people think and why they think what they think. So I listen to the people who are creative and who can identify the resources we have to turn the enterprise positive.

> *"I am inspired by listening to people who say, 'Let's go.' I cut off the people who say, 'no' because they are negative thinkers, and in the turn-around business, negative thinkers do not survive."*
> —Ben Sachs

ENHANCING RELATIONSHIPS

In emphasizing the value of listening leadership, **Tony Lado**, a Human Resource Management leader of a multimillion-dollar nonprofit organization, observed how listening and leading markedly strengthened the relationships that matter most in his life.

I have learned to model listening behavior, and then to be a listening leader for my family members. This, I can honestly say, has positively transformed our family dynamics. There is such a listening vacuum in our fast culture. As a result, just giving those you love your full attention for meaningful moments is immediately recognized and valued. Listening to the significant people in your life is both attractive and rare.

On a recent trip to Spain, I had a profound experience that illustrated how far Americans have drifted away from truly listening to one another. While sharing lunch with a large group, I opened my mouth to speak, and immediately, all other conversation stopped. A table of 10 became exclusively focused on me. They were totally listening with their ears, their eyes, their posture, their expression, and more. To be honest, it was initially a bit uncomfortable and something inside of me reacted with, "Wait a minute. I really don't have anything that important to say. I did not mean to command the attention of the entire table." But then I realized I had become accustomed to being half-listened-to for so long, that I had grown to accept it. That is when it really hit me. My experience in Spain illustrated they have a culture that promotes listening. When you talk, with 10 to 20 people crammed together at a table, everyone is respectful. People are quiet. They look and listen, and they are waiting to hear what you have to say. At first, it was disconcerting because I had created a habit of expecting people to keep ignoring me and continue engaging in their own conversation.

Tony Lado's insight that culture and habits are factors that influence our listening behavior is a significant reminder in our preparation to listen and lead. Tony also observed,

While it may appear to be common sense, it is powerful to realize that by truly listening, you begin to really hear things, really discover things, and really appreciate things about people you have known your whole life. I recently discovered many personal things about our family my mother had never told me. When I asked her why she never told me certain things, she really did not have a good explanation. Her answer was genuine in that she just really hadn't thought about it. I did not know my real father; I'd never met him. I had always heard half-stories, but when I was truly ready and asked with a desire and a willingness to listen, she told me she was engaged to him for three years, they were in love, and had written letters back and forth from the United States and Spain for those years. This was huge information! She shared, and I listened. As a result, our relationship was strengthened.

THE POINT

In his-too short, but dramatically significant life, **Joe Charbonneau** was one of the world's truly gifted speakers and teachers. Joe taught scores of thousands of leaders, around the globe, the importance and value of developing positive attitudes, productive skills, and relevant knowledge through expanded awareness. Legions profited from his advice: "If you want to be a master of anything, study what the masters have done before you, learn what they have done, have the guts to do the same thing, and you will be just as successful as they are."

> *"If you want to be a master of anything, study what the masters have done before you, learn what they have done, have the guts to do the same thing, and you will be just as successful as they are."*
>
> —*Joe Charbonneau*

Or, as **Dr. Al Argenziano** reminds everyone, "If you listen for the whispers, you won't have to hear the screams." The preparation is simple, practice **Golden Rule 2: "Listening Leaders Explore & Execute A-S-K"**, and you will Listen, Lead, and Succeed.

Golden Rule 2

"Listening Leaders Explore & Execute A-S-K"

10 ACTION STEPS

1. Embrace the A-S-K model, and measure how it affects your listening leader success.

2. Demonstrate a consistent positive listening attitude based on your authentic belief that listening is central to your leadership success.

3. Master and teach the eight benchmark facts of listening.

4. Create automatic listening leader behaviors with daily practice of the six-steps of A-S-K.

5. Foster a listening leader mindset that you can learn from anyone.

6. Establish specific emotional, financial, relational, professional, or personal values of listening leadership.

7. Explore the impact of negative attitudes, lack of skills, and limited knowledge on listening and leading.

8. Identify and evaluate the A-S-K source of listening problems.

9. Introduce the practical application of the A-S-K model to those you lead.

10. Build your "Listening Organization" by executing A-S-K on a daily basis.

LISTENING LEADERS™ GOLDEN RULES PYRAMID

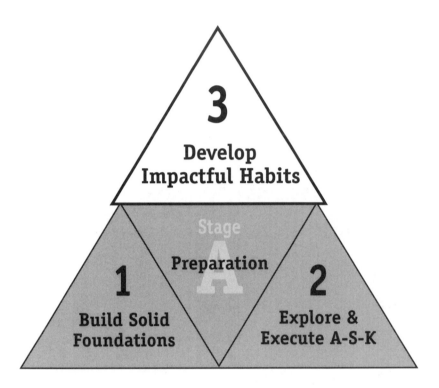

Golden Rule **3**

"Listening Leaders Develop Impactful Habits"

"Habits are strange. Some are positive and serve us well, and some are negative and do us harm. However, we profit when we remember we entered this world with none, and we will depart with none. As habits form silently, constantly, and relentlessly, their pervasive impacts are often unnoticed. Yet they control our life. Although productive habits are invaluable, and bad habits are costly and difficult to break, all the effective listening leaders I know spend an inordinate amount of time studying, consciously shaping, and refining their habits."

—Chuck Maragos

Chuck Maragos is the vibrant, energetic founder and CEO of Valley Dental Arts, Inc. Located in Stillwater, Minnesota, VDA has built a remarkable team of internationally respected dental artisans who are committed to excellence and the highest quality, specializing in serving leading dentists throughout the United States and six foreign countries. For more than three decades, Chuck Maragos has focused on the development of productive business and artistic practices and habits. As a productive practitioner of **Golden Rule 3: Listening Leaders Develop Impactful Habits,"** Chuck observed,

In our artistic and service profession, every team member has listening and leadership opportunities and responsibilities, at every stage. There is no room for bad habits because one person's bad habits adversely impact every other team member in our critical chain of creation and service. Bad habits are very costly. Positive habits serve everyone.

> "…habits form silently, constantly, and relentlessly… and they control our life."
> —Chuck Maragos

Habits are created through constant repetition. Whether they are positive and serve us well or negative and work against our best interests, habits are simply tendencies to act in predictable, easy, spontaneous, and often unconscious ways. Bad habits lock listening leaders into specific, predictable, and unproductive behavior patterns that they may never have thought about. To paraphrase **John Stuart Mill**, "The unending obstacle to individual growth is habit."

> "The chains of habit are too weak to be felt until they are too strong to be broken."
> —Samuel Johnson

Unless we are aware of and evaluate the impact of our habits, they are difficult to address. Thus, enhancing listening leaders' habits begins with awareness and knowledge. More than 200 years ago, **Samuel Johnson** noted, "The chains of habit are too weak to be felt until they are too strong to be broken." Although Johnson's observation continues to be pertinent and valid, present-day effective listening leaders profit by constant and conscious identification of their listening habits.

HOW WELL DO YOU LISTEN?

There are numerous ways to assess your listening habits. For decades, we have asked leaders throughout the world to respond to the following four profiles. Although there are no correct or incorrect answers, there are *accurate* answers for everyone. Your responses will provide a benchmark to advance your insight and understanding of your personal listening habits. In addition, you will see how you compare with hundreds of thousands of other leaders who have completed the same profiles.

Listening Leader Profile I

A. Overall, how would you describe yourself as a listener?

Superior
Excellent
Above Average
Average
Below Average
Poor
Terrible

B. On a scale of 0-100 (100 =highest), how would you rate yourself as a listener?

_____
(0–100)

C. Overall, what five words best describe you as a listener?

_____

_____

_____

Listening Leader Profile II

How do you think specific individuals in your personal and professional worlds would rate and describe you as a listener?

Person	0–100	Descriptive Words
Your best friend	_____	_____
Your boss	_____	_____
A specific colleague	_____	_____
A specific direct report	_____	_____
A specific client	_____	_____
Your spouse	_____	_____
A child	_____	_____
Other	_____	_____

Listening Leader Profile III

A. _____ is the best listener I have ever known. I would rate and describe this person as a listener in the following way:

0–100 **Descriptive Words**

_____ _____

B. _____ is the worst listener I have ever known. I would rate and describe this person as a listener in the following way:

0–100 **Descriptive Words**

_____ _____

Although there are a multitude of listening leader behaviors and habits that can be studied, we invite you to thoughtfully complete the following preliminary listening assessment created more than 50 years ago, by our mentor, friend, and colleague, **Dr. Ralph Nichols**, Professor Emeritus at the University of Minnesota. Widely known as "The Father of the Field of Listening," Dr. Nichols' pioneering and far-reaching research identified measurable characteristics of effective and ineffective listeners. Over the decades, this assessment has been widely utilized, with no significant change in results. In short, despite a multitude of societal changes, productive and unproductive listeners of the present look like their counterparts of the past.

Listening Leader Profile IV

To gain a preliminary insight into your listening behaviors, the following assessment will clarify your tendencies and habits. One way to become a better listening leader is to analyze the habits that separate effective listeners from ineffective listeners. In general, as a listening leader, how often do you find yourself engaging in these listening habits?

Listening Habits	Frequency (Check Only One)				
	Almost Always	Usually	Sometimes	Seldom	Almost Never
1. Calling the subject uninteresting?	❏	❏	❏	❏	❏
2. Criticizing the speaker's delivery or mannerisms?	❏	❏	❏	❏	❏
3. Getting overstimulated by something the speaker says?	❏	❏	❏	❏	❏

	Almost Always	Usually	Sometimes	Seldom	Almost Never
4. Listening primarily for facts?	❏	❏	❏	❏	❏
5. Trying to outline everything?	❏	❏	❏	❏	❏
6. Faking attention to the speaker?	❏	❏	❏	❏	❏
7. Allowing interfering distractions?	❏	❏	❏	❏	❏
8. Avoiding difficult material?	❏	❏	❏	❏	❏
9. Letting emotions arouse your personal antagonism?	❏	❏	❏	❏	❏
10. Wasting the advantage of thought-speed (daydreaming)?	❏	❏	❏	❏	❏

Listening Habits Profile Scoring Key

▶ For every "ALMOST ALWAYS" checked, add 2 points.

▶ For every "USUALLY" checked, add 4 points.

▶ For every "SOMETIMES" checked, add 6 points.

▶ For every "SELDOM" checked, add 8 points.

▶ For every "ALMOST NEVER" checked, add 10 points.

Add up all 10 items for a Total Score of _____.

WHAT YOUR PROFILE ANSWERS AND SCORES MEAN

Listening Leader Profile I

A▶ Eighty-five percent of all the listeners we have surveyed over the last 50 years have rated themselves as Average or less. Fewer than five percent rate themselves as Excellent or Superior. Yet listening leaders have little difficulty in rating themselves significantly Above Average with respect to other leadership activities and traits.

B▶ On the numerical scale of 0–100, we find the extreme scores range from 10–90. For most listeners, the general range is usually 35 to 85, with an average rating of 55.

Listening Leader Profile II

An interesting pattern emerges from the thousands of listener responses we have analyzed. Comparing the listening self-ratings with the projected ratings of others, we find that most individuals believe their best friend would rate them highest as a listener. Moreover, they believe such a rating would be substantially higher than how they rated themselves in Profile I, where the average rating is 55. Perhaps there is a tendency to assume that best-friend status is a special relationship that could not exist without the commitment to listen. In addition, over the years, we have discovered a general correlation of descending scores. When considering their boss, most people believe their boss would rate them higher than they rate themselves. Perhaps that perception is based largely on wishful thinking. On the other hand, we find most individuals generally do listen better to their leaders rather than to others because of the consequences if they don't. Projected scores for colleagues and direct reports generally mirror how people rate themselves, on average 55. When considering their spouse, most people believe their spouse would rate them significantly lower than they rate themselves. Compared to self-ratings, a strange and disturbing picture emerges where overall projected scores of spouses are significantly lower than the average score of 55. Interestingly, newlyweds tend to believe their spouse would rate them significantly better than they rate themselves, comparable to how their best friend would rate them, but the assumption generally declines dramatically in proportion to the years of marriage.

The descriptive words listeners believe others would use to describe them run the gamut of exceedingly positive to neutral to extremely negative. As you can imagine, the projected descriptions generally correspond to the numerical score and the nature of the relationship.

To gain a deeper insight into your actual listening leader behavior and habits, you can extend your assessment by actually asking the important people in your life to rate and describe you as a listener. You may be surprised, as some whom you believe would rate and describe you better than you see yourself, do not. On the other hand, some may perceive you as a better listener than you think. In either case, you will gain greater clarity and create a real benchmark to modify and establish more productive listening habits.

Listening Leader Profile III

Consideration of whom you envision as the *best* and *worst* listeners you know provides two advantages. First, your judgment will provide a high and low standard to which you can compare yourself. Second, you will have a broader and deeper set of criteria to utilize as you undertake the refinement and establishment of productive and profitable listening leader habits. As our **Golden**

Circle of Listening Leaders have identified, the importance of studying the productive habits of role models has been, is, and will continue to be extremely valuable and important.

Listening Leader Profile IV

Results from the thousands of leaders who have completed this Listening Habits Profile produced an average score of 62. As you evaluate your answers and your score, consider the impact of your habits. If you scored:

92–100   Congratulations! You are a superb listener who understands and utilizes the power of listening. Your listening habits serve your leadership well and deserve conscious repetition.

80–90   Well done. You are significantly above average in practicing effective listening habits. As you continue to engage your productive habits, you will enhance your leadership impact. Additional focus on your listening limitations will provide additional gains worth your investment.

70–78   Consider yourself an above-average listener. Your habits serve you better than most; however, you have specific negative listening habits that negate your positive and productive leadership habits. With special attention, willingness, and practice, you can quickly increase your score.

60–68   Get ready to work, because you fall into the land of average. As a listener, the bad news/ good news should be clear. The bad news is the simple fact that average listening will relegate you to the average rank of leaders. The good news is, you have identified specific opportunities for development. Moreover, your conscious investment will provide significant returns. Average listeners hold the potential and opportunity to benefit from quantum gain. By putting your energies into building new listening habits, you will profit immensely.

Below 60 The further you score below the average of 62, the greater your challenge. Your task is formidable, yet clear and simple. First, identify your limited areas of listening strengths and solidify and hone your positive habits. Second, focus on the critical areas where you scored lowest. Third, recognize the negative impact and establish a specific game plan to move the negative behaviors and habits to neutral and then to positive. Finally, track the results and rewards of changing the negative habits to positive habits.

In sum, regardless of how you scored on any of the Listening Profiles, your challenge lies in affirming the items on which you scored the highest and building on your success. In addition, it is equally important to focus on the areas in which you scored the lowest.

William Wordsworth said it best, "Habit rules the unreflecting herd." Three steps will serve you as you step outside the herd of listening habits. As always, the first step is awareness and recognition. What are your positive and negative habits? The second step is acknowledging situations wherein negative listening habits cause leadership problems. Of course, the third step is identifying workable solutions and taking action.

> *"Habit rules the unreflecting herd."*
> —William Wordsworth

Jack Bitzer is a former executive with Sawtek Corporation. One of his avocational passions includes coaching softball. Extending his professional and fine-tuned vocational skills, Jack shared the importance of building positive listening habits with his young players. As Jack clearly understands, "It absolutely takes time to change. It is not like turning a light switch on; maybe it's more like a dimmer switch. As I put a set of expectations together for our team, I reinforced the importance of listening." Jack Bitzer's commitment to creating productive habits from the outset is a leadership model worth emulating.

FOLLOWING WISE LEADERS

An old proverb speaks to the relevance of awareness, habits, and development.

"Some know not, and
Know not that they know not.
They are fools…shun them;

Some know not, and
Know that they know not.
They are simple…teach them;

Some know, and
Know not that they know.
They are asleep…wake them;

Some know, and
Know that they know.
They are wise…follow them."

To follow the wise and better understand the process of listening leadership, we invite you to apply the following specific action steps. As you do, your listening behavior will be enhanced. As noted, **Dr. Ralph G. Nichols** identified a number of approaches to improving listening behaviors. Over the years, as we have expanded the "Minnesota Model," we have helped listening leaders build their skills and, in turn, profit by diligently practicing the following 10 proven habits of effective listening.

1. Find areas of interest.

Listening leaders are searchers and seekers. They cultivate a listening habit of curiosity. Although they recognize the simple reality, 'We cannot listen to all people talk on all things at all times," productive listeners are careful not to turn off their listening prematurely. They listen optimistically and seek to share the speaker's enthusiasm for and interest in the subject. Ineffective listeners prejudge certain topics as boring or uninteresting, and quickly tune them out. Skilled listeners realize that no matter how dull the subject may appear at first glance, it may contain valuable "**nuggets of gold**." Effective listeners are selfish in the best sense of the word. They understand and utilize the **Value Moment of Listening (VM of L)** reality. It has been said, "If you want one ounce of gold, you discard 200,000 tons of rubble. If you want one karat of flawless diamond, you also throw away 200,000 tons of rock. If you want the oil, you have to discard the sludge. If you want the wheat, you must separate the chaff." In listening, you will never find the value moments until you fully listen. So the searchers and seekers are constantly listening for messages and ideas of interest. They ask, "What's in it for me?" "How can I relate this message to something I'm already interested in, and how can I use it?"

Poor listeners prematurely tune out speakers, and may carelessly lose opportunities for personal growth or for new perspectives. There is a great difference between the behaviors of listening leaders and poor listeners when they are confronted with supposedly dry, dull, and boring material. As Listening

Legend, **Carole Grau** so aptly observed, "Like the gold miners of the past, present-day listening miners discover untold treasures of information and insight by simply listening and digging."

> *"Like the gold miners of the past, present-day listening miners discover untold treasures of information and insight by simply listening and digging."*
> —Carole Grau

The 20th Century industrialist, known as the "captain of industry and king of steel," **Andrew Carnegie** held a similar view. "When you mine gold, you don't go into the mountain looking for dirt. You look for gold, no matter how small, or how much dirt you have to push aside." This single consideration, the factor and habit of interest, distinguishes the behavior of effective listeners and provides many clues for methods of improving your own listening behaviors. Following

INTEREST FACTOR CHART

Listening Leaders	Nonlistening Leaders
▶ *Look for the VM of L*	▶ *Are Not Interested*
▶ *Search for Areas that Excite*	▶ *Decide it's Boring or Dull*
▶ *Tune In*	▶ *Tune Out*
▶ *Keep an Open Mind*	▶ *Prejudge Topics*
▶ *Listen Whole-heartedly*	▶ *Listen Half-Heartedly*
▶ *Stay with the Speaker*	▶ *Daydream*
▶ *Create Interest*	▶ *Tell Themselves they are Bored*
▶ *Sit Close & Stay Alert*	▶ *Sit Far Away & are Disconnected*
▶ *Plan to Report Back*	▶ *Have Nothing to Report*

is an **Interest Factor Chart**, which clarifies the contrasting attitudes of effective listening leaders and poor listeners.

The lesson in this striking contrast is that you must be aware of your behavior when your interest is at a low level. If you continually catch yourself calling a topic, speaker, or presentation dry, dull, boring, or uninteresting, you are moving toward the habitual behavior of poor listeners. If you consistently behave in an uninterested manner, you will consistently hear less, process less, understand less, evaluate less, and respond less to potentially valuable messages. If you choose to lead others, break away from these nonproductive behaviors and listen with interest. **David Erickson**, the energetic second-generation President of Erickson Oil, has discovered the value of searching, seeking, and positioning for many years. As David noted,

> *"For the last 15 years, I have always sat in the front or second row of presentations, even though I'm not hard of hearing. It shows consideration for speakers and lets them know I am interested in what they have to say."*
> *—David Erickson*

"For the last 15 years, I have always sat in the front or second row of presentations, even though I'm not hard of hearing. It shows consideration for speakers and lets them know I am interested in what they have to say. It sends a message that I am ready to learn." Listening and learning go hand in hand, and it all starts with interest. In addition, interest and listening lead to excitement, influence, and impact."

A perfect example of expressing interest in others was highlighted by **Dale Carnegie** in his popular book, *How to Win Friends and Influence People*, which has sold more than 10 million copies and continues to reinforce the importance of listening. Reflecting on the constant interest and attention displayed by his childhood dog, Tippy, Carnegie made the important observation, "You can make more friends in two months by becoming genuinely interested in other people than you can in two years by trying to get people interested in you." As Carnegie noted, "Most people are not interested in you. They are not interested in me. They are interested in themselves—morning, noon, and evening."

> *"It's not so much technique as it is her gift of focus, attention and presence. In the presence of such people, you feel fantastically complete."*
> *—Richard Anstruther*

In the same vein, when asked to identify the very best listener he had ever met in his life, listening leader **Richard Anstruther**, responded, "A good friend of mine stands out because she doesn't interrupt. She doesn't correct and she doesn't edit. She's really pleasant, and she's curious. For example, if you gave her a gift, she would stay with the gift and be curious about it, curious about the context of it, and where it came from, and who made it. She has the ability to be able to clear her mind. It's not so much technique as it is her gift of focus, attention, and presence. In the presence of such people, you feel fantastically complete."

2. Judge content, not delivery.

In this world of more than 6 billion people, there are effective speakers and ineffective speakers; those who express themselves fluently, and those who have difficulty expressing a coherent idea. Effective listening leaders focus primarily on the content of a message and consider the delivery as secondary. The charismatic speaker may have nothing profound to say, even though he or she may say it in a very appealing manner. The person who impresses us with the air of authority may still be wrong.

On the other hand, the unpolished speaker, the one with irritating mannerisms, the one who speaks too slowly, the one with the bizarre appearance, may have something of great value to say. As speakers' content varies, so will our attention to other things that have nothing to do with the content. These are called noncontent items. Poor listeners become distracted on these noncontent items. They focus primarily on the speaker's appearance, accent or dialect, mannerisms and delivery style, or what the speaker is wearing. Poor listeners are unable to focus on the main thing, the message content. They consistently pay attention to nonessential items such as the peculiarities of the speaker, the distractions of the room or area, the other people in the room, their inner thoughts and ideas, and their own physical condition. Listening leaders consistently and primarily focus on the content. They are aware they will not be held accountable for non-content items. They seek the value in every message they choose to listen to, no matter how it is delivered. What do you do? Practice focusing on the content and catch yourself when noncontent dominates your behavior in listening situations. As you focus on content, you will discover the important "value moments of listening."

3. Don't jump to conclusions.

We all have opinions about almost everything we hear. Sometimes they are weak opinions we are barely aware of. At other times, they are strong opinions about people and topics and we make quick judgments, both positive and negative, about what we are hearing. We quickly respond with our own opinion to others, or to ourselves. Listening leaders act quite differently than do ineffective listeners when it comes to jumping to conclusions. Poor listeners often become overstimulated when the subject hits their pet bias, favorite subject, or pet peeve. They may get angry and respond by arguing. They become preoccupied with their own enthusiasm for or against the speaker or topic. They may daydream. They may interrupt the speaker. Jumping to conclusions seriously blocks effective listening because it stops the listening process.

Listening leaders avoid making judgments until they fully comprehend the message. They don't let their enthusiasm or anger or any other emotion blur their focus on hearing the speaker through. Listening leaders do not become overstimulated. They maintain control; their motto is "Understand first, make judgments later!" To what extent do you become overstimulated easily when you listen to others? Are you able to withhold judgment until you have received and understood the entire message? Listening leaders recognize the speaker's message may be totally opposed to their own viewpoint. They develop the patience to truly understand the intent and meaning of the speaker's message before making their ultimate evaluation. The listening leaders' perspective is, "Withhold your judgment until your comprehension is complete."

4. Listen for the main point of the message.

The incessant flow of daily messages includes a mixture of ideas, facts, truths, half-truths, principles, statistics, information, and anecdotes. Effective and ineffective listeners listen to the same message, but they focus on different things. Poor listeners have a tendency to listen only for facts and often miss the central ideas. Principles and concepts are often ignored. As ineffective listeners conclude there are too many facts to remember, they become frustrated, overpowered, and quit.

Listening leaders have an entirely different focus. They listen for central ideas. They identify the speaker's purpose and listen for main themes. Listening leaders also hear the factual information, but since they organize it around the main theme, they usually remember many more facts than the ineffective listeners. Effective listeners understand speakers' facts and details are not meant to be ends in themselves. They lead to and support the main point. Thus, listening leaders search for the framework of the speaker's message. For example, when listening to a message, the effective listening leader may reflect, "Why am I being told that fact? What does it lead to? Does this idea relate to any other?" Such active searching for the main point becomes crucial when you're listening to speakers who love detail and who pile on one fact after another without making the main points clear. Here we find one of the listening leader's greatest challenges. Poor listeners drown in details and never get the larger message. Effective listening leaders concentrate on refining the habit of listening for main points.

Of course some listening leaders have an extraordinary capacity to listen to the total message for sustained periods of time. In his Air Force flying days, four star **General Jack Chain** was known as "Fang." Over the course of his distinguished career, General Chain rose to serve to lead the U.S. Strategic Air Command (SAC) and had the rich opportunity to listen to, and be listened to, by a multitude of highly positioned leaders. In Jack's words, no one listened as well, and with such rapt focus, as **Secretary of State George Schultz**. "We had the opportunity to listen to each other for hours-on-end, and Secretary Schultz had the capacity to capture both the main message and the minutest of details. His eyeballs had a way of boring into your skull and he never missed an item of importance. Everyone was honored to talk with George because he truly listened. He cared about your point of view and focused on the total message. In turn, other leaders made a concentrated effort to listen to him."

Listening leader **Dr. Phan Quoc Viet** of Vietnam formerly served as the Director of HanoiPetro. He vividly remembers a three-day personal meeting with the former Vietnam Prime Minister, Mr. Vo Van Kiet.

He is my role model of an excellent listening leader. I had an unforgettable encounter with him that demonstrated his listening and feedback power. When he became Prime Minister of Vietnam, I was an employee of the Vietnam Oil and Gas Corporation and had an

> *"It still amazes me that for three full days, Mr. Kiet mostly listened. As a consequence, he made important decisions in personnel relocation in Vietnam's biggest state-owned Oil and Gas Corporation."*
> —*Dr. Phan Quoc Viet*

invitation to speak to him about our operation. It still amazes me that for three full days, Mr. Kiet mostly listened. As a consequence, he made important decisions in personnel relocation in Vietnam's largest state-owned Oil and Gas Corporation.

Regardless of their position or rank, listening leaders constantly focus on the main points. In the process they capture the basics of every message.

5. Take notes, but adjust your note-taking to the speaker.

While listening, most individuals usually take notes in their head. When effective listeners make a mental note to do something or remember something, it generally works quite well. A productive member of our **Golden Circle of Listening Leaders** is **Larry Humes**, Vice President of Collegis, the leading provider of comprehensive business, technology, and curriculum services to higher education.

Larry is an outstanding communicator and leader and observed firsthand the ability of a quiet leader we all knew well, **Mr. Rogers,** to make mental notes.

> *"Fred Rogers was more than a great listener to children. He was really a great listener to all people. When you were in his presence, he was totally focused on you."*
>
> —*Larry Humes*

A person who impressed me with his listening skills was Fred Rogers, the star for more than 30 years of the extraordinary television show, "Mr. Rogers' Neighborhood." When you were in his presence, he was totally focused on you. It is uncanny how much he focused on what you were saying and how he gave you feedback. He would come back to you a year later and tell you things from that previous conversation. Fred Rogers was more than a great listener to children. He was really a great listener to all people.

As a testament to his note-taking skill *The World According to Mister Rogers*, was published in 2003 and highlighted some of Fred's profound thoughts including, "The purpose of life is to listen—to yourself, to your neighbor, to your world, and to God and, when the time comes, to respond in as helpful a way as you can find...from within and without." Note-taking preserves great thoughts.

Obviously, when it is necessary to listen to an extensive amount of material, when the message is complex, and when the stakes are very high, most leaders cannot depend on mental notes alone. Written notes are the answer. The act of taking written notes rivets listening. Moreover, taking written notes reproduces information that can be reviewed at a later date and can enhance learning. Our research is clear; some individuals are more skilled at note-taking than others. In addition, we have discovered leaders' effectiveness increases dramatically with training and advancement in listening and taking more effective notes. Finally, there are observable, measurable, and definite differences in the way listening leaders and poor listeners take notes. The single major difference is, effective listeners actually take notes; ineffective listeners do not. In addition, when poor listeners do take notes, they are ineffective for five main reasons: 1) they are not aware of speaker patterns; 2) they do not adapt to the speaker's organizational structure; 3) they attempt to take too many notes; 4) they take full-sentence notes and attempt to write down too many facts; and, 5) they do not review their notes.

Progressive and effective listening leaders understand that poor note-taking and poor listening are interrelated, and consciously and continually engage in activities that refine their note-taking skills. Listening leaders profit from being good note-takers, as they typically take fewer notes than poor listeners, but their notes are more meaningful. They are flexible and adapt their notes to the speaker's organizational structure. They seek and find the patterns and main ideas and fit the supporting facts into place. They also review their notes later to review, refresh, and recapture the key points. Learning how to take pertinent and relevant notes will help you listen and lead more effectively.

6. Pay attention.

It is difficult to give all of your attention to all of the people all of the time, as total attention requires a great deal of energy. However, listening leaders give genuine, sincere, and heightened attention to every listening situation in which they choose to engage. Effective listening leaders expend a great deal of energy paying attention. They work hard at diligently tracking the speaker; not just appearing to listen attentively. They develop a learning mindset built around authentic interest and a legitimate orientation of other-centeredness. They truly see each person they come in contact with as having potential value.

Listening leader, **Dick Knowlton**, is a native of Austin, Minnesota, where he went to work at Hormel Corporation at the age of 16. Over the years, Dick became President, Chairman and CEO, led more than 10,000 employees, and grew sales to more than $4 billion. Along the way, Dick received numerous awards and honors. Now retired, Dick Knowlton remembered a listening leader role model who paid authentic attention and greatly affected the careers of many.

Bob Grey was the President of Hormel and a wonderful man. When I was still in high school, he called me up and said, "I'd like to have you come over." I put on my old corduroys with a patch on them and went over to his office. In those days, Hormel had a large open corporate office, and Mr. Grey sat right out there amongst all the people. He wanted to talk to me about my future. He knew I had worked in the plant and had some interest in the company. Mr. Grey also knew I was a member of the National Honor Society and played football. He wanted to know what I was going to do. I thought, "Wow, what a guy, to take an interest in little me." I was just a nobody with seven brothers and sisters who lived in a four-room house near the packing plant. Although I was young, I wondered, "Why does a man at his level take such an interest in others?"

> "I thought, 'Wow, what a guy, to take an interest in little me.' I was just a nobody, with seven brothers and sisters who lived in a four-room house near the packing plant. Although I was young, I wondered, why does a man at his level take such an interest in others?
>
> Over the years, I learned both why and how… [He] was a perfect role model of a leader who cared, paid attention, and listened."
>
> —Dick Knowlton

Over the years, I learned both why and how. As he listened to me, he took notes. He didn't really tell me what to do, but his interest and attention affected my life and career. Over the years, I watched him listen to others as he changed the ethics of the business. Bob Grey was a perfect role model of a leader who cared, paid attention, and listened.

On the other hand, poor listeners drift in and out, depending on their level of focus. Obviously, when they are "out," they lose potential value moments of listening. They do not expend the effort necessary to pay attention. They can look you in the eye and not hear a word. Faking attention is a bad habit that will rob your understanding. Keep in mind, when you "pay" attention, in exchange, you "receive" the value in return. Don't let yourself fake it.

Pastor **Mike Stone** is Senior Pastor of Mt. Pisgah Lutheran Church in Hickory, North Carolina. He understands the value and importance of paying attention. Moreover, he has a strategy that serves him and the numerous individuals to whom he listens to well.

> *"It's impossible to listen to other people without taking the time to do it. Listening leaders make and take time to listen, time to digest what has been said, and time to respond."*
> —*Pastor Mike Stone*

It's impossible to listen to other people without taking the time to do it. Listening leaders make and take time to listen, time to digest what has been said, and time to respond. Often, one of the worst mistakes pastors or business people can make is to say, "I just don't have time to listen to what the consumers, or customers, or members of the congregation are saying." Of course, from my perspective, a bigger challenge is when we do not make time to listen to God. That would be the worst-case scenario. Attention takes time.

Vicki Lavendol is the Director of Leadership and Training for Gaylord Palms Resort & Convention Center. Over the years, she has served in Human Resource Development roles at Walt Disney World and Charles Schwab, and understands the importance and value of extending full attention to whomever we choose to listen to. Vicki described her General Manager, **John Caparella**, as an incredible listener and told us about her initial interview and the level of attention he showed to her.

John totally focuses his attention on you as a speaker. He listens completely and is very careful to maintain an intense focus on you when you are talking with him. He has maintained this level of focused attention every time I have met with him since. He looks you right in the eye, completely focused on hearing what you say, and listens completely. Because his listening behavior is so different from what you typically receive, it takes you aback a little bit. It is like someone is listening to your inner thoughts. As a speaker, I am very thoughtful about what I say because he is so thoughtful about listening to me.

> *"Because his listening behavior is so different from what you typically receive, it takes you aback a little bit. As a speaker, I am very thoughtful about what I say because he is so thoughtful about listening to me."*
> —*Vicki Lavendol*

Listening leaders find it takes less energy to fully attend to every speaker to whom they choose to listen. Faking attention demands a greater expenditure of energy than simply focusing and attending. More importantly, when listening leaders pay greater attention, they place themselves in a position to lead with positive impact.

7. Resist Distractions.

We live in a world that is filled with distractions, some of which will inevitably be present whenever and wherever we attempt to listen. Distractions overpower and disrupt the unprepared listener. For years, we have observed that effective listening leaders and poor listeners deal quite differently with distractions. Poor listeners tolerate distractions. They do not identify or remove them, and they do not fight them or challenge them. Poor listeners simply allow themselves to be distracted! They are overpowered by the distractions and do nothing. On the other hand, effective listening leaders proactively identify distractions and take action to minimize or eliminate them.

As introduced earlier, an important concept to master and practice is the VM of L (Value Moment of Listening). The required constant search for VM of Ls recognizes that we will never know the precise moment an important fact or idea may be presented in any message. Value moments ultimately reside with the listener, and listening leaders are constantly vigilant. In the process, they reduce the impact of distractions, increase note-taking, heighten and intensify their concentration, and thereby enhance the value they receive.

8. Exercise your mind.

When it comes to challenging listening situations, ineffective listeners and effective listening leaders respond in very different ways. Poor listeners avoid such challenges. They listen mostly to simplistic messages and deliberately avoid difficult material. They listen primarily to easy messages, and when the difficult speakers appear, they cannot handle them.

Listening leaders seek out the challenging and difficult. They consciously and constantly exercise their minds' listening muscle.

Because they practice consistently, they are fully prepared for any difficult listening situation. How challenged are you by difficult and complex topics and messages? To what extent do you avoid difficult listening situations? It is important to remember that listening leaders constantly seek challenging listening opportunities.

Michael Matheny is the Manager of Corporate Media for SunTrust Bank. His team produces instructional media for training, marketing, and employee communications. In addition, Michael is responsible for producing a variety of programs for internal clients, and for the organization's external clients. Headquartered in Atlanta, Georgia, SunTrust Banks, Inc. is one of the nation's largest commercial banking organizations with total assets of more than $120 billion and total deposits exceeding $77 billion. Michael highlights the value of exercising listening strengths and weaknesses.

It is important to be conscious of your listening behavior. Listening leaders understand the importance of knowing both their strengths and weaknesses. When you clarify your specific strengths and weaknesses, you will be in position to focus, take corrective action, and be a better listener and leader. We all need to motivate ourselves to listen to topics that may not be of major interest.

> *"We all need to motivate ourselves to listen to topics that may not be of major interest. It takes preparation to mentally prepare yourself for full-body listening."*
> —Michael Matheny

Often others will give you invaluable wisdom about how to do things better if you just listen. It takes discipline to mentally prepare yourself for full-body listening. Not just with your ears, but with your eyes, with your heart, and all of your senses.

9. Check your emotions.

Effective listening leaders understand that listeners cannot avoid emotional reactions. You can, however, keep them from interfering with your productive listening leadership. One thing is certain, everyone's emotions will, at some time, be triggered by what they hear. Poor listeners, however, allow their positive or negative emotions to undermine their listening effectiveness. They often operate with closed minds. They let emotions take over and interfere with listening. When they are angry with the subject, speaker, or language, they react emotionally and miss both the purpose and message. Likewise, the same thing happens when positive emotions control the listener. Again, emotional listeners miss the purpose and message. Compounding the negative impact of emotionality, we have found that ineffective listeners usually are unaware of their emotional triggers.

Effective listening leaders know themselves, and they know where they are emotionally vulnerable. They know how to keep their positive and negative emotions in check, and thus are more effective listening leaders. They focus on the subject rather than on what they disagree with. Listening leaders withhold judgment until comprehension is complete. To what extent can you control your emotional hot spots when you listen to others?

Hal Kantor is a Senior Partner in the law firm Lowndes, Drosdick, Doster, Kantor & Reed, P.A., specializing in real property practice. Hal's full-service law firm serves statewide, national and international clients, and is a founding member of MERITAS, formerly known as Commercial Law Affiliates. MERITAS is a global network of approximately 200 independent full-service law firms located in major metropolitan areas throughout the world.

Our business is deeply involved with controversial issues affecting large numbers of people, who often are opposed to what we are trying to get accomplished. Our task largely requires convincing our clients, elected officials, and appointed officials to take certain actions. In the process, we are often faced with hundreds of people who may attack us. Although the emotions are obvious, there's often an element of validity to their concerns. It is important to cut through the emotions, to let them drain out of the situation so we can address their concerns and deal with valid issues. This is something we are faced with all the time. Emotional control is difficult but necessary.

There is no acceptable win-lose situation in our business. We must reach win-win conclusions. There are always three or more groups that must be satisfied. First is those who are opposed or hostile to our position. Second is the elected and the appointed leadership individuals. Third is our clients. In addition, the press is often engaged, with its tendency to "stir the emotional pot." In some cases, there are individuals who are so emotional they do not listen and cannot agree, be convinced, or convince others. In these cases, no one wins. If you can get people to sit down with each other and recognize and listen through their emotions, good things usually happen.

> *"If you can get people to sit down with each other and recognize and listen through their emotions, good things usually happen."*
>
> —Hal Kantor

10. Utilize the Gap Between Speech Speed and Listening Speed.

For more than 50 years, technology has existed to "compress or speed up speech." Whether by systematic or selective deletion, research indicates the average person can listen and comprehend up to 400 words per minute without substantial loss of comprehension. That is nearly three to four times faster than the average person speaks. Frenetic speech used in radio advertisement qualifiers notwithstanding, most individuals speak at a rate between 125 and 180 words per minute, averaging around 160 words per minute. Thus the average listener has "extra" time to either waste or utilize. If you listen at the rate of a rabbit while the speaker speaks at the pace of a turtle, it becomes easy to waste your listening energy and your precious thinking-time advantage. Listening leaders do not waste it, they use it. Poor listeners loaf when they could be listening more effectively. They do not become active and do not use the thought-speed/speech-speed advantage well. Ineffective listeners daydream. In addition, poor listeners buy into the myth of multitasking and attempt to focus on multiple agendas. They know they can think faster than others speak, so they try to focus on several things. They get bored and often go off on mental tangents while they wait for the speaker to catch up. Daydreaming and tangential activities are common among poor listeners.

On the other hand, listening leaders have developed a variety of strategies to stay with the pace of the speaker and not drift off. Among other things, they evaluate, anticipate, review, and summarize **(EARS).** In addition, they **Plan to Report (PTR).** Listening leaders identify and make a personal commitment to share the essence of what they listen to with a specific individual within 24 hours. They take notes. They question and clarify. In short, they do whatever it takes to use the time on their hands and mind to stay with the speaker, capture greater information, and glean deeper values. In the tortoise-and-hare world of speaking and listening, a key determinant of effectiveness lies in what you do with your thought-speed versus speech-speed advantage. It is the classic case of use it or lose it. You can use it to your advantage and profit, or not.

Misty Haggard-Belford is a great example of a listening leader who, although inundated daily with multiple messages, thoughtfully takes advantage of her thought-speed advantage while listening. Misty is a Campaign Manager with United Way and works with 100 to 150 corporations per year, to educate them about services available in their local communities. In addition, she seeks donations of time and money.

> *"Because I am willing to take the time to listen effectively, I probably have access to more information than most people because people are willing to share."*
> —Misty Haggard-Belford

Misty is focused, works hard, and prides herself on the positive listening habits she has developed over the years.

Because I am willing to take the time to listen effectively, I probably have greater access to more information than most people because people are willing to share. I also think people tend to seek me out and look for my leadership because of my listening habits. In addition, when I take more time and respond appropriately, more consideration seems to be given to my feedback.

HABITS ARE FOREVER

As you choose to follow the lead of effective listening leaders and consciously shape your listening habits, the foregoing 10 habits deserve your daily attention and commitment. Profiles I, II, III, and IV are designed to be completed and reviewed regularly. Like most complex skills, listening can be studied and practiced throughout one's entire life; there will always be room for improvement. Although we will expand on the following thought in Chapter 4, one crucial point remains to be made.

In defining and understanding listening, one must distinguish between the *ability* to listen and the *willingness* to listen. Your ability to listen is one thing, while your willingness to listen is an attitude, which goes beyond the matter of listening proficiency and technique. Many who are highly skilled in listening are unwilling to listen in certain situations. On the other hand, a person who is willing to listen, but has no idea how to fully engage the task, is in a similar position. In both cases, effective listening will not be accomplished. Clearly, both ability and willingness are necessary habits to establish and hone.

THE POINT

As **Chuck Maragos** aptly observed, "As habits form silently, constantly, and relentlessly, their pervasive impacts are often unnoticed. Yet they control our life. Some habits are positive and serve us well, and some are negative and do us harm."

> *"The unending obstacle to individual growth is habit."*
> —*John Stuart Mill*

As you continue to prepare and build your foundations through advanced attitudes, skills, and knowledge, your focus on developing your listening leader habits will pay off. John Stuart Mill, said it best when he clearly stated, "The unending obstacle to individual growth is habit." The preparation is simple, practice **Golden Rule 3: "Listening Leaders Develop Impactful Habits"** and you will Listen, Lead, and Succeed.

Golden Rule **3**

"LISTENING LEADERS DEVELOP IMPACTFUL HABITS"

10 ACTION STEPS

1. Complete, analyze, and frequently review your Listening Leader Profiles I, II, III, and IV.

2. List and consistently practice your habitual positive listening strengths.

3. List and vigorously eliminate your habitual negative listening weaknesses.

4. Seek and record specific Value Moments of Listening (VM of Ls) in every message.

5. Record all specific costs that result from your negative listening habits.

6. Summarize the main point of every communication to which you listen.

7. Apply the "Plan to Report" strategy to all the messages to which you listen.

8. Categorize and raise the level of difficulty of the messages you listen to in a typical day.

9. Develop and activate an action plan to reinforce your positive listening habits and eliminate your negative listening habits.

10. Build your "Listening Organization" by daily teaching and modeling impactful listening habits.

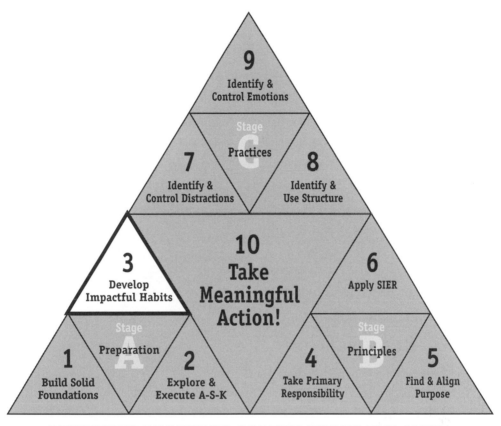

LISTENING LEADERS™ GOLDEN RULES PYRAMID

Golden Rule 4

"Listening Leaders Take Primary Responsibility"

"Accepting ultimate responsibility is the key to effective listening and leading. I have a responsibility to stay motivated, focused and growing as a listening leader because nobody can do it for me. I must become a better listener. In addition, as a leader, I must help my partners grow as listeners as we build a listening organization together."

—Jay Ard

Jay Ard understands the importance responsibility plays in advancing listening leadership. A 24-year veteran of Coca-Cola Enterprises, the world's largest marketer, distributor, and producer of soft drinks, Jay Ard serves as the Vice President and General Manager of the 4,400 employees in the Florida Division of Coca-Cola. Jay believes assuming primary responsibility is the core requirement for leaders at every level. Personal responsibility begins with conscious focus, continues through constant growth and improvement, and ends with heightened action and impact. Taking primary responsibility is the first extension from **Stage A of Listening Leaders Preparation**, to establishing a cornerstone for **Stage B of Listening Leaders Principles**. As Jay observed,

> I constantly try to stay focused to have a positive impact on the people around me by stretching myself to

be the best I can be. When I reflect on how I have managed to advance from working on the trucks of Coca Cola to the General Manager position, I realize that I have been blessed by a Greater Being. Accepting ultimate responsibility is the key to effective listening and leading. I have a responsibility to stay motivated, focused, and growing as a listening leader because nobody can do it for me. I must continually become a better listener. In addition, as a leader, I must help my partners become better listeners and leaders as we build a productive listening organization together.

In every organization, leaders have the primary responsibility to practice what they preach and to help the organization grow. Generally speaking, whatever is important to the leader will be important to the organization. Listening will be a priority for everyone in our organization if it is a priority for me. Listening will be something everyone will want to work on and improve. It is my responsibility to make sure the development of listening is placed in the forefront of our daily activities. To that end, I need to extend my commitment for unending individual and organizational growth of listening responsibility.

Individual responsibility is more important than ever as we seek honest and constructive feedback from employees about how we are doing, where we are going, and how they will be involved in the evolution of where we are trying to take the company. As part of our action plan, each of our Sales Center Managers holds regularly scheduled listening sessions in the field. Each listening session is more than a formality, as each Sales Center Manager is charged with the responsibility for sharing action plans that result from each listening session. Increased responsibility heightens listening accountability on everyone's part. Seventy percent of my managers and sales staff are accepting responsibility; 20 percent are lukewarm; and, 10 percent don't want to play and will be weeded out."

Jay Ard understands that listening consumes a substantial percentage of every leader's day.

Years of research indicates listening leaders spend nearly 80 percent of their working days communicating; with the majority of time invested in listening. Understanding the great amount of time leaders invest in listening raises the importance of assuming primary responsibility.

In his book, *Be Your Own Executive Coach*, **Peter deLisser** reinforces the importance of responsibility with an anecdote about Senator Bill Bradley, the former great New York Knick basketball player. In discussing the main reason for his success, Bradley stated, "I always knew where I was on the court." Like Bradley, all leaders profit when they take responsibility for knowing where they are, at any moment, in every communication. The result is powerful. Assumption of responsibility leads to focus; focus enlarges the listener's perspective; and greater perspective results in more productive action.

This principle becomes clearer for listening leaders when they fully understand and actively manage the nine core components of the communication process. The meaning of "communication" flows from the Latin word *communis*, and simply implies the achievement of "connection or commonality." In its simplest form, communication involves the connection or achievement of common meaning between senders and receivers. However, to illustrate the greater complexity and challenge facing every listening leader, the following model identifies nine elements that are manageable and directly related to the process of listening and leading.

COMPONENTS OF HUMAN COMMUNICATION

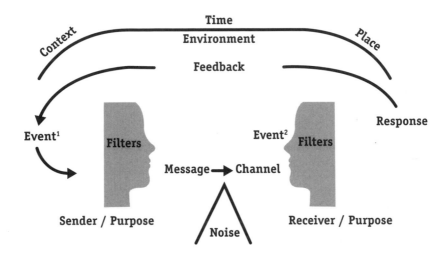

1 & 2. Sender and Receiver: Every communication involves a sender and a receiver. The roles are interchangeable and knowing how often and how well one performs each role affects the responsible listening leader's effectiveness. Although the model of communication illustrates the sender and receiver as two people, it can involve one, two, a few, or many individuals engaging in communication. Sometimes, communication involves only one person, as most leaders periodically talk to themselves. At other moments, the model represents a multitude of individuals listening to a single speaker. Understanding how you respond to various events as either a sender or receiver will enhance your responsible performance in both roles.

3. **Purpose:** Senders and receivers communicate on purpose. Discerning the specific reasons for, and respective purposes of, every communication enhances the focus and affects both sender and receiver behaviors. Listening leaders must assume the responsibility for identifying the purpose of both the sender and receiver. As we will discuss in Chapter Five, identifying, connecting, and adapting to the five different purposes (Phatic, Cathartic, Informational, Persuasive, and Entertaining) is the responsible outgrowth of understanding this element's importance.

4. **Message:** The message element always includes both the message content and treatment. Message content includes the building blocks of concepts, words, ideas, thoughts, and perspectives. Message treatment involves the variability of such factors as verbal and nonverbal delivery, arrangement of ideas, pacing, emphasis, intensity, and volume. When content and treatment are synchronized, message clarity is heightened. When content and treatment are not aligned, the message becomes confusing. Responsibility for synchronizing and aligning message content and treatment resides with both senders and receivers.

5. **Channel:** In every communication, messages move through identifiable channels. Like pipelines, channels actually carry the message and are related to senders' and receivers' sensory mechanisms of sight, sound, smell, taste, and touch. The responsibility and challenges for connecting meanings change as the channels of transmission vary.

Because listening face-to-face is different from listening by telephone, webcast, or recording, it is important to recognize the numerous implications of the channel or medium component. As channels change, the message content and treatment also change. Responsible listening leaders understand the impact and implications of channel or media changes.

6. **Filters:** All senders and receivers communicate through a set of personal filters. These filters are crucial as they trigger how we respond to events, create and capture messages, sense, interpret, evaluate, and provide meaningful feedback. All leaders filter messages based on their individual roles, positions, past knowledge, experiences, prejudices, opinions, attitudes, beliefs, emotions, personalities, intelligence and language abilities. Working in combination, listening leaders' personal filters will impact senders' messages, positively, neutrally, or negatively.

Opportunity for productive communication increases when senders' and receivers' respective filters are closely aligned. As senders' and receivers' filters become measurably more different, the communication process becomes more difficult. A good example of matching filters lies in the use of language. If two individuals of the same gender, education, and socioeconomic level are born and raised in the same time frame and the same geographical area, the probability exists for a close alignment of their language filters. On the other hand, if two individuals are raised in different parts of the country with dramatically different backgrounds, the alignment of their language filters might vary greatly, even though they both speak English. Carry this one step farther and you can see the difficulty in communication between people who speak completely different languages, or between those who have significantly different attitudes, emotions, opinions, and experiences. Responsible and effective listening leaders must understand the inherent challenges that reside in trying to communicate without understanding and accommodating the impact of individual filters.

7. **Response:** The ultimate feedback loop of communication involves the necessary element of response, which brings the process of communication full circle. The fact is, we cannot not respond because no response *is* a response. Thus, responding is the ultimate responsible act of listening leaders! Due to the very private, quiet, and internal nature of listening, the ultimate observable measure of every effective listener is productive, constructive, appropriate, and profitable response and action. Assuming responsibility, and developing and refining the "response-ability," for action-oriented listening, are the keys to every leader's success. Listening leaders understand the key is to move from passivity to activity.

8. **Context:** Of course, all communication occurs in a context of time, place, and occasion. In addition, the social, physical, organizational, political, and environmental context shapes the impact of every

message. Responsible listening leaders maximize their control of time, place, and occasion of communication whenever possible. Choosing the correct context for maximum sending and receiving effectiveness inevitably improves communication. With careful thought, concrete planning, expanded focus, and assumed responsibility, listening leaders can have a positive effect on many communication contexts. Whenever possible, take responsibility to select your time, choose your location, control the environment, or alter the setting. Leaders are often in a position to affect context.

9. **Noise:** Any internal or external factor that interferes with the success of communication is considered to be noise and is important, as we live in a noisy and interruptive world. Obviously, these interferences are varied and numerous and cause costly communication breakdowns. As we will discuss in Chapter Seven, noise includes distractions as simple as mechanical or human noise, interruptions, dialectical differences, age differences, dress and appearance, and positional differences. Responsible listening leaders create and engage a proactive strategy to reduce or eliminate anything that interferes with productive communication.

OBSERVATION

Thoughtful consideration of the individual communication elements or components will serve you well as a listening leader. Moreover, every effort you make to take responsibility and manage each of the nine complex components of the communication process will pay off in measurable ways. As a result, listening leaders who focus and assume responsibility put themselves in a position to control their destinies in numerous ways. Each of these nine components is open to your answer to the question, "Who holds the primary responsibility for successful communication?" Of course, "You do!"

THE LAW OF LISTENING AND LEADING

We have discovered that everyone listens and leads the way they do because of their innate nature and years of conditioned practice. Listening and leading is a result of both innate forces and learned behavior. As a consequence, your listening and leading attitudes, skills, and behaviors are habitual and predictable. Thus, your listening and leading behaviors are also observable and measurable, and you can improve your effectiveness by embracing the responsibility to identify and build your strengths while reducing and eliminating weaknesses. Thirty-five years ago, the "Steil Listening Law," was created to illustrate the requirements of effective listening: $L = (A \times W)^2$. Originally "L" only represented Listening. In recent years, we added effective leading to the equation. **L equals Listening and Leading. A equals Ability. W equals Willingness.** Simply put, effective Listening and Leading require both Ability and Willingness. Ability without Willingness or Willingness without Ability results in ineffective listening and leadership. Leaders, at any level, may have all the Listening Ability in the world; without Willingness, it will make little difference. On the other hand, leaders may have boundless good intentions and "Willingness" to listen to those they lead; however, without "Ability," it will not matter. Obviously, supreme listening leaders combine both "Ability" and "Willingness" as they assume the responsibilities of leadership. In the process, everyone is served.

THE QUESTION OF RESPONSIBILTY

For years, we have asked leaders around the globe the simple question, "Who holds the *primary responsibility* for successful communication—the sender or receiver?" To eliminate the natural and easy answer of "Both," *we define primary responsibility*

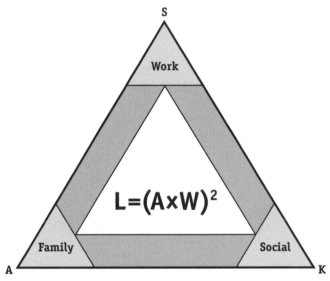

Steil Listening & Leading Law

as *"a Minimum of 51%."* Obviously, both senders and receivers have the ability to control various components in the communication process, so who should hold the primary responsibility for success? Or, put another way, who is to blame when communication breaks down? On a consistent basis, 70 percent of those asked believe the primary responsibility for communication success resides with the speaker. Twenty-five percent believe the primary responsibility lies with the listener. Five percent express no opinion.

A SENDER'S VIEW

Those who believe senders/speakers hold the primary responsibility for successful communication advance the following cogent reasons:

▶ Senders initially control the communication act and contact.

▶ Senders have the primary vested interest in the communication's success.

▶ Senders determine the primary purpose of each communication.

▶ Senders develop the message for each receiver.

▶ Senders control the context and channels for communication.

▶ Senders read the feedback and adjust message.

▶ Senders have initial control over several elements of communication and therefore are primarily responsible.

As the dynamic **Pastor Roger Eigenfeld**, the Senior Pastor of St. Andrew's Lutheran Church in Mahtomedi, Minnesota, who leads a staff of 185 and a growing congregation of nearly 9,000 members, explains,

> *"If people do not hear what I am saying, it is not their fault, it is my fault. I am the communicator, and if they do not get it, then I have to figure out another way to communicate."*
> *—Pastor Roger Eigenfeld*

I live in the world of communication, and if people do not hear what I am saying, it is not their fault, it is my fault. I am the communicator, and if they do not get it, then I have to figure out another way to communicate. My job is that of setting the climate. I have to set the climate so that listening will take place. The desired goal of all our communication is that everyone leaves here in better shape than they came. As a creator and sender of messages, that responsibility is mine.

A RECEIVER'S VIEW

Those who believe receivers/listeners hold the primary responsibility for successful communication advance the following rationale:

▶ Receivers ultimately control the communication act and connection.

▶ Receivers determine the primary and final purpose of each communication.

▶ Receivers can decide to tune-in or tune-out.

▶ Receivers control the choice of channels, context, and response.

▶ Receivers determine the ultimate and final meaning of the message.

▶ Receivers provide the controlling judgment of and feedback for every message.

▶ Receivers have ongoing control over several elements of communication and, therefore, are primarily responsible.

Dr. Clark Taylor, Director of the Institute of Facial Surgery in Missoula, Montana is so highly skilled he is known by many as a "Doctor with Golden Hands." Dr. Taylor supports the position that primary responsibility for successful communication resides with the receiver.

If the responsibility for communication ends with the sender, you will never get beyond the level of the sender. We follow an old and simple rule in my office, "Don't believe anything you hear and only half of what you read," which requires everyone to become a more skeptical, focused, and responsible listener. As we engage in life-altering activities in our enterprise, we have no room for error. Ultimately, we must critically evaluate every bit of spoken information we receive. It puts the primary burden on the receiver and takes it away from the sender.

> *"Without assuming responsibility as a listener, my career path would have been very different, and less fulfilling."*
> —Dr. Clark Taylor

At a very young age, I became aware that I needed to filter every communication that was delivered to me, whether it be from teachers, authority figures, or whomever. My healthy skepticism and refusal to mindlessly accept some communication was developed as I listened to some of my guidance and vocational counselors. Without assuming responsibility as a listener, my career path would have been very different and less fulfilling. Ultimately, I believed little at face value and chose to focus on developing my skills as a critical listener.

Many times, when I followed the advice of others, I was misguided, misdirected, and consequently disappointed. Looking back, I realize in spite of good sender intentions, many times little meaningful communication occurred. They failed to listen to me, and I failed to listen to them. They did not have an understanding of who I was and where I wanted to go. Moreover, I operated under the false assumption they knew who I was and what my strengths were. A significant amount of the advice I have been given in my lifetime was based on the assumptions of others that were rarely, if ever, correct. In this process of self-discovery, I became a critical listener. As a result, I train those I lead to listen accordingly. They are required to critically interpret and evaluate through their own filters. That process highlights any flaws in the sender's reasoning as we develop our program of continuing quality improvement. Thus, every communication and every suggestion holds the opportunity for ensuing discussion, justification, and agreement on the desired action. I believe the ultimate responsibility for successful communication resides with listeners.

Pete Lilienthal, founder and President of InTouch, a company specializing in employee feedback systems, also places the primary responsibility on listeners.

I believe that, ultimately, the receiver is more important than the sender. It is an interesting challenge since we see so many different kinds of senders. For example, some senders are neither concise nor efficient in their communication. Their chatter is verbose and unending. There are senders who are totally unorganized or worse, disorganized, in their presentations. In addition, some senders are quite emotional. As there are so many styles of speakers, effective listeners must assume the primary responsibility and filter through all of the chatter and static just to pick out the real message.

> *"As there are so many styles of speakers, effective listeners must assume the primary responsibility and filter through all of the chatter and static, just to pick out the real message."*
>
> —Pete Lilienthal

RELATED IMPLICATIONS

Over the years, we have listened to the opinions of many and have observed a pattern of predictable behaviors. The related implications are both obvious and troubling. When senders/speakers are viewed to be the primary responsible party, receivers/listeners automatically assume a secondary role. The resulting assumption leads to passivity on the part of listeners. In this scenario, the nonresponsible receiver relaxes, remains passive, and when the communication breaks down, blames the speaker. And one thing is clear, the non-responsible, irresponsible, inactive, passive listener is always ineffective. Ineffective listeners are lazy, uninvolved, and detached as they wait for the speaker to ensure communication success. On the other hand, placing the primary responsibility for successful communication on the receiver enables senders to become passive, irresponsible, and blameless for any breakdown of communication. In either case, productive communication suffers.

ANOTHER VIEW

So who holds the major responsibility for successful communication? Is it the sender or the receiver? Supporters of both sides have valid arguments, but both views place either speakers or listeners in passive positions. In either case, the two viewpoints have one common characteristic: each accepts the responsibility for success, while charging failure to others. Thus, those who hold either view allow others to control their behavior and destinies. As leaders in a wide variety of setting and situations know, there are millions of people who place the primary responsibility for communication success on others. Yet, in the spirit of "If it is going to be, it is up to me!" there is only one individual who can legitimately be held responsible for successful communication.

THE MINIMUM 51% RESPONSIBILITY RULE

Successful listening leaders profit by using a workable and proven strategy of assuming the **"Minimum 51% Responsibility Rule" whenever they are in the role of either the sender or receiver.** Of course, productive listening leaders usually assume more than 51% responsibility, but **never less than 51%.** The key is to assume the major responsibility for the success of every communication, whether you are speaking or listening. The charge is to be responsible and actively engaged in your communication success.

The value of assuming the "minimum 51% responsibility" for successful communication as we constantly move between the role of sender and receiver is reinforced by **Craig Struve**, Director of Television Operations for Vail Resorts, Inc. in Vail, Colorado. As a successful professional and seasoned communicator, Craig confirms the value of assuming individual responsibility,

The fact of the matter is, if the sender does not do a good job of clearly communicating the intended information, the listener is not going to get the desired message. Conversely, if the listener is not effectively sensing, interpreting, evaluating, and responding to the speaker, everyone suffers. As it relates to business, listening requires the ability to truly understand what the other person is saying in order to make important decisions. We need to discern what is important in the greater context of making business successful and balance that with what others are saying.

Craig Struve believes his acceptance of responsibility for heightened success as both a speaker and a listener, springs from the maturing of his personality over the years.

I think I have become a far better communicator because I am simply more mature than I was 10, 20, or 30 years ago. I used to believe I had all the answers, but today I know I do not. In fact, I am still working on creating better questions. Responsibility calls for asking better questions and listening to as much information from carefully selected sources as possible.

> *"I used to believe I had all the answers, but today I know I do not. In fact, I am still working on creating better questions. Responsibility calls for asking better questions and listening to as much information from carefully selected sources as possible."*
> —Craig Struve

With a large ego, I have not found this an easy transition to make, but it is one that has paid off. The fiscal responsibilities of today's business are essential. Leaders have a responsibility to listen well to everyone. The major responsibility of every business is fiscal health. The second major leadership responsibility is building a team that communicates well. The key is that everyone must assume individual responsibility for communication success, whether they are the speaker or the listener.

RESPONSIBILITY AND COSTS

Lavina Smith is a former pilot with PEOPLExpress, co-pilot with Comair, and presently a flight instructor with SimCom, Inc. Lavina highlights the costs incurred when responsibility is abdicated to others in the world of aviation.

In a classic case of failed communication, a Captain and First Officer were not listening effectively and mindlessly accepted the instructions of Air Traffic Controllers who led them along an instrument approach to another airport. As ATC vectored them to an airport 20 miles away from their actual destination, the Pilot and Co-pilot had uncritically accepted everything.

> *"Had all parties assumed the primary responsibility for successful communication, all costs could have been avoided."*
> —Lavina Smith

Although they landed safely, the professional embarrassment and financial loss was significant, as the Captain was downgraded to First Officer for a year. Had all parties assumed the primary responsibility for successful communication, all costs could have been avoided.

PASSIVITY ➤ RESPONSIBILITY ➤ ACTIVITY

Nancy Tallent, Vice President of Human Resources at CNA Insurance Worldwide Processing Operations, identified how important it is to move from passivity through responsibility to activity, by providing an example of how significant costs can quickly mount up when no one assumes responsibility.

I had a meeting with a member of my staff who was engaged in a very time-consuming staffing activity. She was interviewing every single candidate for all the entry-level jobs that we have in our organization. Perplexed, I asked her why

> *"...It taught me to confirm what you think I said by listening to what the person thinks they heard."*
> —Nancy Tallent

she was engaged in such costly and, to me, nonsensical activity. Her answer was incorrect but quite sensible: "I thought that is what you wanted me to do. I thought that is what you told me I had to do." Such a simple example, but it taught me to confirm what someone thinks I said by listening to what the person thinks he or she heard. Knowing what she thought she heard would have been very valuable and saved us a lot of grief because I was frustrated with what she was doing, and she was frustrated that she was being required, in her mind, to do it. If she had just asked me, "Are you saying that you want me to talk to every single applicant for these entry-level jobs in person?" or if I had said, "Now tell me how you are going to handle the application process for these entry-level positions." If either of us had practiced the simple step of confirmation—we would have saved more than 100 hours of valuable time.

The key to successful communication is to be responsible and actively engaged in the entire process. In sum, the **MINIMUM 51% RESPONSIBILITY** for listening and speaking success resides with each individual; you and those you lead.

TAKING RESPONSIBILITY BUILDS TRUST

Recognizing that listening leaders absolutely must accept responsibility has helped **Susan Sears**, the Director of Publishing Operations at AAA (American Automobile Association) build trust with her professional associates. Susan is in charge of the creative production work that is required for publishing the AAA tour books and maps. Susan has more than 40 team members in her department and has discovered the importance of assuming the primary responsibility for effective communication. As a **Golden Circle Listening Leader**, Susan noted, "Listening has helped me to build trust with my associates and the people I lead. They know I will honestly listen to them, respond, and do something about their concerns. As I listen to them, I gain their trust and support and, in turn, they listen to me."

> *"Listening has helped me to build trust with my associates and the people I lead."*
> —*Susan Sears*

TRAINING RESPONSIBLE LISTENERS

Rock Kousek formerly served as a human intelligence operative with U.S. Army special operations units, and presently is a Senior Producer/Director of WFTV Channel 9, an ABC Affiliate. In both roles, Rock quickly learned the communication value of assuming primary responsibility.

Excellent listening is one of the main skills I absolutely must have in my job as Senior Director/Producer. The challenge in listening is to figure out such things as whether the microphone works, whether the satellite shot is prefect, and whether things go together as they should. This job has forced me to become a much more intent listener than I think I would have been otherwise. In addition, I work with several part-time Production Assistants who are learning to be studio crew members. They are extremely young and inexperienced. They are expected to be both initiators and good followers. They need to be very good listeners because during the live shows, they are in the

> *"So my leadership challenge is to be patient enough to explain and show them why assuming responsibility for listening does matter."*
> —*Rock Kousek*

studio connected to me by nothing more than a wireless headset. As the Director and Producer, I am often revising the show as we go and making suggestions regarding changes and correct camera shots. However, many of these young assistants are not yet very good listeners, and I have discovered listening is a real challenge for them. They will say things like, "Oh yeah that's right, I heard you say that," or "I didn't think you were serious," or "I didn't think it mattered." So my leadership challenge is to be patient enough to explain and show them why assuming responsibility for listening does matter. They must understand why this job literally depends on their ability to listen. Like the rest of us, they must accept that responsibility, which, to a large degree, will determine whether they will succeed and whether we keep them on as part as our station family.

TARGET 25 & BULLS-EYE 5

Responsibility for effective listening and leadership is recognizing the fact that no one can listen to all of the people who want to be listened to. World population milestones illustrate the extraordinary growth and related challenges all listening leaders face. According to the United Nations population accounts, the world numbered its first billion human inhabitants in 1804. By 1927, 123 years later, the world's population had doubled to 2 billion. By 1960, 33 years later, we numbered 3 billion. In 1974, just 14 years later, we reached 4 billion. It took just another 13 years, until 1987, to grow to 5 billion. A world population of 6 billion was reached in 1999, a mere 12 years later. Today, with almost six and a half billion people in the world, the numbers become mind-boggling. However, it is clear that no one can listen to all the people talk about all things at all times. Thoughtful and responsible choice is imperative. To advance listening leadership, it is important to decide who the most significant and most important people are in your world. Whom should you listen to more? Whom should you listen to less? Where and how should you invest your time and energy?

On a monthly basis over the next calendar year, we invite you to identify the most significant and important people in the world to you.

In the space on the following page, list in priority order by name and relationship, the 25 individuals who are most important and significant to you in your life.

Name	Relationship	Name	Relationship
1		14	
2		15	
3		16	
4		17	
5		18	
6		19	
7		20	
8		21	
9		22	
10		23	
11		24	
12		25	
13			

Once you have identified the 25 most significant people in your life, locate them in the following five-ring Bull's-eye Target: place the five most significant individuals in bull's-eye ring one; the next five in ring two; the next five in ring three; etc.

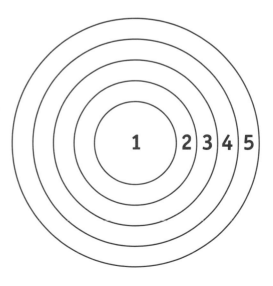

Target 25 Analysis

As you choose to enhance your individual and organizational listening attitudes, skills, and knowledge, you will profit significantly from continually asking and answering the following big question: **What responsibility level will you take when you listen to the most significant and important people on your personal T-25 list?**

RESTORING CONFIDENCE THROUGH LISTENING

Dennis McGrath is an internationally respected public relations and communication executive who experienced the responsibility and challenge of listening and leading people who spoke a language he did not. Dennis and his talented wife ran the Japanese office of a multimillion dollar global agency in Tokyo, Japan.

We were challenged with a Japanese company President who resented our assigned involvement in reshaping his business, which had been losing market share. Of the nearly 100 employees, only half spoke English and the quality of that English varied greatly. The other half of the staff did not speak any English except hello, good-bye, and thank you. This organization was one of the great old names of Japanese public relations, although by comparison with the way public relations and communication counseling is practiced in the United States, it was, in the main, relatively primitive. There was a lot of ill will in the office because the older men held the positions of authority and made the money, while the young people did all the work. Like mushrooms, they were kept in the dark and fed manure. We discovered problems with quality, morale, and the loss of clients. I interviewed every professional in the firm, and because my Japanese language skills were no better than their English, I used an interpreter with those who did not speak English. This, of course, created another problem because the quality of interpretation varied greatly. However, I listened to every professional in the firm and discovered I had to listen with an intuitive ear. In this time-consuming, but important process, we learned a number of things that helped us restructure the firm. Although, at that time, it was difficult to terminate people in Japan, we managed to eliminate a high-ranking individual who was a real problem in the organization because the employees totally resisted his leadership. As we demoted him, took away a great deal of his responsibility, and lowered his salary, he lost face.

Of course, he was not a bad human being, so that was not a fun thing to do. However, the key lesson was if we wanted to restore confidence among our employees, then we had to take the responsibility to listen to those we were leading. In addition, regardless of the culture, we also had the responsibility to take appropriate action, as we desired to lead with impact.

> *"If we wanted to restore confidence among our employees, then we had to take the responsibility to listen to those we were leading."*
> —Dennis McGrath

THE $5 MILLION ERROR

Rhonda Glover is an insightful College Administrator and corporate consultant who has observed how her professional associates experience great leadership success as they listen with assumed responsibility. On the other hand, Rhonda periodically has observed expensive consequences when leaders have not listened responsibly.

Several years ago, during a consulting assignment, I was working with the CEO of an organization that provided advanced training for professionals. The CEO decided he was going to embark on a $5 million CD-based training program at his institution. Unfortunately, use of technology was new and he did not invite a broad group of people to provide any helpful input. He did not ask past or potential future participants how they would respond to such a concept. He did not establish any focus groups for feedback. Of course, he asked a few people within the organization what they thought, and they responded very positively. However, in retrospect, I do not know how authentic their responses were. As he decided to go forward with his plan despite the minimal input, a couple of people came to him and said, "You know, this might be a quick response and too expensive. Maybe you should slow down before you go to the board with it." Regardless of the expressed concerns and with no further listening, he impatiently moved forward.

> *"Unfortunately...*
> *he did not invite*
> *a broad group of*
> *people to provide*
> *any helpful input."*
> —Rhonda Glover

The result was negative and devastating. Students did not want the CD-based learning program. They desired to continue with the proven face-to-face learning method. More importantly, the organization lost potential students, its sterling reputation, and an investment of $5 million. In turn, within two years, he lost his job as he was asked to step down from his position. Although small and incremental components of CD-based instruction might have worked well, we will never know. Had this CEO been a more responsible and better listening leader, he would have listened to a broader group of individuals who may have uncovered the limitations of the plan. Shared responsibility and extended listening hold the heightened opportunity to avoid costs and reap rewards.

GRANDIOSITY DESTROYS RESPONSIBILITY

Former Vice President of Florida's, University of Miami, and the present President of Rollins College, in Orlando, Florida, **Dr. Rita Bornstein**, has seen her share of effective and ineffective listeners and leaders. In her new book, *Legitimacy in the Academic Presidency*, Dr. Bornstein, highlights how "grandiosity" threatens responsibility and therefore can stifle leadership legitimacy.

Grandiose behavior is a characteristic of leaders who have been in office a long time and think they know what is good for their organization, so they do not feel the need to consult with anyone. They just act independently on behalf of the organization. Although they operate with good motives, they never last very long as leaders. Effective leaders cannot operate independently very long and still

> *"Effective leaders cannot operate independently very long and still retain legitimacy with stakeholders."*
> —Dr. Rita Bornstein

retain legitimacy with stakeholders. I know a College President who had a very successful run for about nine years, was well known on the national scene, and then became very involved in a local urban development project. In the process, although he became disconnected from his key constituents, he continued to make big decisions on their behalf. Grandiosity took over and, unfortunately, he is no longer the President.

THE RESPONSIBILITY FOR BUILDING RELATIONSHIPS

Larry Tyson is President of Trailwood Transportation, LLC, the Truckload Division, of the third generation of privately held Tyson Companies. Trailwood Transportation currently operates 100 tractors from North Dakota to New York and is a prime service provider for major food and candy manufacturers. For decades, the secret of successful working relationships centered on the mutual assumption that shippers and transportation service providers would take individual responsibility for establishing and maintaining productive business relationships. However, Larry has recently observed a major change that has had a negative impact on the industry.

There's a trend in the trucking industry causing major changes and challenges. It used to be that everybody knew everybody else in the business, and we all worked together for the common goal of moving goods in an efficient and productive way. Although pricing was important, it wasn't always the pricing that dictated how the goods were moved. It was based on a combination of factors like fairness, reasonableness, friendships, timeliness, and simply getting the job done. As a result, service levels were very high. In the last 10 years, however the major manufacturers

> *"Although everybody told them it wouldn't work, they didn't listen. Worse yet, they refused to engage in any meaningful dialog."*
> —Larry Tyson

have been are hiring employees directly out of colleges. The new breed seems to be less interested in assuming responsibility for creating, or allowing the development of, important personal relationships with their vendors. Today, we are basically treated as a transportation service provider—a supplier. Today's business relationship seems to be based more on the manufacturer's dictatorial nature and pricing strategy. There is a well-publicized case involving a major manufacturer that independently and arbitrarily implemented a new software process.

Although everybody told them it wouldn't work, they didn't listen. Worse yet, they refused to engage in any meaningful dialog. They simply implemented their software package and basically said this is the way it's going to be. As a result, they literally had to shut down their plant and ultimally lost multimillions of dollars. Although their computerized spreadsheets had indicated they would derive significant cost savings by reducing their carrier base and implementing this new strategy, their real-world results were different. Because of the Halloween and Christmas fluctuations in the candy business, they could not move their products to market and lost millions of dollars in sales. Clearly, they did not assume the responsibility to listen because they were driven by computerized statistics and bottom-line spreadsheets. Everything was about software and not relationships. Without a single phone call, they discontinued doing business with us. One day, the loads simply did not show up, and they never told us a thing. They literally could have put us out of business, but we survived. When we asked for an explanation from them, they said, "It was all about cost control!"

MY HEALTH...MY FUTURE...MY RESPONSIBILITY!

Carole Grau is a longtime educator, trainer, and consultant and a perfect role model for any leader who desires to listen better. Carol believes that speakers can always recognize when they've had an impact by observing listening leaders' authentic inquiry and integration of their ideas. Skillful and responsible listeners understand there is a world of difference between *claiming* you understand someone and *demonstrating* it with a response that proves the depth of your comprehension. Reflecting on a significant personal medical experience, Carole vividly remembers a pivotal moment of listening with responsibility.

No one wants to be confronted with a life-threatening illness. However, when it happens, responsible listening allows intelligent decisions. Following detection of a lump in my breast, a needle biopsy and a second opinion, a doctor recommended surgery. Although he did not say it was malignant, he sent me to the hospital and scheduled the procedure for the next day. That evening, he arrived at my room with waivers to sign as he revealed the preliminary tests had identified cancer cells, and he wanted a release to do a radical mastectomy.

The immediate shock of hearing this new information was overwhelming. I needed time to digest, question, and research it, so I could make meaningful choices on how best to proceed. The doctor did not listen to my concerns and kept urging me to sign the papers. He threatened that postponement would result in his and the hospital facility's unavailability. Nevertheless, I postponed the immediate surgery and engaged in research of my options. It was my health and my life and my responsibility. Following significant research, exploring, reading, and listening I opted for a lumpectomy and radiation. Of course, we need to listen to experts; but there are numerous experts. The listening challenge is to slow down events when possible, reduce intimidation by gathering more information, and take appropriate action.

In retrospect, two lessons stand out. First, after 25 years, I remain grateful for the support of loved ones who provided a climate in which I could listen and sort through options, none of which was appealing. Second, responsibility lies within. Leaders must listen and lead themselves before we can lead others. It is our responsibility.

THE POINT

Of course, as Jay Ard, Larry Tyson, Craig Struve, Rita Bornstein, Clark Taylor, Carole Grau and every effective listening leader know, the ultimate power for success resides with individuals who build, refine, and maintain relationships based on assuming the primary responsibility for listening.

As **Jay Ard** so aptly noted, "Accepting ultimate responsibility is the key to effective listening and leading." The principle is powerful, Practice **Golden Rule 4: "Listening Leaders Take Primary Responsibility"** whenever you are listening or speaking and you will Listen, Lead, and Succeed.

Golden Rule 4

"Listening Leaders Take Primary Responsibility"

10 ACTION STEPS

1. Learn and manage the nine core components of the communication process in your professional and personal life.

2. Learn and regularly apply the Steil Listening & Leading Law $(L= A \times W)^2$.

3. Take charge and assume the Minimum of 51% Responsibility as a sending or receiving Listening Leader.

4. Complete your personal T-25 list on a quarterly basis.

5. Complete your Bulls-Eye 5 list on a quarterly basis.

6. Publicly avow your assumption of primary responsibility as both a sender and receiver.

7. Practice raising your responsibility level when listening to individuals on your T-25 list.

8. Identify, measure, and record specific results and benefits you achieve when you and those you lead assume primary responsibility as a sender and a receiver.

9. Identify, measure, and record specific costs that occur when you and those you lead fail to take primary responsibility as a sender or receiver.

10. Build your "Listening Organization" by teaching those you lead the practical value of taking primary responsibility for the success of all communication activities.

LISTENING LEADERS™ GOLDEN RULES PYRAMID

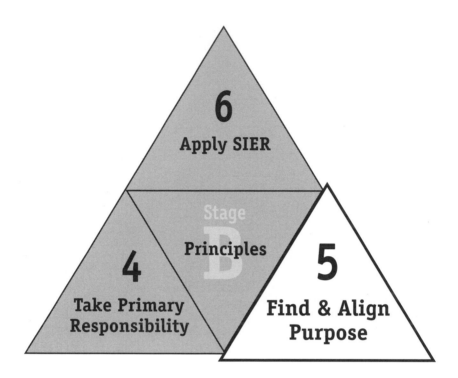

Golden Rule 5

"Listening Leaders Find & Align Purpose"

"Somewhere I learned that everyone speaks and listens on purpose. Their purpose! Sometimes the purposes are clear and precise. Sometimes they are fuzzy and muddled. However, when we listen on purpose and connect to the speaker's purpose, we will always achieve more and serve better."

—George Knutsen

George Knutsen, founder and President of WhisperGLIDE Swing Company, is serving the social and physical needs of thousands. George lives, listens, and leads on purpose, and is one of the most positive and upbeat listening leaders you will ever meet. For 35 years, he was a very successful insurance agent. As a life member of the "Million Dollar Roundtable," George listened to and positively served scores of thousands of clients. However, in spite of his success, George Knutsen listened to his larger purpose in life and concluded that "most people are driven to the *what*; few are driven to the *why*." As George noted, "Our *beliefs* are what we carry around. Our *convictions* are what carry us around. So I enjoyed my first 35 years because I found purpose in my profession. But in the last 10 years, I have found purpose in my calling."

Through listening and leading, George Knutsen's purposeful calling resulted in the development and production of the therapeutic state-of-the-art WhisperGLIDE Swing used by senior care centers and retirement communities across America. Because they listened on purpose, George and his team are providing glide swings and "social therapeutic motion," which dramatically enhance relationships and provide a sense of purpose, belonging, and meaning to their users.

Whether speaking or listening, we have discovered that all effective listening leaders identify, differentiate, and adapt to the linked and multiple purposes of communication. Skilled listening leaders recognize that we communicate at different times for different purposes. They recognize the critical importance of achieving congruence of purpose between speakers and listeners. The four primary communication purposes of phatic, cathartic, informative, and persuasive, are essential for every listening leader's personal and professional success. Moreover, as the following Communication Purpose Model indicates, each purpose potentially affects the opportunity for success of each higher level communication purposes.

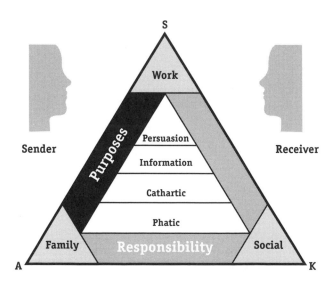

Communication Purpose Model

THE BINDING PURPOSE—PHATIC COMMUNICATION

Phatic communication is the "small talk" of life, which builds binding relationships. Whenever you are involved in small talk, chit-chat, or conversation that is focused on building relationships, you are engaged in phatic communication. It might be communication about the weather, the week-end, the ballgame, the new tie, the kids or grandkids, or many topics that simply help you to connect and get to know others on a personal basis. Phatic communication is the most basic purpose of communication and provides a foundation for higher level communication. Unfortunately, for many, listening to others discuss their vacation, their health, their pet hobby, or what's new in their world seems trivial, unnecessary, and a waste of time. However, effective listening leaders understand that the primary purpose of phatic communication is to establish a relationship platform with those they serve. They also discover the value and power of building binding relationships.

> *"I find most of life is small talk. Small talk is critical because you can't get to the big talk without the small talk."*
> —George Knutsen

As a rule, we generally communicate better at higher levels of purpose with people with whom we have "created binding relationships" than with those we have not. As George Knutsen insightfully noted, "I find most of life is small talk. Small talk is critical because you can't get to the big talk without the small talk." Phatic communication simply focuses on the small talk which builds binding relationships. Without such relationships, communication for other purposes generally becomes more difficult and less effective.

As many of our listening leaders observed, although phatic communication is important, it is not always simple and easy. In discussing valuable members of their teams, different listening leaders had a variety of comments.

One said, "I find it very difficult to connect with her. We've worked together for the past three years, and, yet I don't know her." Referring to a colleague's avoidance of phatic, chit-chat, relationship-building small talk, another leader observed, "He's as cold as a freezer. I respect his abilities, but I'd rather not work with him." Another noted, "I can't seem to reach her. She never pays any attention unless she wants something." Speaking of others, one prominent listening leader commented, "My boss thinks small talk is a waste of time. Unfortunately, he suffers at higher levels because he is not interpersonally connected and people don't think he cares." Another explained, "She fails to persuade others because she has never created a real sense of personal connection and relationship. She is too busy talking and trying to impress others. As she openly states, she has no interest in listening to minutia. If she did, she would find that what she perceives as minutia, others may consider monumental. Time invested in listening to small talk would pay her great dividends at other levels of communication." These views indicate serious failures of phatic attitudes and behaviors wherein no meaningful relationships were established. In each case, little relationship-binding or sharing was attempted or achieved.

Without phatic communication, it becomes more difficult to communicate at any higher level. Effective listening leaders understand that communicating for impact requires the formation of relationships, which means engaging people as individuals. In that respect, phatic communication must be considered a prerequisite to every other purpose. In many fields, tight-lipped, objective-driven professionals who consider chit-chat a waste of time are sometimes puzzled by their inability to connect at other important communication levels and purposes. The truth is, when no relationship has been established, it is more difficult to succeed in any kind of communication.

At the other extreme, we all know egocentric individuals who spend an inordinate amount of time engaged in phatic communication. They are extreme time-wasters. They are never succinct and seldom get to the point. They give a complete play-by-play of their weekend, explain a dream they had the night before in extraordinary detail, go into every element of what happened to them that morning, and never quite get around to the reason for visiting. These are the folks who supply us with endless jokes before they make a substantive statement. Effective listening leaders know how to assume control when the speaker goes beyond the point at which phatic talk serves a beneficial purpose. They realize meaningful relationships are the foundation of all productive communication, and neither the listener nor the speaker can afford to discount them.

Matt Koehnen has been the Lexus Master Certified General Sales Manager for eight consecutive years at the Elite Lexus of Maplewood, Minnesota dealership, and he clearly understands the importance of all communication purposes, starting with phatic communication.

We're ranked 18th in the nation for "Overall Customer Satisfaction," and we know listening is a lot more than simply sitting across from somebody and passively taking in what they're saying. Listening requires creating a climate of purpose. Every day, it begins with the way you greet the people you work with, and the people who grace us with their business and trust. In my leadership role, I consciously establish purposeful opportunities every day to schedule a few moments with a select set of employees and check in with them. We will focus on

> *"I always try to find a few current events in an employee's life I can focus on. The result is an atmosphere of mutual caring and trust in which everyone feels comfortable communicating.*
> *—Matt Koehnen*

small things just to enhance our relationship.

For example, I just had a conversation with an employee which, although it was filled with information, would not have been effective if we had not established a solid relationship through ongoing small talk. Because I knew what was important to him, I simply asked, "How did everything work out with your car accident last Friday? I know you weren't hurt, but what are you doing to get your car fixed? Is everything going to be okay?" Although this communication included an opportunity for his emotional release and informational update, my primary listening purpose was to engage in small talk and expand our connection. I always try to find a few current events in an employee's life I can focus on. The result is an atmosphere of mutual caring and trust in which everyone feels comfortable communicating. The same is true with our customers. On the other hand, there are people who engage in small talk with the wrong motive. They spend time in small talk just for the sake of small talk. They are not really engaged. Listening has to be genuine. I do care about each and every person who works here, and I try to demonstrate that by building meaningful relationships with everyone. In today's business climate, meaningful and purposeful small talk is imperative to everyone's success.

As a leader committed to leading by listening, Matt Koehnen and his Lexus colleagues have discovered that the key to building an award-winning sales and service team begins with creating and maintaining relationships through purposeful and invaluable small talk. All other communication purposes and success flow from the phatic platform.

Consider the wisdom of **Norbert Wiener**, who developed the field of cybernetics and authored *The Human Use of Human Beings*, when he wrote, "There is one quality more important than 'know-how.... It is 'know-what' by which we determine not only how to accomplish our purposes, but what our purposes are to be." In that vein, **Michael Abrashoff** understands the tremendous importance of purpose and the benefit of phatic communication. Mike is the President of Grassroots Leadership, author of the best-selling book, *It's Your Ship*, and the former Commander of the USS Benfold, a guided-missile destroyer armed with $1 billion worth of sophisticated weapons and a crew of more than 300 men and women. At the age of 36, Commander Michael Abrashoff was the most junior commanding officer in the Pacific Fleet. As a new and very young leader his challenges were obvious and staggering, with exceptionally low morale and unacceptably high turnover. Few thought this ship could improve. In some ways, Mike's challenge was an example of the same problems facing many organizational leaders today. Mike only became more resolved.

From the moment of my induction ceremony, I knew command and control leadership was dead. A leader's job has to be all

> *"A leader's job has to be all about growing people. You cannot order people to be cohesive. You cannot order great performance. You have to create the culture and climate that makes it possible. You have to build the bonds of trust, and I found that the only way you can do that is one crew member at a time.*
> —Michael Abrashoff

growing people. You cannot order people to be cohesive. You cannot order great performance. You have to create the culture and climate that makes it possible. You have to build the bonds of trust, and I found the only way you can do that is one crew member at a time. The first week after I took command, I saw my first sailor who was leaving the Navy. He came up to see me, and I asked, "So why are you leaving?" He simply said, "Nobody ever asked me to stay." It made no sense to me. It was then I decided to sit down and listen to each man and woman individually in my quarters.

> *"It all starts and continues with small talk, but when you take a real active interest in who someone is as a person, it affects all communication."*
> —Michael Abrashoff

As the ship's leader, I wanted to get to know each of them as an individual. So although it probably started out as a retention tool, after the first couple conversations, I realized these kids were so bright. That's when I started asking, "What do you like most? What do you like least? What would you change if you could?" From there, it took on a life of its own. Eventually, I knew the name of every sailor, their spouse's names, their kids' names, their hometowns, and who their favorite football teams were. We built rapport. It all starts and continues with small talk, but when you take a real active interest in who someone is as a person, it affects all communication."

Like all effective listening leaders who create listening action plans, Commander Mike Abrashoff witnessed the positive impact of building binding relationships through purposeful phatic communication. During his command, he increased retention rates from 28 percent to 100 percent, reduced operating expenditures, and improved readiness. Most importantly, he grew his people into a cohesive unit, bound to one another through small talk and loyalty.

C. William Pollard is the former Chairman and CEO of the ServiceMaster Company. ServiceMaster has been recognized by *Fortune*, the *Wall Street Journal*, and *The Financial Times* as one of the most respected companies in the world, and is ranked the number-one service company among the Fortune 500. Pollard speaks, writes, and teaches on management and ethics, and is the author of a bestseller, *The Soul of the Firm.*

> *"I've found the commitment to listening has been a continuous learning process for me and a continual reminder that I don't know everything. In that way, it has been very exciting for me because as you take time to listen, you learn."*
>
> —C. William Pollard

I've found the commitment to listening has been a continuous learning process for me and a continual reminder that I don't know everything. In that way, it has been very exciting for me because as you take time to listen, you learn. There are obviously some times where I can be impatient. If a person is exceedingly verbose and not getting to the point, sometimes my impatience comes into play. But I think the more patience you have in the process, the more it becomes a learning experience. I'll tell you an experience I had which reaffirmed the importance of listening for me. I was recently with **Peter Drucker**, who is 93 years old. I had visited with him in his home and then we went out to lunch. When you are around a person like Peter Drucker, you listen carefully. What fascinated me most was the great effort he made to listen to me. More amazing, most of his questions dealt with what was going on in the personal side of my life, not in the business side of my life. He asked me questions about what was going on in the life of my family, and in the process of listening he continued building a relationship with me. Not only was I listening to him, but he was really listening to me. Listening is part of relationship building.

The purpose of binding communication lies at the heart of every listening leader's ability to reach others. It is a basic and mandatory requirement for achieving higher levels of communication. Moreover, it lies at the foundation of all effective leadership. To advance your attitudes, skills, and knowledge as you build your phatic communication strengths, we invite your thoughtful response to the following five questions:

ASSESS YOUR PHATIC COMMUNICATION

1. *List three individuals with whom you experience productive phatic communication.*

2. *Why do you experience productive phatic communication with these individuals?*

3. *List three individuals with whom you should, but do not, experience productive phatic communication. Why not?*

4. *What specific action can you take to improve your phatic communication?*

5. *What concrete and specific measurable value will it bring to you and others?*

THE VENTING PURPOSE—CATHARTIC COMMUNICATION

Throughout the history of the world, people have had, have, and will continue to have a need to exercise both positive and negative emotional release. The need to find caring outlets for emotional release is universal and perpetual. Everyone lives on a teeter-totter. Imagine your own teeter-totter with an Emotional rider at one end, a Social fulcrum in the middle, and a Rational rider at the other end. At our listening best, we are in balance. On the other hand, at our worst we are out of balance, with Emotionality high and Rationality low. Because no one listens, leads, or follows productively when out of balance, the importance of understanding, developing, and engaging skilled cathartic listening is invaluable for listening leaders.

More than 4000 years ago **Ptahhotep**, an Egyptian Pharaoh, wrote:

> An official who must listen to the pleas of his clients should listen patiently and without rancor because a petitioner wants attention to what he says even more than the accomplishing of that for which he came. Not all one pleads for can be granted, but a good hearing soothes the heart.

Ptahhotep understood how effective listening leaders provide opportunities for emotional release. Catharsis is the second purpose of human communication and involves the opportunity for and process of releasing emotions, ventilating feelings, and sharing problems and frustrations without being judged. Listening to cathartic communication allows others to get their emotional, social, and rational teeter-totter rebalanced.

Like the need for phatic communication, the importance of allowing catharsis is often underestimated. Many leaders simply expect their charges to "stop whining, suck it up, get over it, or move on with it." Whenever unloading is required, catharsis is as essential to human beings as any other purpose of communication. As **Dr. Elton Mayo** of Harvard observed, "One friend, one person who is truly understanding, who takes the trouble to listen to us as we express our problems, can change our whole outlook on the world."

Jeulene C. deMatheney is a leading business development and marketing executive with Dynac, Inc. Dynac is a U.S. based aerospace company providing high-end engineering services to the space and defense industries. As a listening leader, Jeulene believes that, at times, everyone needs to cathart to a nonjudgmental listener if he or she is going to relieve tension and move to higher communication purposes.

On a recent Monday morning, I was in the office early to get caught up from a recent three-day, off-site meeting. I checked my calendar and noticed that one of my staff members had blocked out one hour for a meeting, without stating a purpose for the meeting. I knew she'd had a very important meeting the previous week with a senior client, and I assumed she wanted to bring me up to date.

At 2:00 p.m. she arrived in my office, closed the door and sat down. She looked pale and lifeless, unlike the dynamic, high-energy, star performer I knew her to be. I took notice and said, "You wish to talk with me?" She immediately looked relieved and said, "As you know, my wedding is scheduled for next April." I nodded, said "yes," and quickly adapted my listening, for I realized this meeting was not about her client. She apparently just needed to vent.

She went on to say her best friend was dying from cancer and was not expected to live through the end of the month. I expressed my sorrow and continued to listen. She explained that her friend had two little girls whose father had been killed in an automobile accident by a drunk driver five years earlier, and the dying mother had no living relatives to care for the girls. Their custody would be awarded to the state.

I listened quietly for a moment and, with empathy, asked her if she had any love for these children. She looked so relieved and replied: "Yes." Saying they had long been a part of her life, and she could hardly bear the thought of them being awarded to the state, as the girls would be separated from each other and from her.

Her emotional release was obvious, so I asked her what her fiancé thought. She replied that he loved children. I just smiled and continued to listen. She went on to say she was at her wit's end with her work, her upcoming wedding with over 200 guests, relatives and friends flying in from all over the world, her best friend dying, and the children possibly being cast into foster care.

I just listened. Then I asked her how she could help the children given the challenges of a new marriage. With less emotion, she leaned back in the chair and thoughtfully said, "You know, we had been discussing adopting after our wedding, but never in my life did I think about this." She paused, and looked at me for an answer. Quietly, I said, "I cannot advise you, but please know that whatever your decision is, you have my full support."

All of a sudden, the employee I knew came back; she stood up, placed her hand firmly on my desk and said, "That's it! The children's mother will die knowing her girls will have a home, be loved, and will graduate from college." I simply said, "May God bless you many times over." She looked and me and said, "He already has." Then she started to dash out of my office, stopped in mid-stream, turned to me and said: "Oh my

> *"As I sat there, I realized that by simply listening, I had helped make a significant difference in my team member's life. Sometimes the best leadership just calls for a quiet and empathic listener."*
> —Jeulene deMatheny

gosh, there is so much to do now, the children's mother, the attorney, the wedding, and I need to order two more flower girls' dresses...can I leave early?"

I just looked at her with a smile and said, "God-speed!" After that conversation, I kept the doors closed and just took a few moments for myself. As I sat there, I realized that by simply listening, I had helped make a significant difference in my team member's life. Sometimes the best leadership just calls for a quiet and empathic listener.

Like all long-term listening leaders, Juelene deMatheney understands that the opportunities to serve others through cathartic listening are perpetual. As Juelene continued,

The opportunity for purposeful listening never ends. On the following Wednesday, the dynamic employee I knew, bounced into my office with the news of her decisions. She was so excited, she could hardly talk. She did not sit this time; instead she almost danced in front of my desk. She glowed as she shared the decisions she'd made since we had talked on Monday. She and her fiancé had met with the mother of the children to let her know they wished to adopt the little girls. As the mother sobbed with tears of joy, she and her attorney arranged to take care of all the necessary paper work, including the last will and testament, and the adoption papers. Then they all made arrangements for the girls to officially move in with her over the weekend. In addition, she had decided the children would be flower girls in her wedding. As I listened, she added more. She had shared her decision and the impending challenges with her mother, a retired child psychologist, who was coming to help everyone move through the transition.

That day, I took a long lunch and just reflected. I had witnessed, and in a small but significant way had contributed to, a significant transformation of a valued colleague by simply listening. In the process, I watched her move from despair to exhilaration. The key is, I listened with authentic empathy. I understood there are times when we all need someone to listen to us.

The lesson for all listening leaders is crystal clear: Whether the emotional release is negative or positive, catharsis is critical when needed. As the brilliant author **David Augsburger** states so eloquently, "Being listened to is so close to being loved that most people don't know the difference." One thing is certain, the ordinary, and sometimes extraordinary, stresses of life build up on occasion, and it is important that everyone

> *"Being listened to is so close to being loved that most people don't know the difference."*
> —David Augsburger

has the opportunity to unload their emotions to an attentive, authentic, and caring listener. This is what the cathartic purpose of communication provides, but unfortunately it is often overlooked or misunderstood.

Everyone has encountered family members, friends, associates, co-workers, customers, and others with a need to vent: their faces are tense, their eyes clouded, their muscles tight, just waiting to explode. But someone intervenes and simply invites catharsis. Few like to keep hurtful garbage within, so when a listening leader provides authentic opportunity for release, they immediately unload. Common reactions include such statements as, "Everything has gone wrong... The world is turned against me... The sky is falling... People do not understand me... You and everyone else are in a conspiracy to make my life miserable."

If you understand and value the significance of catharsis to all communication, and if you choose to serve those you lead, you will not respond with impatience, or anger, or even with irrelevant cheerfulness. You will listen and let catharsis flow. Usually, the storm will pass.

Listening leader **Rabbi Fred Reiner** is the Senior Rabbi of Temple Sinai in Washington, D.C. Approximately 1200 families attend the Temple, providing Rabbi Reiner with ample opportunities for listening to catharsis.

Some people are reluctant or even hesitant to tell you what they really think or feel. If you listen very carefully to their messages, you may understand what they are attempting to convey, or perhaps attempting *not* to convey. For example, if I sit down with the parents and a young girl who is going to have a bat mitzvah in a year and I say, "So, you're going to have a bat mitzvah, how do you feel about it?" She may reply, "Well, I don't know." I may pursue that, by asking: "Do you feel excited, nervous, like you can't wait?" and so forth. She may take one of those cues, and then I may be able to probe a little deeper. So I may ask, "Well, what are you nervous about are in particular?" and try to reassure her by saying, "We are here to help you and make you feel more confident, and what we are trying to accomplish is to have you succeed at an important moment in your life."

They may not be able to articulate what they are thinking so one needs to listen actively, and give them some partial answers to help

> "They may not be able to articulate what they are thinking, so one needs to listen actively, and give them some partial answers to help them articulate what they are thinking or feeling."
> —Rabbi Fred Reiner

them articulate what they are thinking, or feeling. They may come in with a jumble of feelings and advice that a half-dozen people have given them. They are trying to sort everything out, and you can sit down and organize their thoughts with them.

However, as valuable as listening to Catharsis is, listening leader **Gary Johnson** reminds us there are special challenges. Gary serves as the Director of Public Works for Seminole County, Florida and leads nearly 250 employees who manage a system of 800 highway miles in the state. Although Gary has learned to listen with empathy when required, he offers a caution.

> At times, empathy can be perceived as agreement. However, at times, the listener's empathy can convey a very different message than intended, when the listener is not able to take action in the way the individual venting their emotions would like. I have had a couple of unfortunate incidents when people came back to me and said, "But you agreed with me." It is a small thing, but it can be devastating when people mistake your heart-felt caring and empathy for agreement and concurrence.

Gary Johnson provides important counsel. Wise listening leaders must make sure their caring and valuable service of listening to catharsis is not perceived as approval of, or agreement with, specific actions or requests.

In sum, catharsis is simply the process of releasing emotion, the ventilation of feelings, the sharing of problems and frustrations with an empathic listener. Catharsis basically requires an understanding listener who is observant of the cathartic needs, cues, and clues. Individuals who have a need to vent their feelings will often give verbal and nonverbal cues, and effective listening leaders will be sensitive enough to recognize them and provide opportunities for release. Satisfaction of catharsis is required for successful fulfillment at all other communication purpose levels. To advance your attitudes, skills, and knowledge as you build your cathartic communication strengths, we invite your thoughtful response to the following five questions:

ASSESS YOUR CATHARTIC COMMUNICATION

1. *List three individuals who serve your cathartic communication needs.*

2. *How important is their listening to your venting?*

3. *List three individuals who should, but do not, serve your cathartic communication needs. Why not?*

4. *Whose cathartic communication needs do you serve as a listening leader?*

5. *Whose cathartic needs can you serve better? Why? How? Where? When?*

THE DATA PURPOSE—INFORMATIONAL COMMUNICATION

The purpose of sharing information is considered by many to be the most important communication activity on which our social, business, educational, governmental, financial, military, and health-care systems are built. It is the activity that gives us data, knowledge, and power, yet depends completely on the ability to listen. Informational communication includes the developing, packaging, and transmission of information, and is a rapidly growing industry. More time, effort, energy, and money is spent on educational and informational services than on any other product or service in our economy. The simple result is that all listening leaders face a major problem of information overload. In 1950, "The Father of the Field of Listening," **Dr. Ralph Nichols**, astutely observed that "We are drowning in a sea of paper." Today we are drowning in an deeper sea of instantaneous data and information. Dr. Nichols also noted, "The effectiveness of the spoken word hinges not so much on how people talk, but mostly on how they listen." Yet, any attentive leader in today's world will recognize that greater focus has been placed more on talk. Our society concentrates more than ever on our ability to add to this overload—our ability to speak, to organize thoughts and put them into language that is clear and meaningful, and to express what we have to offer. The problem is intensified by the constant flow of information that pours from the Internet, television, and other media, which has increased the amount of information aimed at us daily by a factor of 10 to 1,000.

> *"The effectiveness of the spoken word hinges not so much on how people talk, but mostly on how they listen."*
> —Dr. Ralph Nichols

Verlyn Klinkenborg writing in the *New York Times* spotlighted a report entitled "How Much Information? 2003," completed at the University of California at Berkley's School of Information Management and Systems. The findings estimated the rate at which production and storage of information is growing. In 2003, they concluded, we transmitted 17.7 exabytes of information and stored about 5 exabytes, 30 percent more than the previous year. An exabyte is 1 billion gigabytes, or 1 trillion megabytes.

The Berkeley Report includes another startling conclusion: U.S. radio and television stations generate 23 million hours of "original" programming per year. A simple example of this increase is seen in the phenomenal growth of "talk radio." Prior to 1990, there were approximately 300 news talk radio stations in the United States. By the year 2003 the number of stations exceeded 1500. In today's world, the multitude of informational messages produced daily has increased geometrically within every individual's life span.

In the initial days of television, **Newton Minnow**, Chairman of the FCC, aptly described television as consisting primarily of "mind candy." In his famous 1961 "Vast Wasteland" speech to the National Association of Broadcasters, he spoke as a protector of the public interest of the then 180 million Americans. In the intervening years, many claim the "vast wasteland" has simply grown. However, today approximately 300 million Americans have a dramatically greater choice, and the potential richness of information and entertainment is virtually endless. Due to the technological advancements of cable television, satellites, the Internet, and more, we are awash in channels and messages. Although many of the messages remain "mind candy," any perceptive listener who assumes the Minimum 51% Responsibility will find "mind vegetables" of benefit.

In addition, technology has expanded the reach and speed of information flow to a point of real overload. With speech compression technology, voice mail, the Internet, cell phones, PDAs, wi-fi, and more, we are bombarded, inundated, and overloaded with a flood of information. It is ironic that, as technology and the potential connections for obtaining meaningful information increase, real communication decreases. In a world of more than 6 billion inhabitants, more and more information is thrown to the wind, and the multitudes are left to selectively choose, attend, process, and deal with it. It raises the question of "What is the effect on listener leaders?

Adam Aron serves as Chairman and CEO of Vail Resorts, Inc., and proudly explains how the company has grown significantly in size, scope, and profitability during his tenure of nearly a decade.

When I arrived, we were basically an uphill transportation company with two wonderful ski resorts in Colorado. Now, we are more than four times larger and have five wonderful ski resorts. In addition, we have a new Hotel Division and a Mountain Resort Division that is very active in lodging, retail stores, and restaurants. Our summer revenues have increased more than six-fold. All this occurred during a time that

> *"Twenty-first century leaders will find the job of listening to be more important and more difficult because information flows continuously."*
> —Adam Aron

listening increased in its importance and complexity. Over the last 20 years, the pace of life has sped up, not slowed down. Twenty years ago, there were no fax machines, cell phones, Internet, or wireless connections. If you wanted to send information in a document to someone, it took two to three days to be delivered. Today, information can be delivered in seconds. As a result, listening leaders will have few moments of rest or peace. 21st century leaders will find the job of listening to be more important and more difficult because information flows continuously.

More to the point, Adam Aron highlights the significant value of listening to information.

In a two-minute phone call with a member of our Board of Directors, I gained insight into the Board's desire that Vail Resorts should look at broader opportunities. A casual informational response to a simple question, "Would you be open and supportive if I did that?" eventually led to actions resulting in more than $500 million of acquisitions and expansion. Had I not been listening that day, Vail Resorts would not be the company it is today.

Likewise, commercial real estate executive **Edward O. "Ed" Wood, Jr.**, the Chief Operating Officer responsible for property management of the Florida portfolio for Trammell Crow Residential Services, observed the challenge of listening to the increased flow of information. With leadership responsibilities for more than 30 properties and more than 400 employees, Ed shared his thoughts on the impact of the explosion of information and technology.

Think about our ability to move information. We can take a picture and transport it anywhere in the world in one second through the Internet. We can send information to anybody in the world instantaneously with a cell phone and other technological marvels. Yet, we experience extensive breakdown of relationships; an inordinately high divorce rate; people who stay mad at each other for decades; organizational leaders who fail; and ongoing multiple wars throughout the world. Communication breakdowns are widespread. People refuse to listen to each other. We have marvelous tools to exchange information and enhance communication, yet we fail more often than we can afford to. What is wrong with this picture? We have to listen first and then teach others to listen if we hope to lead in a new way.

> *"We have to listen first and then teach others to listen if we hope to lead in a new way."*
> —*Edward O. Wood Jr.*

As the flow of information continues to grow, we must become more efficient. To do so, we must learn how to listen better.

To this end, **Pete Lilienthal**, a Harvard MBA and the creative founder and President of InTouch, developed a brilliant system and service to enhance the informational listening that is critical for the success of all leaders. Through his experiences in a variety of leadership positions, in a variety of organizations, Pete discovered that a serious informational disconnect exists between employees on the front line and the organization's leaders.

It is the flying-at-35,000-feet syndrome, where many leaders are focused on the organization's vision, mission, culture, values, strategies, and stock value, while their employees just want to get their jobs done. The employees want the tools, knowledge, and information they need to succeed. They also hold the information about how they can do their jobs better. I also discovered that there often is an informational disconnect between many members of the Board of Directors and Management. Board members seem to be continually surprised by information that is common knowledge around the water cooler. So we started to examine why

> *"The key to the system's success is that leaders must make themselves available to receive information. The next challenge is to effectively interpret, evaluate, and respond to the information."*
> —Pete Lilienthal

information flow is stifled in its journey within the organization. Eventually, we created InTouch, a company and a system that provides the unfettered flow of information up and down the organizational chain. As a result, leaders who are committed to listening have a mechanism and a conduit to receive information from all quarters. The key to the system's success is that leaders must make themselves available to receive information. The next challenge is to effectively interpret, evaluate, and respond to the information. Simply put, we enable employees at all levels to share their thoughts, their fears, their concerns, their feelings, their ideas, and suggestions on any issue.

The world's great caravan of information moves on, and listening leaders who choose to fully profit from it must keep their listening gates open. Listening leaders who consciously and continually enhance their information-processing ability will succeed. To help build your strengths in listening to information, we invite your thoughtful response to the following five questions:

ASSESS YOUR INFORMATION COMMUNICATION

1. *List five key individuals with whom you communicate for purposes of exchanging information.*

2. *List three individuals with whom you should improve your informational communication.*

3. *To what extent do you suffer from either a lack or an overload of information?*

4. *What steps do you need to take to streamline your information intake?*

5. *What tools do you use to strengthen your Information Communication needs?*

THE IMPACT PURPOSE—PERSUASIVE COMMUNICATION

TV infomercials, telephone solicitors, fast-talking salespeople, political candidates, and multilevel marketing promoters come to mind when thinking about persuasive communication; yet everyone persuades and is persuaded. Our environment is inundated with a multitude of persuasive appeals, ranging from family pictures on office desks, computer pop-up advertisements, airline mileage offered for switching long-distance phone service, to people's apparel and dress. Persuasive messages come in many and often unnoticed forms.

Persuasive communication attempts to do one or more of three things: 1) reinforce existing beliefs (REB); 2) change existing beliefs (CEB); or, 3) to achieve action (AA). All communication is essentially persuasive, as we all want our ideas to be embraced. However, the success of persuasive communication depends on a person's conscious or unconscious listening. Many commercials appeal to unconscious buyers, who are unaware persuasion took place even as they enter checkout lines with items in hand.

Communication purposes rarely operate independently of each other and are often difficult to isolate. However, senders and receivers of messages usually have, at any given moment, a primary goal and purpose of communication. A civic organization may think a guest speaker who has a financial planning background has come to discuss the economy, when actually his primary purpose may be to sell the audience on one of his investment products.

Steven Leuthold, a deep-thinking, analytical contrarian and leading financial expert, has a special perspective on listening and persuasion. Steve is the founder and CEO of the Leuthold Group, an Institutional Investment Research firm that provides research information to 230 institutions and 15,000 individuals throughout the United States and Europe. In addition, the Leuthold Group serves most of the major mutual funds and largest banks in the United States. As a regular guest on CNBC and "Wall Street Week," Steve believes that most communication is intended to persuade. Thus, in listening to persuasion, Steve highlights the value of listening beyond the big picture and the averages. Steve's focus and recommendation is to "listen to the excesses."

In our business, you must listen for clues about people and what they are thinking outside the mainstream box because the majority of people are usually wrong. So you listen to find out what everyone thinks, but you are really listening from a contrarian's perspective. Listening is very different when you are trying to please the client. In the financial world, you listen for the "group think" because when an idea becomes commonplace, it's pretty well built into the market, whether it's stocks or bonds. For example, in 1999 and 2000, many experienced people were saying, "Internet stocks were going to go to the sky." On the other hand, there was a group of investment leaders who had been through this kind of experience before and took the opposite position and did not buy or recommend the Internet stocks. Unfortunately the majority of investors did not listen and they lost a lot of money.

> *"In our business, you must listen for clues about people and what they are thinking outside the mainstream box because the majority of people are usually wrong. So you listen to find out what everyone thinks, but you are really listening from a contrarian's perspective."*
> —*Steven Leuthold*

It is well-known that listening is important to persuasion. Examples abound of the high-pressure marketers or sales professionals, the aggressive vendors of projects or ideas who do not listen. They have become largely ineffective in today's complex world, primarily because they miss clues about the individuals they are trying to reach. As a consequence, they end up advancing ideas that others consider against their interests. The many elements that compete for the busy person's attention today demand that great care must be taken before making proposals. When a sampling of people who had accepted proposals were asked why the persuasion had been successful, they gave the following reasons:

 He recognized I had a problem with the difficulties in this proposal. However, he indicated how we could overcome some of the roadblocks that loomed ahead.

2▶ She answered my questions patiently and completely and seemed to understand what we were getting at.

3▶ He listened carefully to the difficulties involved and did not try to evade or play down my fears and reservations. As I explained the issues to him, I found there might be ways around my reservations if he would make certain changes and modifications.

4▶ I found I liked working with her. She was a good sounding board, and in a big program like this, I really needed someone I could hash it out with. I needed someone who could listen intelligently.

Identifying the purpose of any speaker's communication will enhance your opportunity to adapt your listening behavior and be more productive. In addition, your insight regarding the various purposes of both senders and receivers will provide an extra bonus as you refine your speaking skills. Understanding different purposes will enable you to understand the circumstances in which your ideas can best be presented. You will make fewer counterproductive attempts to persuade someone, when they need first to establish a relationship, or release emotions through catharsis, or gather information.

In sum, the purpose of persuasion involves the sender's intent to: 1) *reinforce* listeners' existing attitudes, feelings, opinions, and beliefs; 2) *change* listeners' existing attitudes, feelings, opinions, and beliefs; or, 3) *impact* listeners' behavior and elicit action. Effective leaders know it is difficult to persuade others when their phatic, cathartic, and informational needs have not first been satisfied. In addition, leaders who listen better to the persuasive efforts of others become more productive. To advance your attitudes, skills, and knowledge as you build your persuasive communication strengths, we invite your thoughtful response to the following five questions:

ASSESS YOUR PERSUASIVE COMMUNICATION

1. *How frequently, and with whom, do you engage in persuasive communication?*

2. *How skilled are you in listening to attempts to persuade you?*

3. *How well do you understand the persuasion strategies of those who persuade you?*

4. *List three ways you will improve your ability to listen to the persuasion of others.*

5. *List three ways you can profit by improved listening to persuasion.*

THE GIGGLE PURPOSE—ENTERTAINMENT COMMUNICATION

Entertainment, the fifth purpose of communication, is presented in numerous venues, is important, and contributes to the success of the well-balanced listening leader. Although we will not discuss it in great depth, entertainment is a key aspect of life, is many-sided, and is necessary. It includes the primary elements that make us most human. Operating at various levels, entertainment ranges from great literature and the arts, to the entertainment of sporting events, to comedy, to water-cooler and office humor. All the everlasting works of the world's outstanding playwrights were conceived to entertain. The lasting benefit of such creative works as poetry, drama, films, television, radio, tapes, and more, are measured by the degree they contribute entertaining moments to our lives.

Workaholic leaders who take little time to listen to communication intended to entertain—who rarely attend the opera or theatre, laugh at jokes, or exchange entertaining pleasantries with others—shut themselves off from many of the deepest joys and most profound experiences of life. Enjoyment of entertainment requires listeners to invest in activities of deeper sensing, deeper understanding, and more profound evaluation. At other times, listening to entertainment requires listeners to suspend belief and simply giggle. As **Lord Chesterfield** wrote in *Letters to His Son* in 1752, "Whenever I go to an opera, I leave my sense and reason at the door…and deliver myself up to my eyes and ears." Regardless of the level, listening for purposes of entertainment has the benefit of evoking deep responses and pleasure.

To build your strengths in listening to entertainment, we invite your thoughtful response to the following five questions:

ASSESS YOUR LISTENING TO ENTERTAINMENT

1. *What are your favorite types and forms of entertainment?*

2. *How much time do you invest in listening to entertainment?*

3. *Do you explore opportunities to listen to new forms of entertainment?*

4. *What specific values will you find in listening to entertainment?*

5. *How will listening to entertainment positively affect your leadership skills?*

ALIGNMENT OF PURPOSE

Productive listening leaders profit from their ability to distinguish among the five communication purposes, as each purpose requires different listening strategies. Phatic communication requires time, patience, selflessness, and recognition of the larger value of relationship building. Cathartic communication requires attentive, caring, concerned, and nonjudgmental listening. Truly empathic people suspend evaluation and criticism when they listen to others. The challenge is to enter into the private world of the speaker and to understand emotional release without judging actions or feelings. Listening to information is a never-ending endeavor, as information is imbedded in all communication purposes. However, the challenge is to identify the sender whose purpose is primarily to share information. In contrast, the task of listening to persuasion requires a higher level of evaluation which affects agreement, disagreement, and productive listener action.

Howard Dayton, CEO of Crown Financial Ministries, leads an internationally acclaimed organization that operates in nine countries. Crown's vision is to teach 300 million people, including 30 million Americans and 270 million people internationally, how to handle money from God's perspective by September 2015. As a listening leader, Howard Dayton is committed to service.

When I listen, my purpose is two-fold: 1) to express to the other person that I really care for them and, 2) to learn what's in their heart. At times, I find myself in a position where I am inadequate for the job, and realize I need the input of others. Over time, I have intuitively realized that listening is more and more important. In fact, we have an intern program at our ministry, and I recently told our young leaders about a friend's expression regarding listening and time. My friend counseled, "Always be sure you finish your meal before the other person. If you are asking the questions and listening, you will." I think it has become habit and a deep part of my life, which I probably did not realize was happening. Listening is one of the ways you can express your appreciation for others. When you lead in a ministry environment, where most of the people who work with you are volunteers, the single most important thing you can do is to express your love and care for them. Listening is the relational glue that holds everything together.

Significant failures in listening result when the speaker and listener communicate at cross-purposes. All leaders have experienced individuals who attempt to persuade before providing the necessary information needed to make a rational decision. By the same token, when people engage in catharsis while others desire hard data about a problem, communication suffers. Without successful listening at the information or persuasion levels, everyone suffers. It is important to remember that, with the exception of the entertainment purpose, the other four purposes are hierarchical in nature. Building relationships through phatic communication provides the basis for the other three purposes of communication. Small talk often lays the groundwork for catharsis, information, and persuasion. Similarly, a person desperately needing catharsis will not be able to effectively transmit information or persuade others until his or her emotional needs have been met. Finally, we know persuasive communication must be based upon evidence and information before it can be truly successful. Listening to entertainment enhances the development of a well-rounded leader.

> *"Always be sure you finish your meal before the other person. If you are asking the questions and listening, you will."*
> —Howard Dayton

THE POINT

In sum, listening leaders will profit by constantly applying **Golden Rule 5: "Find and Align Purpose,"** since everyone communicates to: 1) establish relationships; 2) relieve emotional tensions; 3) inform; 4) persuade; and 5) entertain. Understanding and adapting to the speaker's purpose and intent will result in more productive listening and leading.

As **George Knutsen** so aptly observed, "...everyone speaks and listens on purpose. Their purpose! Sometimes the purposes are clear and precise. Sometimes they are fuzzy and muddled. However, when we listen on purpose and connect to the speaker's purpose, we will always achieve more and serve better." The principle is simple, practice **Golden Rule 5: "Listening Leaders Find & Align Purpose"** and you will Listen, Lead, and Succeed.

Golden Rule 5

"Listening Leaders Find & Align Purpose"

10 ACTION STEPS

1. Raise your awareness by recognizing that everyone communicates at different times for different purposes.

2. Learn and apply the five purposes of communication at work, home and in social settings.

3. Consistently strengthen your relationships with others by improving your listening to their phatic (binding) communication.

4. Serve and support others by improving your listening to their cathartic (venting) communication.

5. Refine your ability to listen for specific information to improve your processing skills.

6. Exercise your ability to identify each of the three sub-purposes (REB, CEB, AA) of others' persuasive efforts.

7. Identify and record specific opportunities for listening to entertainment communication.

8. Calculate and record the percentage of your typical work day that is spent listening to each of the five specific communication purposes.

9. Identify specific and significant failures that occurred when speakers and listeners communicated at cross-purposes.

10. Build your "Listening Organization" by teaching those you lead the significance of identifying and aligning speakers' and listeners' purposes.

LISTENING LEADERS™ GOLDEN RULES PYRAMID

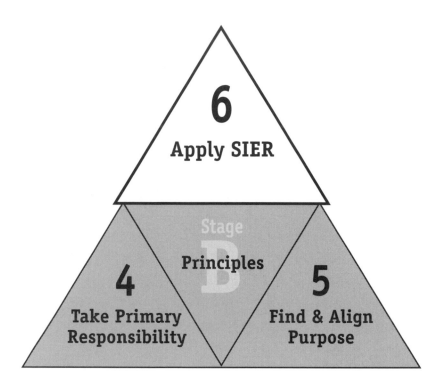

Golden Rule 6

"Listening Leaders Apply SIER"

"Listening has become my career. I am the daughter of a mother and father who each had their own brand of listening skills. My mom taught me to listen for the unspoken emotion. My dad taught me to watch while I listen since body language speaks so loudly. I believe being a good listener has made me a better marketer because, whenever I am faced with a new product, ad, or service, 'I hear' through the ears of others before 'I hear' for myself."

—Mary Lou Quinlan

For 25 years, listening leader **Mary Lou Quinlan** has been listening to people's desires and translating those desires into successful marketing strategies. In 1999, after 20 successful years in sales, marketing communications, and advertising, Mary Lou created Just Ask a Woman. Her firm is a strategic marketing consulting company that specializes in new ways of listening and interpreting women's needs for major corporations. Mary Lou was hailed by the *Wall Street Journal* as the "Oprah of Madison Avenue," and by *Continental* magazine as "The Ask Master." Mary Lou interviews women for clients like General Motors, Lifetime Television, Johnson & Johnson, CitiGroup, Toys "R" Us and Estee Lauder. Mary Lou began her career at Avon Products, where for 10 years she achieved great success as a motivator and sales coach to 500,000 Avon representatives. As a listening leader, she became Avon's Director of Advertising for the United States. Listening remains a constant in Mary Lou's ongoing success. Her insightful book, *Just Ask a Woman: Cracking the Code of What Women Want and How They Buy* discusses how to listen to women.

Fostering listening in our organization is a constant agenda. A woman I work with has a great saying, "You don't get to be the smartest one in the room!" In other words, let someone else have a chance to speak while we listen and learn from them. I try to reinforce the quieter people by repeating what they say like, "Wait, and listen to what Sally just said..." It makes everyone realize I am listening hard and they should also. I try to lead by example. When I listen, my eyes are totally focused on the person I am with. I am distracted by nothing. I even say up front, "I don't care what anyone else wants me for in the next hour; I am only interested in what you have to say." I find people are amazed by the focused attention and a simple bit of respect.

> *"I try to lead by example. When I listen, my eyes are totally focused on the person I am with. I am distracted by nothing. I even say up front, 'I don't care what anyone else wants me for in the next hour; I am only interested in what you have to say."*
> —*Mary Lou Quinlan*

Mary Lou understands that for all effective leaders, the process of listening begins with attention and ends with action. The process is complex, but it need not be overly complicated if you engage the four sequential and hierarchical stages of listening as outlined in **Golden Rule 6: "Listening Leaders Apply SIER."** By applying the SIER Model (the listening stages of Sensing, Interpreting, Evaluating, and Responding) leaders position themselves to positively control their listening and leadership destiny.

THE LISTENING LEADERSHIP SIER PROCESS

In exploring the **Ten Golden Rules of Listening Leadership,** you have learned the importance of the **Preparation** in **Stage A**, consisting of the Golden Rules 1, 2, and 3 ("Listening Leaders Build Solid Foundations"; "Listening Leaders Explore and Execute A-S-K"; and, "Listening Leaders Develop Impactful Habits"). In addition, in **Stage B** you have focused on the Principles of Golden Rules 4 and 5 ("Listening Leaders Take Primary Responsibility" and "Listening Leaders Find and Align Purpose"). It is now time to learn the last rule of **Principles** in **Stage B, "**Listening Leaders Apply SIER."

Listening leadership is a complex process that can be simplified and mastered by dissecting, understanding, and applying the four multidimensional stages, or blocks, that make up the activities of listening. These four basic stages must be connected in an hierarchical sequence, appropriate to the existing communication purpose.

To review, effective listening requires: **1) Sensing**, or receiving the message; **2) Interpreting**, or understanding the message; **3) Evaluating**, or judging the message; and, **4) Responding**, or reacting to the message. Taking the first four letters of each stage creates the "SIER Listening Model" that has profitably served international leaders for over forty years. Listening leaders, remember the SIER Model by focusing on achieving "Success In Everyday Relationships."

SIER = Success - In - Everyday - Relationships

Listening leadership must be viewed in a sequential and hierarchical order. Like building any structure, movement must proceed from the foundation up. In building the "effective house of listening leadership," leaders must listen through four stages. First, productive listeners must satisfy the completion of the **Sensing** foundation before they focus on constructing the second stage, **Interpreting**. Sensing and interpreting are required for all purposes of communication (Phatic, Cathartic, Informational, Persuasive, and Entertainment). Although the third stage, **Evaluation**, is inherent in all informational, persuasive, and some entertainment communication, evaluation destroys the basic purpose and intent of phatic and cathartic communication. In addition, any premature interpretation, evaluation, and response activity will short-circuit most communication. The fourth stage for productive and profitable listening leaders, **Responding**, is an ongoing and ultimate activity. As such, it assumes the final position of the four stages of listening. When viewed sequentially, the SIER Model flows from Sensing to Interpreting, then to Evaluating as required, and finally to Responding. Any attempt to complete any stage out of sequence will lead to listening leader failure. As the SIER Model is fully utilized, we will explore how it can serve you in three ways: first, as a Planning tool; second, as an Application tool; and, third, as a Diagnostic tool.

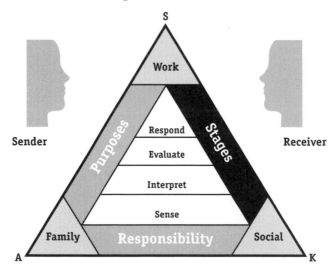

SIER Listening Leadership Model

THE IMPORTANCE OF *SENSING*

As noted, the foundation of all effective listening is based on accurately receiving senders' messages. Although listening is not synonymous with hearing, it begins with sensing. Sensing engages the entire range of sensory mechanisms, sight, sound, smell, taste, and touch. Effective listening leaders focus first and foremost on sensing a sender's relevant messages. With a plethora of forces competing for our sensing attention, it is imperative to focus on "first things first." In the United States, the challenge is heightened as the population is aging and experiencing greater hearing loss. According to the National Center for Health Statistics, in 1997, 20.4 percent of 45–64-year-old individuals reported that they suffer from at least mild hearing loss. That represented a 14.8 percent increase since 1988. And, of course, when the sense of hearing is diminished, listening is adversely impacted. When sensing is incomplete or inaccurate, all other stages of listening will be affected adversely. Sensing is the single most important stage of listening, until it is satisfied; then it is time to move to each higher, and more important, stage.

Listening leader **Sharon Walker** is the Chief Operations Officer of Insight Financial Credit Union, a $350 million organization. Sharon is responsible for planning, organizing, and managing overall credit union operations for 10 branch offices and a call center, and she coordinates operational support. In her leadership role, she understands the importance of successful sensing.

> *"You have to use all of your senses to really capture what someone is saying."*
> —Sharon Walker

Listening requires all of your senses. It is not just hearing what someone is saying. You have to listen to verbal and non-verbal cues. You have to listen to what you see. You have to listen to the tone of voice and the complete message. It is not just what they say, but how they say it. What is their purpose? What are they trying to say? What words are they using? What words are they are not using? You have to use all of your senses to really capture what someone is saying.

Although sensing is critical, many leaders are often quick to move prematurely to higher stages. It is important to constantly remember two things about sensing. First, sensing is the foundation for the rest of the listening leadership process. If sensing is incomplete, nothing else can be or will be productively accomplished. Second, as important as sensing is, it is wise to remember sensing is only the first stage of the total SIER Model.

Listening leader **Nancy Tallent** Regional Vice President of Human Resources for CNA Insurance, appreciates the importance of focusing on the first stage of listening leadership.

> Listening requires focusing on each stage of the communication process. It requires receiving all of the messages sent your way, being silent, and letting your ears listen. Listening is being able to tune in to all the other things people do, including their pattern of breathing and their body language. How is someone sitting, and how do they move? Sometimes, when I hear other people talk about communication during our meetings, I am impressed with how they pick up on all the subtleties. I am reminded of the importance of capturing the full message.

"Listening is being able to tune in to all the other things people do, including their pattern of breathing and their body language."
—Nancy Tallent

Another listening leader, **Dr. John Davis,** enjoyed a widely respected career as the Superintendent of Minneapolis Public Schools, President of Macalester College, Chair of the Federal Reserve Board, and too many other leadership roles to list. For John, the importance of sensing was developed at the beginning of his distinguished career, nearly 60 years ago.

The President of the University of New Hampshire was my first academic administrator. He hired me to be his assistant in 1945, when I had just gotten out of the military service. Fortunately, he was a very astute leader and taught me a lot. He said, "John, I am not going to call upon you to make my decisions, but I would like you to be my eyes and my ears as you move around the campus. I don't want you to be a spy; I just want you to sense what is going on and bring me ideas as to how we can improve the situation." Since then, I have been a wanderer and a roamer. I always visited a school once a week and just popped in unannounced. When I visited classrooms, I would always think, "One mouth and two ears." I think that is significant. I have sat in many situations and listened and wondered when should I cut this off? Sometimes you are in a situation where there are many people who want to be listened to, and one of these speaker's thoughts might trigger somebody else's. So the topic you are discussing gets translated through a number of mentalities, attitudes, and prejudices represented around the table. I was always amazed that, because of listening, I would see the situation

> *"He said... 'I don't want you to be a spy; I just want you to sense what is going on and bring me ideas as to how we can improve the situation.' Since then, I have been a wanderer and a roamer."*
> —Dr. John Davis

changing quite significantly, often without the knowledge of the person who first introduced the idea. Listening often gave me the ability to anticipate what was likely to be said. I feel fortunate to have developed the ability to focus my energies on total listening. I also think it is important to be able to sense when speakers are speaking out of what they have carefully thought through, or whether it is some idea pulled up at random or stolen from somebody because it impressed the speaker. Artificiality has to be determined in light of the prospect of the speaker being able to execute the point he or she is advocating.

As Dr. Davis discovered, truly active and productive sensing listeners are alert for clues being transmitted by senders. Listening must be your primary activity at the time. You will always profit when you face the speaker, adapt to the nonverbal cultural norms, and give the speaker your undivided attention. Focus on the speaker's posture, gestures, and facial expressions. Listen to the speaker's tone of voice. Is it agitated or calm, uninspired or enthusiastic? What about the speaker's intensity? Is the speaker pleasant, upset, or furious? Is the speaker relaxed or excited; is he or she speaking slowly or fast? Is the vocal volume soft, moderate, or loud? Does the speaker emphasize specific words? Is the tone low or high? As there are numerous additional variables that leaders must sense, the challenge of complete sensing becomes evident.

Sensing these elements will shape the ultimate meaning of the message, but first and foremost, one must be sensitive to their presence. Although ineffective leaders place the cart before the horse, effective listening leaders always place the horse before the cart. Ongoing sensing must precede all other listening activities. When leaders fail at the sensing stage, they will fail at each subsequent stage. When leaders fully sense senders' messages, they have a chance to succeed at the following stages of interpreting, evaluating, and responding.

DEVELOP YOUR SENSES

Thomas T. (Tom) Ross is a prominent real estate attorney who has been practicing law for nearly 40 years. Listed in the 2001–2002 Edition of Woodward/White, Inc.'s "The Best Lawyers in America," Tom believes that listening is the key ingredient in the legal process. "The lawyer's function is to create a road map to help people achieve a mutually desired objective. Whether it is a consummated transaction, a sale, a lease, a lending, or a borrowing, Tom believes, "Listening is, in my view, a critical ingredient." Tom Ross's view on sensing takes on added meaning when you learn that, just two years ago, Tom experienced a major medical mishap in which he lost his sight.

There is a common misconception that when you lose your sight, your other senses are suddenly going to be enhanced or there is going to be a physiological change that makes your fingers more sensitive so you can read Braille. I have learned that is absolutely untrue. What *is* true is that you can no longer rely and depend on sight. When you engage in an everyday event, like walking down the street, an enormous portion of your ability to physically accomplish that task is sight-dependent. Balance is enormously sight-dependent. Direction, guidance, speed, and everything you learned through a lifetime and take for granted, happen almost unconsciously. Everything from eating, dressing, walking, and all the things people normally do. We're not aware of how much of what we do on a daily basis is in fact reliant and dependent upon sight. With sight, you can hear the same thing I hear, but you don't care, you don't need as much of it. If you are standing on the edge of a street you can look up and down both ways. Think about it, we teach our children to "look both ways." You don't say to your child, "hear both ways when you cross the street."

We learn to use the sense of sight, touch, taste, smell, or sound that is most effective for whatever we're doing, and we tend to be less dependent upon our other senses. In my case, I don't have sight anymore, so when I step off a curb, if I haven't listened, I'm likely to get run over. So I had better listen very carefully. Similarly, if I am walking down the street, if I don't have my cane out in front of me to help me feel my way along, I'm going to bump into a lot of telephone poles. So, physiologically, your senses don't improve. But you improve your ability to rely upon senses that were there before that weren't needed as much as they are now. And you learn to use them better. I think I'm learning to hear and listen better than I did before. I know when I listen to tapes, go to movies, and talk to people, I listen to the tempo of their voice. I listen to their breathing. I listen to their volume and more.

> *"In my case, I don't have sight anymore, so when I step off a curb, if I haven't listened, I'm likely to get run over."*
>
> —*Tom Ross*

Now I just tend to assimilate and evaluate sensory perceptions with a slightly different priority and arrangement. It's like wine tasters. Most people have similar taste buds, and yet when you initially start drinking wine, you may believe cheap wine is good wine. However, if you drink wine over the years, your senses become more discriminating, and you will be able to distinguish good wine from bad wine. I don't believe wine tasters have taste buds that are better than mine. I just think they have learned to discriminate and focus their power and existing senses. The bottom line is, I believe everyone can train their senses.

THE CHALLENGE OF INTERPRETING

Greg Steil's Quality Control leadership responsibilities at Toro, Inc. requires disciplined and detailed listening. In the world of quality control, precise measurement and understanding is basic. There is no room for error, so imagine Greg's amusement when he related the following story.

A man walked into a medical clinic and the receptionist asked him what he had. He said, "Shingles." So she took down his name, address, and told him to have a seat. A few minutes later, a nurse's aid came out and asked him what he had. He said, "Shingles," so she took down his height and weight and took him back to the examining room. Ten minutes later, a nurse came in and asked him what he had. He said, "Shingles." So she asked a few more questions, gave him a blood pressure test, told him to take off all his clothes and wait for the doctor. Fifteen minutes later, a doctor came in and asked him what he had. Exasperated, he said, "Shingles." The doctor looked him over carefully and asked, "Where do you have them?" to which, the man answered, "Outside on the truck."

Although it's challenging, every thinking leader knows it is critically important that the speaker's message be interpreted to match the speaker's meaning. Listeners must be sure that speakers' and listeners' meanings are synchronized. Leaders must ask the basic question, "Do the words mean the same to both of us? Are we talking about the same thing?" Interpreting is the second stage of the SIER listening process, and like sensing, is essential to the following stages. When you fully sense any message but misinterpret the sender's meaning and intent, you will fail at each higher stage. Each stage builds and depends on the stages that precede it.

Listening leader **Anne Knapp** is the thoughtful and purposeful Executive Vice President of Corporate Development at GMAC-RFC. Anne expends great effort in correctly interpreting and understanding what others mean.

I have worked hard to develop the ability to listen to really understand what people are saying. As a result, I focus on making sure my interpretation of what people are saying is closely aligned to what they are actually saying. Then I analyze and feed it back. I believe my strength as a strategist is a combination of hearing and understanding what people are saying, and mixing their insights and experiences with my own creative thoughts. The key is to listen, collect, and understand the ideas of many. Restructuring GMAC-RFC was positively impacted as a result of listening to the voices of many. By interpreting and sorting through a multitude of ideas, I was able to write a white paper outlining a proposed process of organizational change. Our organization was about twice the size it is now, but as we listened and understood where the organization needed and wanted to go, we successfully decentralized a fair amount of what we did. By correctly interpreting what many of our employees were saying, we managed to positively move through that change process and come out healthy at the other end.

> *"I listen very carefully when people talk about what not to do, because I do not have any need to repeat other people's mistakes."*
>
> *—Anne Knapp*

Correctly interpreting and understanding what everyone really means is very difficult, but imperative. I try very hard to listen and understand what others believe is going on. I listen to what people are feeling about things and what is coming up. I try to pay the most attention to, and understand, what might go wrong, as opposed to listening to people who agree with me. I have found I learn much more from other people's mistakes, and not repeating them, than I do from people's successes. I listen very carefully when people talk about what not to do because I do not have any need to repeat other people's mistakes.

Like all outstanding listening leaders, Anne Knapp understands that interpretation requires the careful matching of sender and receiver meanings. In some ways, the second stage of interpreting is the most challenging stage of listening. Considering the complexity and variety of meaning in language, and the variety of nonverbal behavior, the ongoing task of matching meanings can boggle the mind. But, as in the old story of the three baseball umpires who were discussing the differences between balls and strikes, it is important to remember that, "Words have no meaning; people have meaning." The first umpire said, "Some pitches are balls and some are strikes, and I call them the way they is." The second umpire said, "I disagree, because some are balls and some are strikes, and I call them the way I see them." The third and wiser umpire listened and simply said, "Gentlemen, get real. Some are balls and some are strikes, but they ain't nothing until I call 'em."

In the larger game of life, misunderstandings can be trivial or monumental, inconsequential or catastrophic, meaningless or extraordinarily costly. Major misunderstandings always become apparent. On the other hand, it is often the seemingly small differences of meaning that get us in trouble. Vague generalities often lead to misinterpretations. For example, what is meant by, "I'll take care of it as soon as I can," or, "Give me a little more of that," or, "It's up the road a ways," or, "I will be ready in just a few minutes," or, "This won't hurt much." In such cases, senders always know and understand what they mean; listeners usually don't. However, as listeners accept the "Minimum 51% Responsibility," the pursuit of connected meaning begins. Long ago, Socrates argued in Plato's *Cratylus* that, "It is not enough to try to understand what a thing is based on its name because the name givers may have been living in ancient times, and the name only reflects what the name givers thought was the nature of reality then."

Or as **Lewis Carroll** wrote in *Alice in Wonderland*, "'When I use a word,' Humpty Dumpty said in a rather scornful tone, 'it means just what I choose it to mean—nothing more or less.' 'The question is,' said Alice, 'whether you can make words mean different things? 'The question is,' said Humpty Dumpty, 'which is to be the master—that's all.'" Or, as President Bill Clinton strongly argued, the veracity of his sworn statements depended upon what one understood the words "is" or "alone" to mean. Successful listening leaders profit by remembering, "Words have no meaning; people have meaning."

More than half a century ago, the distinguished educator **Edgar Dale** counseled, "Beware of the COIK fallacy." COIK stands for "Clear Only If Known," and skilled listening leaders profit by probing for the complete meaning when background information is missing. The listener's task is to make sure his or her listening interpretation and understanding matches that of the sender. When sensing is successful but interpreting fails, the listening stages of evaluating and responding will automatically fail. When both sensing and interpreting are successful, listening leaders have a chance to succeed at the stages of evaluating and responding.

> *"Beware of the COIK fallacy. COIK stands for 'Clear Only If Known.'"*
> —*Edgar Dale*

THE COMPLEXITY OF EVALUATING

The third stage of listening, Evaluating, can occur only when leaders have completely sensed and correctly interpreted the speaker's message. Only then is the listener in a legitimate position to evaluate the message. At its simplest level, listeners will like or dislike, agree or disagree, accept or reject speakers' messages. At a deeper and more complex level, evaluating challenges the listener to judge whether the speaker's message is: consistent or contradictory; fallacious or well reasoned; complete or incomplete; fact or opinion; supported by substantial evidence; and objective or biased.

Evaluating is enhanced by those who follow the advice, "Withhold your judgment until your comprehension is complete." Effective listening leaders who avoid premature evaluation generally reap more productive results. Profitable listening results when the process of evaluation determines whether the speaker's message is factual or opinionated, if the content development is complete and sound, if the evidence supports the message, and if the reasoning is valid. These are the more complex judgments that are required by productive listening leaders.

Listening Leader **Jim Poling** is the successful Head Coach of the men's tennis program at the United States Military Academy at West Point. Poling arrived at West Point with 16 years of head coaching experience at the college level, serving additional highly successful terms at Rollins College and Tulsa, South Alabama, and Mississippi State Universities. Coach Poling, who was named Wilson Intercollegiate Tennis Association Division II National "Coach of the Year," stresses the importance of listening to his athletes.

Listening is more than just listening to the words. You are looking for the story behind the story because sometimes you don't always get all the facts. You have to be able to dig in and look behind what someone is saying before evaluating and devising the consequence. I have learned a

> *"Listening is more than just listening to the words…*
> *the first step… is to ask for clarification before making a judgement."*
> —Coach Jim Poling

new way of evaluating athlete behaviors at West Point. The Academy has an honor code, which dictates that a Cadet will not lie, cheat, or steal, nor tolerate those who do. If a situation occurs, the first step in dealing with it is to ask for clarification before making a judgment. Cadets do not say, "Did you cheat yesterday?" or "I saw you cheating." Rather they say, "There was a situation that happened, and I just want to hear your side." As a result, clarification is always sought before evaluating and responding. This process provides greater opportunity to evaluate in a more thoughtful and fully appropriate way. To me, that really makes a lot of sense.

The Evaluating stage of the SIER Listening Model must be engaged primarily in the informational and persuasive purposes of communication. Although evaluation may be involved in the process of listening to phatic, cathartic, and entertaining communication, it is of far greater importance in listening to communication that is intended to inform or persuade. As significant as evaluating is in every productive leader's listening process, it is important to remember that evaluation is generally out of order in the purposes of phatic and cathartic communication. Other than being judged as authentic and sincere, most senders are not interested in being evaluated when they are "building relationships through small talk" or "dumping their emotional bucket." On the other hand, listening to informational, persuasive, and some entertaining communication demands skillful evaluating.

By completing the first three stages of sensing, interpreting, and evaluating as required, listening leaders are in position to engage in the profitable fourth stage, Responding.

THE RESULT OF RESPONDING

Responding, the fourth stage of listening leadership, is often overlooked as a part of listening. Without completion of the Responding stage, your communication will be incomplete. Without response, there is no measure of success at the stages of sensing, interpreting, or evaluating. On the other hand, as we live and listen in an action-oriented society, many leaders believe their responsibility is to respond quickly by taking action. During years of observing and coaching listening leaders, we have noted a widespread pattern of leaders skipping some combination of stages one, two, or three and of moving directly to the Responding stage. That is, taking action on what they think is called for. But as communication expert **Dr. Robert J. Walker** has so astutely observed, "Preemptive responses are perilous."

At times, leaders may not actually sense or understand what is being said because they have already moved toward a predetermined course of action. At other times, leaders fail because they simply don't bother to respond. Effective listening leaders recognize the importance and order of responding, in some clear fashion, to all communication. The responding stage of the SIER model requires that, ultimately: "The Listening Leader must be a Responding Listener."

TIMING IS EVERYTHING!

Listening leader **Andy Greenshields** is a highly successful Venture Capitalist (VC) with a long and rich history of listening to individuals with ideas in search of money. As Andy explains, "In my world, everyone is listening and looking for the ultimate response that will serve everyone."

When a young entrepreneur or a management team comes in with a business plan for the first meeting, the ven-

> "If you are not fully listening, and listening well, the end response will serve no one."
> —Andy Greenshields

ture capitalist has to listen for little items based on their history. Outstanding venture capitalists seem to develop a "special antenna" that enables them to pick up clues to good and bad possibilities that lead to a series of focused questions. Listening to entrepreneurs' responses allows understanding, evaluating, and deciding if you want to pursue their project further. If you are not listening well, the end response will serve no one. I have participated in meetings wherein entrepreneurs have presented their ideas to more than one venture capitalist and they would not let the entrepreneur fully express what they wanted to accomplish or who they were going to build a business for. Rather, the focus would quickly move to how they would build the business.

I have found that when people come to you to describe an opportunity, everyone is served better if you let them fully express their ideas, hopes, and dreams, even if you already know the solution. If you have seen the problem enough times, you probably do know the solution. But, it is always wise to let the person describing the opportunities and challenges finish before judging and responding. Of course, you ultimately have to evaluate and respond, but first you must let them describe the total problem and how they are thinking about resolving it because that will help you better understand that person. They are going to be responsible for executing the plan and running the business, so it is important to gain a deep insight into what kind of person you will be working with. When you prematurely respond and say, "Hey, I know the solution to that problem; this is what you have to do," you have just absolved them of any responsibility. They have been given your prescription, so if the solution fails, it will be because of your bad advice. Over the years, I have participated in numerous board meetings wherein members will respond and cut somebody off before the entrepreneurs have completed their presentation or fully described their issues and problems. This could be the first business they have ever started in their life, and it is a huge learning experience for them. It is important to find out how they are going to run the business and work themselves out of problems. Everyone is looking for constructive responses, but the timing has to be right. As someone said, "Timing is everything."

LISTENING EQUALS AIRCRAFT SAFETY

Harry Mitchel is the Director of Aviation for Magic Carpet Aviation. His major responsibility is to ensure the safe transportation of the Orlando Magic NBA team players, executives, passengers, and the flight crew on the corporate Boeing 737 aircraft. In addition, Harry sees that all pilots, flight attendants, maintenance department employees, and scheduling staff are properly trained, are currently qualified in their individual areas of responsibility, and have the tools and support to execute their jobs in a professional manner. Harry recognizes the importance of listening as one key to his leadership growth, as he has always believed that, "It takes a team that listens." In addition, Harry recognizes the obvious, that within the aviation industry, many airplanes have crashed and too many people have died because of a flight crew's failure to listen well.

Years ago, there were many accidents that were attributed to mechanical failure. Today, with the technological advancements of avionics, the wings, the structure of the aircraft, the engine, and the radios, the current number of accidents that can be attributed to mechanical failure has dropped dramatically. Accidents attributed to human error, on the other hand, have increased significantly. To address this problem, the industry and the Federal Aviation Administration (FAA) developed the acronym "CRM" which originally stood for "Cockpit Resource Management." CRM included a process to help the cockpit crew communicate more effectively with each other. The primary focus of the training was listening. Listening to what other people were telling you, particularly in emergency and stressful situations. It was reasoned that if pilots had better listening skills, there would be fewer serious accidents. The FAA expanded the process to include the entire crew, emphasizing how to listen in stressful situations.

Harry has taken the process one step further at Magic Carpet Aviation by expanding CRM to stand for "Company Resource Management," and he includes virtually all employees (i.e. pilots, flight attendants, maintenance crews, schedulers...) in the process. As Harry discovered, "Listening is the central factor."

A TRAGIC CASE

A tragic case of failed sensing, interpreting, evaluating, and responding that occurred more than a quarter of a century ago resulted in the worst disaster in the history of aviation. On March 27, 1977, two Boeing 747s, KLM Flight 4805 and Pan Am Flight 1736, collided on takeoff from the Tenerife Airport in the Canary Islands, resulting in the loss of 583 lives and hundreds of millions of dollars in damages. Although the crew members were experienced and highly regarded, the official investigation and report of this tragedy focuses on human error—specifically the faulty listening at all four stages of sensing, interpreting, evaluating, and responding. A review of recorded cockpit and control tower communication pointed to the failure of sensing the full messages, specific misinterpretation regarding taxi-way exit points and clearance for take-off, faulty evaluations, and inappropriate and ultimately tragic responses. Like most human communication failures, every breakdown could have been avoided with complete and effective listening at every stage.

The significance of the sequential and hierarchical order of the four stages of the SIER Model is clear. When we fail at the stage of sensing, we fail at every higher stage. What is not fully sensed cannot be properly and fully interpreted, evaluated, or responded to. If the failure of listening begins at the stage of interpreting, then evaluating and responding will be impacted negatively. When failure of listening begins at the evaluation stage, responding will fail. Of course, listening failure can also begin at the responding stage, regardless of the success of sensing, interpreting, or evaluating. In sum, there is "no room for error."

CHOOSING APPROPRIATE RESPONSES

Ultimately, effective leaders are responding listeners. Responses may be as simple as a nod or shake of the head, frowning or smiling, taking notes, a verbal answer, or a physical action appropriate to the purpose, message, and request.

In the process of responding, there are three levels of listening responses. First is **Passive Listening,** which involves the least amount of observable response. Listeners are not responsive in any significant way. Consequently, it is difficult to know if they have sensed, interpreted, evaluated, or stored the message. Second is **Acknowledgement Listening,** which involves a variety of non-verbal responses (listeners smile, nod, hold direct eye contact) that indicate the message may have been sensed, interpreted, evaluated, and stored to some limited degree. However, it is still hard to be certain. Third is **Responding Listening,** which involves the highest level of involvement and ultimate response. Responding listening leaders engage and utilize all the attitudes, skills, and knowledge developed to this point. They respond by interactively engaging SIER through sensing, interpreting, evaluating, storing, and responding to selected senders. Responding listeners are not passive, nor do they simply acknowledge, they are fully engaged. They restate, they clarify, they question, they paraphrase, they check matched meanings, they carefully evaluate, and they respond. Effective listening leaders are responding listeners.

Responding listening requires ongoing patience, understanding, and observable feedback, which can be demonstrated through paraphrasing and questions. Questions and paraphrasing are critical in discovering the speaker's thoughts, opinions, feelings, and attitudes. Some people are more comfortable sharing their thoughts and opinions rather than feelings and attitudes. But feelings and attitudes are more important for the listener to understand, as they impact and drive the speaker's thoughts and feelings. Effective listening leaders will always consider the speaker's purpose before responding.

Listening Leader **Paul Niccum** has developed a very effective SIER-oriented strategy to enhance his and his colleagues' listening.

> *"People are moving so fast these days, and everyone seems to follow a 'Cliff Notes' version of listening… As a result, listeners' responses often miss the mark."*
> —*Paul Niccum*

People are moving so fast these days, and everyone seems to be following a "Cliff Notes" version of listening, wherein, they do not take time to fully and effectively capture, understand, or judge what someone is trying to communicate to them. As a result, listeners' responses often miss the mark. With that in mind, my managers and I have adopted a simple strategy, "Repeat." "Repeat" is a process of restating the essence of the sender's message as the listener heard it, understood it, judged it, and is prepared to respond to it. That really helps bridge any gap, as the sender can say, "Oh, no, that's not at all what I said or meant," or, "that was what I was trying to communicate." So it is very important that every response is done in a way to ensure common connection.

Listening leader **JoAnn Barnett** is Vice President of Infant Swimming Resource, the internationally acclaimed organization dedicated to prevent infant drowning. Listening and questioning form the basis for their entire instructional curriculum. As JoAnn explains:

We have actually built listening into our protocols for training instructors. You don't talk, you ask; you don't preach, you inquire. All of our training materials are formulated in the form of questions. Our training protocols all are based on listening and all begin with questions. At first, it is a little frustrating for the Master Instructors, to whom it may seem easier to just go in and tell and teach what you know. As everybody comes with such different backgrounds, I first teach the Master Instructors to create dialogue with the student instructors. We ask them, "Are you comfortable being coached through this?"

Because most of our students are infants, all of our instructors have to learn to listen to and read body lan-

> *"We have actually built listening into our protocols for training instructors. You don't talk, you ask; you don't preach, you inquire."*
> *—JoAnn Barnett*

guage. To fully listen, you have to be completely keyed in to what the student does in the presence of various stimuli. Since the average age of our students is 18 months, much of the instructors' listening must be done with their eyes. Also, we train the instructors to listen to the parents in a questioning format as well. "What about this bothers you?" "Did you see what he just accomplished?" "Do you realize...?"

Although swimming instruction was taught in a very structured way for 30 years, our revised, listening-oriented method of instruction began in 1999 and is very new. So from the time we began incorporating listening into our organization, the changes have been exponential and monumental. We believe that encouraging listening and questioning provides a measure of safety. The objectives of our organization are reinforrced when we listen and reinforce instructors who really want to learn. We don't have an instructor thinking: "It's taking me four weeks to get all my students to roll over and float; I hope nobody finds this out." Because we are committed to listening, they are much more likely to pick up the phone and say, "Something is wrong. Can I send you a videotape?" So listening and questioning helps us create a productive learning atmosphere in which we can provide another measure of safety as we expand.

Another listening leader **Dan Carricato** is Vice President of Human Resources for the Hilton Grand Vacation Corporation and a member of the Executive Committee. Dan understands the importance of each stage of the listening process and traces his listening development back to his childhood.

I can clearly see myself as a little kid, lying on the floor in my living room and just listening to my parents talk to friends and family members. I would track conversations in my mind and think, "How did we get to this topic?

How did we get to talking about this? What led from one topic to another to another?" It was interesting because I learned how to listen and move a conversation along by

> *"We can be honest with each other because we know we are going to be listened to and respected."*
> —Dan Carricato

watching and listening to my parents. My parents never said, "A child is to be seen and not heard." I could jump in anywhere I wanted to and respond. I remember when I was 13 or 14 years old, an age when you have strong opinions, the neighbors would come over every night and we would engage in lengthy conversations. It was a time when people used to enjoy extended conversations. That experience has extended into my adult life, both at work and at home. As a result, my wife, children, and I have established a very cohesive and trusting family. We can be honest with each other because we know we are going to be listened to and respected. My wife and I have been married 32 years, and we still have so much to talk about because we know how to fully listen and carry on a conversation.

Like all effective listening leaders, Paul Niccum, JoAnn Barnett, and Dan Carricato are profiting from listening through the four stages of SIER. As you learn to utilize the SIER model, it is critically important to remember:

1. ▶ Each stage of the listening process is important.
2. ▶ Each stage must be completed in sequential order.
3. ▶ Each stage involves different skills and activities.
4. ▶ Each stage can be mastered with conscious practice.
5. ▶ The success of each stage can be observed and measured.

In addition, it is imperative that listening leaders remember:

> 1. *Sensing alone is NOT listening;*
>
> 2. *Interpreting alone is NOT listening;*
>
> 3. *Evaluating alone is NOT listening;*
>
> 4. *Responding alone is NOT listening.*
>
> *Taken together, these four elements foster listening leadership.*

THREE WAYS TO PROFIT BY APPLYING THE SIER MODEL

In your pursuit to build your listening foundation; to enhance your listening attitudes, skills, and knowledge (A-S-K); to develop positive and productive habits; to take responsibility; and to identify and adapt to purposes, the SIER model can be utilized as a future-tense *Planning Tool*, a present-tense *Application Tool*, and a past-tense *Diagnostic Tool*. Individually and collectively, the stages of SIER will provide valuable direction as you and your colleagues choose to become better listeners.

1. Using SIER as a Future-Tense Planning Tool.

Like great orchestra leaders, winning coaches, military geniuses, and outstanding business strategists who establish detailed plans for action, effective listening leaders *create* strategic listening game plans to ensure greater success in their future communications. As **Napoleon** observed, "For everything, you must have a plan." In addition, no one has highlighted the value of planning better during our time than **Yogi Berra**, who noted, "If you don't know where you are going, you could wind up someplace else."

The SIER Model has value as a planning tool for both senders and receivers. Productive senders will plan to send a message that heightens the listener's success at sensing, interpreting, evaluating, and responding. Equally important, productive listeners will plan and position themselves to succeed at each SIER stage as required. For example, productive listening increases when listeners position themselves to sense completely, interpret with matched understanding, evaluate with skill as required, and respond appropriately. *Planning* will be enhanced when you:

▶ Identify and deal with potential listening distractions.

▶ Control your environment to ensure complete sensing.

▶ Study the subject and match the speaker's language and intended meaning.

▶ Request repetition when you do not hear or remember the speaker's message.

▶ Seek clarification when you are unsure of the meaning of any message.

▶ Identify and control your emotions.

▶ Withhold judgment until your comprehension is complete.

▶ Evaluate a speaker's message content, support, and reasoning.

▶ Respond and provide helpful and relevant feedback.

2. Using SIER as a Present-Tense Application Tool.

In addition to planning, effective listening leaders *consciously apply* every stage of the SIER Model as they are engaged in every communication. During the present-tense process of listening, it is important to constantly, consciously, consistently, actively, and sequentially focus on each of the SIER stages:

▶ Am I fully and completely sensing the speaker?

▶ Does my meaning match the speaker's meaning?

▶ Am I asking questions to clarify?

▶ Am I withholding evaluation until warranted?

▶ Am I controlling my personal prejudices and emotions?

▶ Am I evaluating in a complete and thorough fashion?

▶ Am I responding in a timely, clear, and relevant manner?

The present-tense ongoing application of the SIER Model can be a very valuable tool in any leader's quest for ensuring and enhancing dynamic communication.

Bill Orosz, President of Cambridge Homes, highlights the value of planning and engaging the stages of the SIER tool in establishing and reinforcing a positive listening workplace.

> *"Once members of your management team know you want to listen to what they have to say, they come to meetings much more prepared than otherwise. They realize their input is meaningful."*
> —*Bill Orosz*

Once members of your management team know you want to listen to what they have to say, they come to meetings much more prepared than otherwise. They realize their input is meaningful, will be respected, and will be used to help to craft a solution to whatever problem or opportunity is being addressed. Whenever I have a meeting, I like to open by "setting the stage" or "setting parameters for discussion" and then let everyone give their input before I offer mine. It makes for a very collaborative atmosphere.

As has been said many times, "Wise men and women in all arenas profit when they plan their work and work their plan." Planning and applying the plan, namely to listen more effectively at every stage of SIER is guaranteed to enhance the end result for listening leaders. The primary requirements are an appropriate attitude and a planned strategy of proactivity. By planning and applying SIER, proactive listening leaders leave little to chance. They assume the Minimum 51% Responsibility for successful listening and work through the required sequential stages.

3. Using SIER as a Past-Tense Diagnostic Tool.

Finally, SIER can be applied in the past-tense, as an after-the-fact diagnostic tool. A careful diagnostic review of the fulfillment of each stage of SIER will help listening leaders *assess* what worked and what did not work. In a case of communication breakdown, the use of SIER as a diagnostic tool will identify at which stage the breakdown began. Communication breaks down because of specific faulty listening habits and behaviors, and listening leaders will profit by isolating the "starting point" of the breakdown. By identifying where listening and communication failures begin, you will discover predictable failures at higher stages. Over the years, we have observed numerous leaders waste their time by primarily focusing on the costly end results. If the failure begins at the S, or Sensing, stage, the negative impact will always be noted at the I, E, and R stages. In turn, if the failure begins at the I, or Interpretation, stage, the negative impact will show up at the E and R stages. When the failure begins at the E, or Evaluation, stage, the negative impact will be seen at the R stage. Of course, the failure can begin at the R, or Responding, stage, in which case the negative impact will be measured at the R stage. In short, any past-tense diagnostic utilization of the SIER model should begin at the lowest level of the SIER Model to discover where the failure originated. Sequential diagnosis of the four stages will aid your orderly consideration of the following:

▶ Did you fully and correctly sense the speaker's message?

▶ Can you repeat the essence of the message to the speaker's satisfaction?

▶ Did your interpretation match the speaker's? Did the meanings coincide?

▶ What was the extent of your and the speaker's agreement or disagreement?

▶ Was there evidence of logical evaluation?

▶ Did you respond in an appropriate, timely, clear and measurable way?

By sequentially analyzing the successful or unsuccessful activities at each stage, you will isolate the source and point of any communication breakdown. Two major benefits result from using SIER as a past-tense diagnostic tool. The first benefit is the opportunity to correct the problem at the micro level, as that is where the breakdown originated. The second benefit is the opportunity to learn how to avoid the problem in additional future-tense planning and present-tense application activities. Viewed in a 3-dimensional time frame, you will find profit in applying the pragmatic 3-D formula.

THE POWER OF 3-D
SIER CAN BE USED IN THREE TIME PHASES

Develop—*Plan—Future Tense*

Deliver—*Apply—Present Tense*

Debrief—*Diagnose—Past Tense*

THE SIER SAWTOOTH MODEL

To this point, the components of communication and the SIER stages of listening have been viewed primarily from a static or a "frozen time" perspective. However, productive listening leaders understand all communication occurs in a dynamic, ongoing, rolling fashion.

To understand the greater dynamics of ongoing, action-oriented communication and listening, the **Sawtooth Model** illustrates the overlapping levels of SIER that exist in every communication situation. The Sawtooth Model also reinforces the ascending-order challenge speakers and listeners face. As the communication time line advances, it becomes clear that, although sensing always holds the primary stage, listeners quickly overlay activities of interpretation, then evaluation, and finally response. At each stage, it becomes easy to put the cart before the horse. As listeners begin to interpret what they have just sensed, or evaluate what they have just sensed and interpreted, or respond to what they have just sensed, interpreted, and evaluated, the challenge to complete each stage becomes great. Again, ineffective listeners tend to put the cart ahead of the horse, while effective listening leaders satisfy one stage at a time.

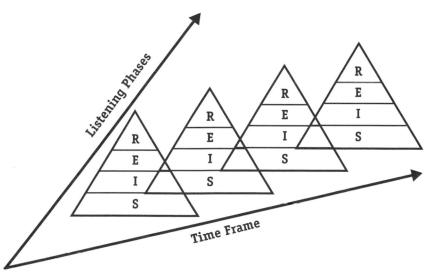

Listening leader **Dwayn Eamer** is the former CEO of Electrical Safety Authority in Toronto, Canada. In his numerous leadership roles over his productive career, Dwayn observed how following the Sawtooth Model can result in listening problems in any organization.

As a visionary leader, I tended to listen carefully to what I thought was going to keep us from achieving our vision. Like all leaders, I experienced moments of great frustration when communication failed at various stages, and we did not achieve the desired results. For example, when I provided direction to an Operations Manager and he, in turn, communicated to a group of Managers, it was interesting to measure the results. I thought the directions were clear, we had a discussion, and everyone made notes and agreed what action was going to be taken. Later, I would sit down with the same group with my notes in hand, and discover nothing even close to what everyone had seemingly agreed upon had resulted. When several individuals at different levels are involved in listening to the same vision, it is quite interesting to track the various failures of communication. It is frustrating when listeners fail to capture, understand, agree with, or act on important visions.

> *"Like all leaders, I experienced moments of great frustration when communication failed at various stages, and we did not achieve the desired results."*
>
> —Dwayn Eamer

THE GOLDEN PAUSE

One way to avoid failed communication is to engage the SIER "Golden Pause." The Golden Pause helps ensure that each SIER stage is fulfilled before moving on to the next stage. Listening leaders will profit by following the sage advice a church member gave to **Pastor Roger Eigenfeld**, years ago as Roger assumed the leadership role in a new church. The advice was in the form of a gift—a desk plaque that read, "Make Haste Slowly." Obviously, some leaders move faster than others, but every leader will serve better by utilizing the Golden Pause.

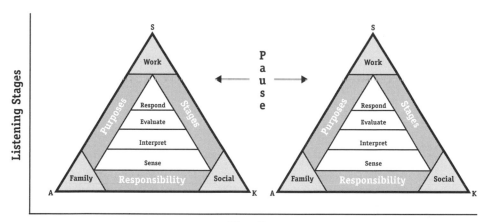

The Golden Pause is a simple and straightforward process that encourages listening leaders to sequentially engage in every stage of SIER as required. When consciously engaged, the Golden Pause calls for a brief pause while listening to provide and ensure completion of each prior stage before moving to the next stage. The result is always positive because listeners do not allow any higher stage to overlap or intrude and diminish the others.

The Golden Pause simply requires the conscious fostering of patience. Listening leader **Dr. John Guarneri** is an outstanding Physician and recipient of the prestigious "Physician Humanitarian Award." John believes leaders in the medical arena must lead by listening and dealing with a patient's body, mind, and spirit.

When you listen to patients, it is easy to think you know where they are going and you will try to anticipate that. I find you really have to lie back and see where they are coming from and going to. It is important that we not be too precocious in our listening. Thorough listening takes patience and time. Listening is a form of giving time, space, focus, and yourself to others. It requires focus on the patient, giving him or her your undivided attention, and listening on the 3-D level. It is certainly fulfilling when patients comment, "I appreciate the time Dr. Guarneri gave me. He made me feel like I was the only patient in his office."

> *"Listening is a form of giving time, space, focus, and yourself to others."*
> —Dr. John Guarneri

As **Dr. Douglas Forde**, co-author of the classic text *"Interviewing and Patient Care"* said so well, "In the field of medicine, if you listen, patients will tell you what is wrong. If you listen hard enough, they will tell you how to treat it."

ANOTHER VIEW OF SIER

SIER with Golden Pause

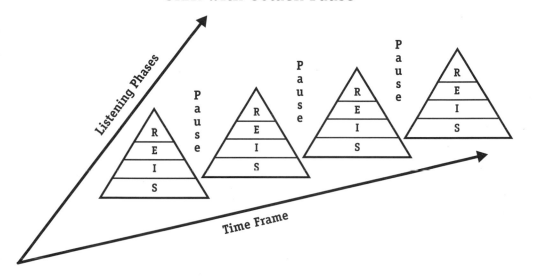

Utilizing the Golden Pauses of the listening process one step at a time, the first part of communication takes place and sensing is heightened. Focused and undivided attention is given to the sensing process in an ongoing way. In step one, effective listeners constantly check that the message is fully sensed before it is interpreted, evaluated, and responded to. Then, and only then, does the second step, interpretation, come into play. At this moment, effective listeners constantly check that their meaning matches the sender's meaning. Are we talking about the same thing? If so, and only if called for, the opportunity exists for the third step, evaluation. This is the moment that requires careful and skilled judgment and clarification of agreements or disagreements. Any conclusive or incomplete judgment prior to this moment is out of order. Finally, as listeners move through the steps of the Golden Pauses, responding is called for. Although effective listeners respond along the way to provide feedback that S, I, and E are satisfied, step four calls for responses that are clear, complete, and constructive. Observing the momentary pauses enhances the completion of each important and necessary stage.

When listening leaders activate the SIER Golden Pause, they create a greater opportunity to capture, understand, judge, and respond effectively to every speaker they choose to listen to. Introducing momentary pauses into the listening process guarantees immediate and dramatic improvement in the success of the listening process. The result of practicing the SIER Golden Pause is a more leisurely, thoughtful, and significantly better communication.

ANOTHER CASE IN POINT

Jerry McCollum is the County Engineer for Seminole County, Florida; he is the listening leader of a team of 60 professionals engaged in a $50-million-per-year transportation-improvement program. He also serves leadership roles on various federal, state, and regional technical committees and in those roles has discovered that everyone is well served when the SIER Golden Pause is observed.

Listening is being able to exist in the moment, which is probably the hardest thing anybody can do. In general, engineers are the world's worst listeners. We are referred to as "gear heads" because our gears are always spinning as we are thinking. We are very analytical, and thus we are always thinking of things we need to do. In most cases, we engage in multiple activities and don't listen well at all. In the early 1990s, my light bulb went off as I realized that, while what I do for a living is not real easy, I make it much harder on myself by not just sitting down and listening. Whether I agree or not is not the main point. The first point is giving others time to express their opinions. By reducing my interrupting, debating, or judging others, I have become a more effective listener and leader. Since I came to that conclusion, my life has become a lot easier. I have seen significant improvements in my work performance.

> *"Listening is being able to exist in the moment which is probably the hardest thing anybody can do. In general, engineers are the world's worst listeners. We are referred to as 'gear heads' because our gears are always spinning as we are thinking."*
> —Jerry McCollum, P.E.

With the old Jerry, by the time any person had gone through the first 30 seconds of the conversation, I would have already known the answer and stated it. And if you disputed me, I would have debated you. The new Jerry will listen and say, "Well, you know, you have a point there. Have you thought about this?" Or, "I never thought of that. Let me think on that." I have discovered that I seldom need to make an instant decision. In fact, delayed understanding and reflection usually lead to better judgments and actions. Engineers have to learn that we have a tendency to constantly think, analyze, and reach solutions quickly. The greater our experience, the faster we analyze and respond. The problem grows when somebody expresses a position on a problem we think we have already figured out and for which we're ready to provide the solution. Unfortunately, many times we have never really heard or understood what they are trying to say. The answer is to think and act like an engineer, but move through the listening process one step at a time.

Ed Bradley, of CBS's "60 Minutes," reinforced the point when he told CNN talk show host **Larry King**, "I learned a lesson from fellow "60 Minutes" commenator **Mike Wallace**, who counseled me, 'Just listen! You don't have to fill space. Just listen!" Although many leaders have a strong tendency to "fill silence or space," effective listening leaders fight the tendency with application of the Golden Pause.

VISIONARY LISTENING LEADERS

Today, thousands of listening leaders are conscientiously applying the SIER model as they plan and meet their daily listening challenges. Business consultant **Betsy Buckley** is a business growth strategist who has served countless leaders and organizations around the world. Betsy believes real leaders think at the broadest possible level, with listening at the center of their leadership strategy and activity.

Effective listening leaders are visionary. They see the present. They have an understanding of the past, and they keep pushing for a clearer holistic picture of the future. The outstanding leaders I work with simultaneously see multiple visions. In addition, I believe the best leaders exhibit three critical and measurable behavioral characteristics. First, although they are extremely confident, they are "other-directed." They know their strengths and weaknesses, but they always think in an inclusive way. They see an inclusive marketplace. They are just as attentive to the janitor as they are to members of the Board. Second, the leaders who achieve are courageous. They take bold steps but always keep the primary focus on the larger whole. The third characteristic of listening leaders who are worth following is their commitment to always follow through. They are responsive and take action.

The bottom line for effective listening leaders is to stay present and adaptive. The driving motto for listening leaders must be: "My ears are open, my eyes are open, my ego is open, and my heart is open."

> *"My ears are open, my eyes are open, my ego is open, and my heart is open."*
> —Betsy Buckley

THE POINT

As it has for **Mary Lou Quinlan**, who noted, "Listening has become my career," diligent application of the SIER Model will help you and your colleagues advance your individual careers through enhanced listening. In the process, you have an opportunity to build a greater "Listening Organization." The principle is simple, practice **Golden Rule 6: "Listening Leaders Apply SIER"** and you will Listen, Lead and Succeed.

Golden Rule 6

"Listening Leaders Apply SIER"

10 ACTION STEPS

1. Become a Master of the SIER Model by applying it to every listening and leadership interaction.

2. Fully sense all messages by utilizing your entire range of sight, sound, smell, taste, and touch mechanisms.

3. Confirm that every important message is interpreted as the speaker intended.

4. Exercise your Minimum 51% Responsibility and Beware of the COIK fallacy (Clear Only If Known).

5. Withhold your judgment when receiving a message until your comprehension is complete.

6. Refine your ability to evaluate if messages are factual or opinionated, complete and sound, have valid reasoning, and if the evidence supports the message.

7. Exercise ongoing patience, understanding, and feedback through paraphrasing and questioning.

8. Apply SIER as a past-tense planning tool, a present-tense application tool, and a past-tense diagnostic tool.

9. Practice the Golden Pause continuously as you listen through the SIER process.

10. Build your "Listening Organization" by teaching the power and utility of SIER to those you lead.

LISTENING LEADERS™ GOLDEN RULES PYRAMID

9
Identify &
Control Emotions

Stage
C

Practices

7
Identify &
Control Distractions

8
Identify &
Use Structure

Golden Rule 7

"Listening Leaders Identify & Control Distractions"

"When I attended Notre Dame, I became a very focused listener, for the simple reason that I had to listen beyond people who were confusing and distracting me. The forces that interfere with your listening are all around us.

—Rudy Ruettiger

In just 27 seconds, and against all odds, **Daniel "Rudy" Ruettiger** carved his name into the famous gridiron history books in South Bend, Indiana in 1975. As a result, he became one of the most famous graduates of the University of Notre Dame. Of course, Rudy's real story resides in the larger story and illustrates the importance of vision, discipline, perseverance, hard work, and dealing with distractions. Rudy was the son of an oil refinery worker, the third of 14 children, who rose from the valleys of discouragement and despair to the pinnacles of success.

In 1993, TRISTAR Productions immortalized Rudy with the blockbuster film, *RUDY*. Written and produced by Angelo Pizzo and David Anspaugh, the critically acclaimed film continues to inspire millions worldwide. As captured in this entertaining and motivating landmark film, it took years of fierce determination for Rudy to overcome a multitude of obstacles, distractions, and criticisms.

At every turn, many told him he would fail. Yet Rudy cut through the numerous distractions, listened carefully to himself and selected supporters, and achieved his dream to attend Notre Dame and play football for the Fighting Irish. As the janitor in the film said, "You're five foot nothin', one hundred and nothin', and you have nary a speck of athletic ability. Yet you hung in there with the best college football team in the land for two years. And you're getting a degree from the University of Notre Dame. In this life, you don't have to prove nothin' to nobody but yourself."

The film culminates with the fans cheering "RU-DY, RU-DY, RU-DY," as he sacks the opposing quarterback with only 27 seconds to play, in his only play of the only game of his college football career. Since then, he is the only player to have been carried off the field on his teammates' shoulders. Yet the real story centers on years of listening and overcoming a number of distractions. Although Rudy always dreamed of playing football at Notre Dame, his high school grades and his athletic ability were only average. He joined the U.S. Navy and later worked in a power plant. However, as he listened to his dream, he knew he had to ignore his detractors.

So at the age of 23, Rudy was admitted to Holy Cross Junior College and supported himself as a groundskeeper at Notre Dame's Knute Rockne Stadium. Although he was eventually admitted to Notre Dame as a transfer student, Rudy was rejected three times in the process. Again Rudy Ruettiger beat the odds and won a position as a practice player on the Notre Dame scout team. Although he did not suit up for an actual game, he persisted for two years, won the respect of his teammates and coaches, and played in the final home game of his football career.

As Rudy fulfilled one dream, he decided to dream another. He decided to see his story made into a film and discovered the road through Hollywood was also filled with numerous distractions; in fact, 16 years of nay-sayers and detractors. In the end, however, distractions can be identified and controlled, and perseverance will win out. As Rudy said,

> When I attended Notre Dame, I became a very focused listener for the simple reason that I had to listen beyond the people who were confusing and distracting me. These are the "intellects" who distract you because they think they are smarter than you. Yet they do not know what is in your heart and soul. On the other hand, I chose to listen to the "smart people" who helped me find answers. What they didn't know, they would help me find and in the process encouraged me to do better. These are the people I listened to and it made a world of difference. I found out it was the common person who has wisdom. If you saw the movie you know that one individual who had wisdom was the janitor. The janitor was someone I really listened to. In the movie, listen to what the janitor is saying because it is powerful. Listen to the little things people say to Rudy throughout the movie. To this day, one of my biggest listening challenges is listening to people who think they know it all, when they really don't. Yet, they may have good information and say something you need to listen to. That continues to be a challenge as I have a tendency to prejudge and evaluate. I am becoming better as I work to overcome this and put everyone on a level playing field.

In short, I don't care what someone has done, and I don't care who they are or who they think they are. I try to live in their moment to find out what they need or want and that helps me. Listening

> *"Listening in today's world is dangerous business. The forces that interfere with your listening are all around us. And these forces are very, very strong!"*
>
> —*Rudy Ruettiger*

in today's world is dangerous business. The forces that interfere with your listening are all around us. And these forces are very, very strong!

THE DEVASTATING POWER OF DISTRACTIONS

Virtually every listener is well intentioned. We begin to listen to the speaker's message, the personal story, the lecture, the sermon, the sales pitch, and the weather report, until something distracts our listening. We live in a noisy and disruptive world, and it is becoming worse. Untold distractions lie in wait, just waiting to capture our attention and dominate our listening. When distractions dominate listening, they dominate leading. The deadly and devastating reality of distractions is they can appear at any moment and from any source. When they do, listening at every stage is destroyed. While some distractions may be small and seemingly inconsequential and some may be large and intrusive, all distractions are devastating as they interfere with our listening. Whatever the size or nature of any distraction, leaders are in danger of missing significant segments of important messages. Listening leaders are in a perpetual search for the "Value Moments of Listening (VM of L), and every distraction holds the potential to destroy the VM of L. Once missed, some messages are lost forever.

Effective listening leaders engage in the constant, refined, and developed practice of identifying, controlling, and minimizing listening distractions. As distractions occur regularly and haphazardly, this is no small task. Unless you become aware of distractions and skilled in combating them, they will destroy your ability to listen with purpose and clarity.

Fortunately, listening leaders are not helpless. The first step in controlling distractions is to understand the devastating impact distractions have on every individual's and organization's listening. The second step is developing the ability and willingness to deal with distractions. The third step requires understanding the nature and sources of what distracts our listening. The fourth step requires the creation and implementation of an action-oriented plan to reduce, eliminate, avoid, or listen beyond any distraction.

THE NATURE OF DISTRACTIONS

A listening distraction is anything that impedes or interrupts the sensing, interpreting, evaluating, or responding to a message. Although all listeners are potentially confronted by a multitude of destructive distractions, good news exists. There are only two general kinds of distractions: Internal and external.

Internal distractions lie within and are influenced and triggered by our physical, psychological, and rational states of being. A listener's *physical* state provides numerous opportunities for listening distraction. In addition, at any specific moment, listeners' *psychological, emotional,* and *rational* make-ups provide negative opportunities for internal distractions. Internal emotional activities (i.e., anger, fear, stress, joy, excitement) provide moments of internal distractions that can occur while listening. In addition, internal distractions (i.e., reverie, daydreaming, nit-picking, drawing conclusions, mental arguments) are often caused by rational thought. Feeling tension about a possible company downsizing and possible layoffs, not getting enough sleep, having an argument with one of your children, suffering a migraine headache, contemplating a daunting task that lies ahead, feeling too cold or too hot, and daydreaming are all examples of sources of internal distractions. All internal listening distractions are known only to the listener, and thus only the listener is in a position to recognize and control them.

External distractions lie without, are everywhere, and often are not under our control. A broad array and variety of external distractions (i.e., ringing phones, sirens, construction equipment, interruptions, latecomers, the speaker's vocal accents and physical mannerisms, visual stimuli, jetliner noise, room temperature) can adversely distract and impair your listening behavior.

Listening leader **Colin McCormick,** an enterprising manager with Tupperware, describes a distraction challenge that almost every listening leader faces.

A challenge in our office is the frequency of interruptions. With the constant flow of information and interruptions, it is amazing that any real listening can be done. I have an office with a door, but like many companies, we have an open-door policy. In addition, the phone is constantly ringing. The e-mail is always available, and the distraction of e-mail is everybody expects a quick response when they e-mail you. Someone may be involved in listening on the phone, but as soon as they see that little envelope icon appear, they become distracted. Often in an attempt to multitask, they will click on the icon and try to read what someone just sent while they continue to try to listen to the caller. When there is no response within ten minutes, the sender will probably call. Such distractions are incessant and potentially deadly. I might be listening to someone who needs to discuss a big project or conduct a brainstorming session, but the interruptions continue. There's an assumption and expectation that anybody can jump into your office at any given moment and grab your attention. It just

> *"A challenge in our office is the frequency of interruptions. With the constant flow of information and interruptions, it is amazing that any real listening can be done."*
> —Colin McCormick

seems like we are being bombarded at work and at home from all directions. It seems as if there is no escape."

Internal and external distractions can function independently or in combination with each other. For example, consider a listening leader who had a 2:00 p.m. meeting with an important client across town. He arrived late because an irate employee had cornered him on the way to the parking lot, and he had gotten stuck in traffic; he hadn't had a chance to eat lunch; and to top it off, just before the meeting began, his spouse had called on his cell phone to tell him the water heater at home was leaking water all over the floor. Distractions like these will understandably hinder the listening effectiveness of the best leaders. As noted, sometimes the distractions to listening are within, sometimes they are without, and sometimes they are a combination. However, one thing is clear. First, they must be recognized and acknowledged. With awareness and careful thought, proactive listening leaders are in a position to reduce and/or eliminate distractions that might seem insurmountable. As distractions affect different people in different ways, it is important to remember that *you* are the one who is in the best position to deal with the distractions that interfere with your listening.

Edward O. "Ed" Wood, Jr., is the Trammell Crow Partner and Chief Operating Officer who is responsible for managing all the company's property in the state of Florida, which includes over 30 properties and 400 employees. As a **Golden Circle Listening Leader**, Ed recognizes the ongoing battle he faces with both external and internal distractions. The key to overcoming listening distractions always begins with awareness and moves to action. Ed knows that overcoming distractions takes focused effort.

> External distractions always result when I don't bother to reserve time or to deal with clutter. When I don't have a clean desk, I find my listening drifting. I am most susceptible when someone is boring or is saying something

that does not seem to pertain to me. The external clutter in my environment is what I have not dealt with well. Of course, internal distractions come into play when I seemingly have a million things on my mind and someone unexpectedly walks in the door with a problem. The distractions are worse when I am listening to someone while also expecting a phone call. Often times, I think I have much bigger problems than anything they could possibly say to me. However, the real

> "When I don't clarify my state of distraction and ask them to schedule a time to come back when I can pay full attention to them, I do everyone a disservice."
> —Edward O. Wood, Jr.

problem is compounded when I don't acknowledge the distractions. When I don't clarify my state of distraction and ask them to schedule a time to come back when I can pay full attention to them, I do everyone a disservice. It is not productive to just blow someone off by giving some half-baked answer as a result of a half-faked job of listening. The challenge I am working on is to eliminate the clutter and distractions.

OVERCOMING INTERNAL DISTRACTIONS

Over the years, we have discovered that productive listening leaders have developed a series of strategies and tactics to proactively combat both internal and external distractions. As every listening leader operates in his or her own arena of life, it is imperative to create and personalize one's own listening strategies and tactics.

In all cases, the *first step to enhanced listening involves identifying all potential internal forces of distraction.* First, and foremost, it is necessary to become aware of all self-induced internal distractions, which are basic barriers to your effective listening and leading. What tends to distract you on an internal basis? Make a list. What triggers your internal distractions? When do most internal distractions occur? What time of day are you most susceptible to internal distractions? What people, places, and messages exacerbate your internal distractions? What are the primary types of internal distractions that cause you the greatest challenge and cost? *Why* do the foregoing things distract you?

The *second step to enhanced listening involves identifying the negative impact and cost of each internal distraction.* Focused insight into the real impact and real costs of internal distractions provides great motivation for action. In calculating costs, it is important to be as concrete and specific as possible. Generalities are interesting, but specifics become compelling. Identify actual moments when internal distractions interfered with one or more levels of listening. What was the impact and cost? To what extent can you afford the cost in the future?

The *third step to enhanced listening involves creating a concrete strategy and action plan to overcome your internal distractions.* Because internal distractions are personal, what works for one leader may not work for another. The key is to have a plan. One listening leader finds it is useful to wear a rubber band on her wrist. When she detects any internal distraction, a simple nonobtrusive snap of the band brings her back to the speaker and message. Not desiring to pay the price of such distractions, and having carefully analyzed and recorded the sources of her internal distractions, she has perfected a simple plan that works for her. Many listening leaders report that they reduce activation of their internal and external distractions by constantly applying the Minimum 51% Responsibility Rule, searching for the Value Moments of Listening (VM of L), and engaging the Plan to Report (PTR).

Listening leader **W. Myron Hendry** is the Senior Vice President of Worldwide Operations, CNA Insurance. A 31-year veteran with the company, he is responsible for CNA's World Wide Processing Operations with primary locations in Chicago, Orlando, Kansas City, London, and New York. Myron understands that distractions come in two deadly forms. The first are the physical distractions you can hear, see, smell, and touch.

But the biggest distractions are the distractions that reside in the available space in your mind, which tend to allow you to do other things while you are listening. However, I have found I can avoid the distractions by using the available time for other things that will enhance my ability to listen effectively.

> "But the biggest distractions are the distractions that reside in the available space in your mind, which tends to allow you to do other things while you are listening."
> —W. Myron Hendry

I have a notepad and pen and write down the key points of every important discussion. No matter how well I think I understand these points, I ask questions during the process to enhance my understanding of what the person is trying to convey. Then I verify what I believe I just heard.

Like numerous other leaders, Myron has discovered that the key to overcoming the negative and costly intrusion of internal distractions lies in the substitution of proactive and productive activities. The focus must remain on the simple fact that all internal distractions are self-contained and self-induced. As such, all internal distractions are open to self-leadership and self-control.

OVERCOMING EXTERNAL DISTRACTIONS

While internal distractions have the soul and nature of quiet, covert killers, external distractions are overt, often boisterous, and equally deadly. Both destroy the effectiveness of listening leaders, individuals, and organizations. However, good news resides in the overt nature of external distractions. There is no mistaking their existence.

The most effective way to deal with external distractions is head-on. Proactive listeners confront external distractions more effectively than reactive listeners. Although it is true that external distractions are not apparent or potentially destructive until they show up, they can be anticipated. Like internal distractions, the listening leader's secret to overcoming external distractions lies in three steps: *First, identify all potential external forces of distraction. Second, identify the negative impact and cost of each external distraction. Third, create a concrete strategy and action plan to overcome every external distraction you can imagine.* Again, the key to success rests upon the assumption of primary responsibility. As many listening leaders say about successful communication, "If it's going to be, it's up to me."

For an ear and mind-opening exercise, select a representative day of your work week, then reference your Target 25 list (see Chapter 4), and identify past and potential future external distractions. Moving through steps one and two, the payoff question centers on step three, "What can you do to thwart any external distraction?" First, what can you do to reduce the reoccurrence of any external distractions? Second, what can you do to control and/or diminish any ongoing external distraction? Reflect on the habits of others. Who are the interrupters? Who has behavioral tendencies that are distracting? What about your environment? Which distractions are predictable? Which distractions are common and constant? Which distractions are uncommon, unpredictable, but possible? Which distractions can be eliminated? Which distractions simply have to be overridden? Repeat the mantra: Identify and control, identify and control." Take action.

Most important, it pays to remember that external distractions appear in many forms. Consider the example of a business traveler who, while sitting at a gate in Chicago's O'Hare airport, observed a failure of listening due to the costly distraction of movement of the masses.

An announcement was made on the public address system that instructed all of the travelers waiting at an adjacent area, which I could easily observe, to move to a different location to get information about their flight. As a few, who had not listened well, moved and led the way, everyone picked up their bags and belongings and followed, even though the leaders moved to the wrong destination. It appeared to me that the majority, who were distracted by the movement of the nonlistening minority, had not listened to or understood the complete message. As the distraction of mass movement became paramount, everyone stopped concentrating on the announcement.

In reality, the message had actually instructed them to go to a Customer Service Desk located on the other side of the gate number that was referenced. There were approximately 60 people involved, and I watched as they attempted to check in at the new gate, along with many other travelers who actually were departing from that gate. What a mess! As I watched, I observed how easy it is for the majority to be distracted by the movement of a few. Listening breakdowns occur so easily.

USING THE CONE OF DISTRACTION

Whether in a busy airport, a private office, a noisy restaurant, a conference room, or a quiet church, listening leaders profit by choosing optimal listening locations within the "Cone of Distraction." Conscious placement within the cone of distraction will help you overcome many internal distractions and avoid most external distractions as it literally moves you in front of most distractions.

Listener location becomes important in avoiding many distractions. Generally speaking, distractions diminish as listeners move closer to the speaker. Picture the cone of distraction in your minds-eye, with the speaker at the apex of the cone. A profitable rule of thumb to remember is the further back the listener is in the cone, the greater the opportunity for disruptive distractions. As you move closer to the source of message, numerous distractions will be put behind you. In fact, it is safe to say that, as one moves closer to the speaker, many distractions will be eliminated. Front-row locations are generally better than back-row locations. With the exception of con-

CONE OF DISTRACTION

SPEAKER

Poten**tial Distractions**

Greater
Poten**tial Distractions**

LISTENERS

cert, theatre, or sporting events where ticket prices are scaled based on proximity to the action, note which listening positions usually fill up first. Typically the back rows fill before the front rows. The seats facing the distractions of windows or doors fill before those close to the speaker. In sum, the locations that experience the most distractions fill before those which experience the fewest distractions. It appears many listeners have a listening death wish.

On the other hand, productive listening leaders control their own destinies. They show up early, scope out the environment with one question in mind, "Where is the *best listening seat* in the house?" and stake their claim. They shut doors and windows and focus on eliminating any external distractions before the fact. In addition, when distractions do occur, they take active steps to eliminate them whenever possible.

THE DISTRACTIONS OF MULTITASKING

Trammell Crow Residential Services Executive, **Edward O. "Ed" Wood, Jr.** focuses on the distraction of the "myth of multitasking" which he believes is one of the major listening distractions in the world of work. Ed is trying to eliminate the myth of multitasking because he believes,

> You can't do two things at once; you can only do one thing at a time. Therefore, I try to stay very, very organized by personally using Microsoft® Outlook and a file system and blocking my time to pay attention to what I need to pay attention to, kill it dead, and then move on to the next thing. Our business has to be very fluid and flexible because interruptions are part of our day-to-day business. In fact, some say we manage by interruption. When you don't manage such distractions, you don't accomplish anything. Although people flippantly use the word multitasking, I am not sure what that means. To me, it refers to people who don't get anything done because they are trying to do everything. I am amused when I read job descriptions that say, "Individual must be capable of multitasking."
>
> We have many wonderful people who can do many different things. Is that multitasking? I don't think that is what people communicate when they promote multitasking. I think they mean somebody who can fly around juggling. Maybe some are

> *"Although people flippantly use the word multitasking, I am not sure what that means. To me, it refers to people who don't get anything done because they are trying to do everything… You can't do two things at once; you can only do one thing at a time."*
> —*Edward O. Wood, Jr.*

good jugglers, but we need to be careful. I simply cannot listen well or have a conversation with you while I check my e-mail. That is what I mean by the distraction of multitasking. I cannot do you justice when I am distracted with my e-mail. Nor do I do my e-mail justice. Of course, I have watched many intelligent people fail because they could not juggle. Distractions must be controlled. When you're in any complex business you have to know when to listen, when to touch, when to move on, and how to keep everything rolling. Focused attention is the key.

SOME DISTRACTIONS CAN KILL YOU

Some distractions are merely bothersome. Listening to a crying baby in the middle of a wedding will likely embarrass the parents and upset the wedding party, but it will probably not materially change the purpose or outcome of the event. On the other hand, as we noted in Chapter 6 regarding the world's worst aviation disaster, some distractions can kill you. Obviously, there are some professions wherein internal and external distractions carry a greater toll. Any listening circumstance that involves and requires a high response level and fast action can be quickly compromised by uncontrolled distractions. When these listening situations require simultaneous listening to multiple messages, the challenge is compounded. For example, air traffic controllers and pilots must develop the refined ability to identify and control distractions and listen to multiple messages.

Listening leader **Jack Barbieri** is a highly skilled training supervisor with the FAA and appreciates that listening is a required key core competency of all Air Traffic Controllers.

In this field, you have to be a great listener. It is something that has to be assessed on a regular basis. You have to

> *"In this field you have to be a great listener. It is something that has to be assessed on a regular basis. You have to be a very competent listener because there is too much at risk if you're not."*
>
> *—Jack Barbieri*

be a very competent listener because there is too much at risk if you're not. When I think about the great controllers I have worked with over the years, two qualities stand out. They can cut through the distractions, and they are conditioned to listen to many messages simultaneously. Even in the break room, someone can be carrying on a conversation and simultaneously hear somebody say something in another corner of the room. It is as though they are listening, and listening well, to multiple conversations at once. It is not distracting because it is part of our training and nature wherever we are."

TOLERATE NO DISTRACTIONS

J. Allen is President of James Allen Consulting and a Founding Partner of the Minneapolis-based Masters Alliance, LLP. For more than 25 years, he has influenced and served leaders in more than 90 client organizations in 17 industries. Coupled with his leadership experience as a U.S. Naval Officer and 12 years of intense corporate responsibility, J. Allen believes effective listening leaders cannot tolerate any distractions. As an example, J. recounts his experience with the charismatic automobile industry leader John DeLorean, who exemplified the skill of controlling distractions.

I worked with Mr. DeLorean on a project for two years when he led the Chevrolet Motor Division. He was one of the most effective Senior Managers I have ever worked with, and one characteristic that stood out was his refusal to tolerate distractions. In addition, he was a model leader because he sought to understand a variety of different disciplines, all of which he did well. He was one of the few executives I've been privileged to work with who was equally adroit at finance, marketing, and engineering. I was a marketing consultant on one of his project teams, which included people from General Motors and outside consultants. DeLorean kicked off the project team by announcing we were team members and responsible for every topic of the project. We were to pay attention, and no distractions would be tolerated. We were expected to know what was going on in each of the other topics because we would be asked from time to time to provide an objective and perhaps naive perspective on other topics.

John DeLorean was a creative and innovative leader who fostered an open-door atmosphere but tolerated no distractions and suffered no fools. During this period, DeLorean never missed a listening trick.

Eventually, however, John left General Motors and started his own car company, and a strange change occurred. In my opinion, during his transition, he lost every listening bone in his body. He seemed to be distracted by his quest to achieve and did not listen to requested marketing advice regarding the probability of success.

The bottom line is, John DeLorean succeeded because he fostered and exhibited admirable leading-edge listening skills; and he failed because he gave them up.

> *"The bottom line is, John DeLorean succeeded because he fostered and exhibited admirable leading-edge listening skills; and he failed because he gave them up."*
> —J. Allen

ATTENTION MAKES THE DIFFERENCE

In every case where listeners have allowed internal or external distractions to disrupt their listening success, they report they were paying attention to the wrong thing. Seldom will you find value in the distraction. Value moments reside within the speaker's message. Moreover, they can pass in split seconds. Distractions can persist for extended periods of time. The key is to pay attention to what counts.

Ann Newhouse is the perceptive Manager of the Energy Efficiency Program for Progress Energy in Central Florida. Her team of 30 professionals serves a diverse customer base of approximately 600,000 people. The focus of her team is to analyze and evaluate residential, commercial, and industrial locations. When discussing the challenge of dealing with distractions and listening to what is important every day, Ann focuses on the practical activities of attention and choice.

> *"I think the key listening requirements are deciding who and what to listen to and for, learning how to pay attention, and not trying to do three things at one time when someone is talking to you."*
>
> —Ann Newhouse

One of the biggest challenges we face is the tremendous amount of information that comes at us from all directions. The number of people in our lives, the unending information coming at us through written materials, e-mails, and verbal communications challenges everyone. The never-ending task of sorting through it all requires skill and the ability to determine which messages are most important. What deserves our attention? How can we take control of our environment instead of allowing our environment to control us? I think the key listening requirements are deciding who and what to listen to and for, learning how to pay attention, and not trying to do three things at one time when someone is talking to you. The real challenge is to take time to determine what your objectives and boundaries are, what your limits are, what is important, and what your priorities are, so that you focus on what is important."

UNDERSTANDING DISTRACTION PATTERNS

At times, most listeners sabotage their listening success by introducing individual distractions to the communication process. As our activities are subtle and ingrained, it is important to understand and deal with distraction patterns. Your listening patterns and tendencies illustrate how true you stay to the speaker's line of communication. "Listening Hall of Fame" member **Dr. Sara Lundsteen** has outlined four typical listening distraction patterns. While each pattern distracts listeners from the line of communication and can result in a variety of costs, some distractions have greater negative impact than others. As outlined in the following figure, each pattern is related to the line of communication. Obviously, listening to some speakers, topics, language, or distractions heightens the challenge of staying close to the line. Committed leaders invest significant effort in identifying patterns of distraction within their listening environment.

FOUR PATTERNS

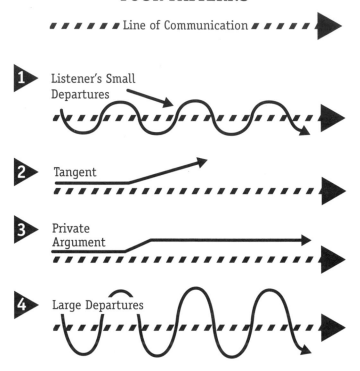

Although all distractions are potentially destructive, the least destructive listening pattern involves *small departures*. The listener stays close to the line of communication with relatively few and slight departures. In addition, return to the line of communication is done in fairly rapid order. Of the four listening patterns, the first is the least destructive.

As listeners progress through the following three patterns, the negative impact of digression and distractions grows. In the *tangent* distraction, listeners begin on the line of communication, but something distracts their attention and they drift off for a period of time, missing more of the message. In the *private argument* distraction, the listener is challenged by the speaker and immediately shifts into a mode of internal rebuttal and misses even more. In the *large departure* distraction, the listener is totally unfocused and drifts far from the line of communication, thus missing the most.

The important question to continually ask yourself is, "What are your repetitive and predictable patterns of distraction? What are the costs? How can you modify your listening behavior? When will you move to action? Who can contribute to your growth?"

POLICE YOURSELF

Rhonda Glover is the Assistant Director of Institutional Research at Valencia Community College. Rhonda is a 29-year veteran of the institution and an effective listening leader who wears several hats. Her team is responsible for gathering and interpreting local, state, and national data. In addition, she teaches Humanities and works with numerous corporations in leadership development programs for the Hartwick Humanities in Management Institute. With multiple leadership responsibilities, Rhonda assumes personal responsibility to control her constant distractions.

I must police myself and control the numerous and constant distractions in my world. My listening strengths and limitations are tied to the fact that I am the kind of person who wants to be there for everyone. So in the past when I had someone with me and someone else wanted my attention, my tendency was to try to respond to both. As I found I created my own distractions, I decided to police myself. As a result, I have made a policy of doing common-sense things like closing my door and not answering the phone. If I am in a large room where a lot of people are talking, I use constant eye contact. This keeps me focused and helps the person understand I am there for them, and they have my undivided attention. Sometimes I will close my eyes, or blink for a moment, to not allow myself to look away. Dealing with distractions takes a special self-discipline. Of course, it requires a lot of effort because there is so much that stimulates us. The bottom line is it is just a matter of discipline.

> *"The bottom line is it is just a matter of discipline. My love of knowledge and people led me to this path of self-discipline, as I really believe there is so much to be learned and so little I know."*
> —*Rhonda Glover*

My love of knowledge and people led me to this path of self-discipline, as I really believe there is so much to be learned and so little I know. I am so excited to learn from others that it is worth giving my time and attention to someone if there is something of value I can learn. In addition, there is great value in listening to others' opinions. People need to be able to express what they feel. Disciplined listening is important if we want to learn and grow and build strong relationships with others.

LISTENING BEYOND NONVERBAL DISTRACTIONS

As established in **Golden Rule 6: "Listening Leaders Apply SIER,"** all stages must be satisfied, beginning with Sensing. Of course, that includes sensing both verbal and nonverbal components of every message. However, a special challenge arises when nonverbal messages intervene and contradict verbal messages, thus becoming distractions. **Professor Albert Mehrabian's** pioneering research in the area of nonverbal communication found that when there is an inconsistency in the verbal and nonverbal message, listeners will place greater emphasis on the nonverbal. The danger lies in the assumption that the meaning placed on the nonverbal message is correct.

The problem with many recent popular "body language" books which encourage the interpretation of certain postures and gestures as always meaning a certain thing is obvious. Sometimes they don't, and the nonverbal component may become the distraction.

Recently, a friend made a presentation to an insurance company and kept her arms folded across her chest during the entire presentation. On the way home, someone who was distracted by her nonverbal communication asked, "What was the matter, were you feeling closed to the questions they had to your presentation?" Our friend laughed at the assumption, and said, "No, my bra came loose when I stood up, and I didn't know what else to do." When anyone crosses their arms, there may be a number of possible reasons. Perhaps they are cold, or their chair may be too small or confining, it may be a habitual posture, or it may just be comfortable. On the other hand, it may mean they are protecting themselves or are closed to other ideas or are stubborn and resolute. Does nonverbal body language always mean what we think it means, or is it just another distraction?

Dr. Daniel Rosenblum is a leading Medical Officer with the U.S. Food & Drug Administration who has focused on the importance of listening. A highly regarded Oncologist, Dr. Rosenblum is the author of *A Time to Hear, a Time to Help: Listening to People with Cancer*. Having studied at the University of Chicago and taught at the Harvard, Washington, and Georgetown University medical schools, Dr. Rosenblum recognizes the potentially distracting impact of technology on nonverbal messages. Obviously, technology serves everyone in the medical profession.

For example, computerization of medical records has a number of advantages for finding and screening information to reduce errors and to serve patients. It provides a very organized way of improving information legibility.

Patient history and records can be reproduced quickly and completely and printed out as required. Errors in prescribing medications are dramatically reduced, as communication with the Pharmacist is enhanced.

In all these cases, the patient is well served. Yet, there is a potential major disadvantage, in that the computer can become a communication barrier when it becomes a distraction between the doctor and patient. Some patients become distracted by the nonverbal activities of the doctor and the computer. In the process, patients may focus more on the doctor's body language and conclude you are more interested in your equipment than in them. As the movement to electronic medical records and technology increases in the future, it will be increasingly important that everyone controls the distractions of the nonverbal elements of communication.

> *"In the process, patients may focus more on the doctor's body language and conclude you are more interested in your equipment than in them."*
> —Dr. Daniel Rosenblum

The key to controlling nonverbal distractions lies in the continual search for verbal and nonverbal congruence. Communication congruence simply means that the verbal message and the nonverbal message match and have the same meaning. When you recognize incongruent messages, it is an opportunity to control the distractions, as you pause and explore the unmatched meanings.

MOVING PAST INHERENT DISTRACTIONS

When it comes to moving past inherent listening distractions, **Michael Matheny**, Manager of Corporate Media for Sun-Trust Bank believes the secret of success lies within every leader.

As Socrates so clearly counseled, it all begins with, "Above all else, know thyself." However, we are reminded that knowledge without meaningful application has little impact. Michael's self-knowledge and practical application has served him and his colleagues well, in moving past inherent distractions.

I know I don't hear as well as I used to, and that fact provides special challenges in terms of listening and overcoming distractions. Now the joy is, I find I have to sit closer to people because I have to make eye contact. I have to look at speakers' lips to really focus. Listening requires a lot more work now. As a consequence, I invest more time and effort in what I call full-body listening. With my inherent listening challenges, controlling my listening environment becomes all-important. I cannot multitask and succeed at full-body listening because listening requires that I use all of my senses. I have to constantly be aware of the noise, the amplitude, and the distractions. Inflection is critical. The key is to move past the distractions and capture what is being said and, even more importantly, what is not being said and why. But to get there, I have to recognize and move past my shortcomings. Like every other leader I know, I am not perfect, but I am a listening work in progress.

> *"I know I don't hear as well as I used to, and that fact provides special challenges in terms of listening and overcoming distractions… As a consequence, I invest more time and effort in what I call full-body listening."*
> —Michael Matheny

HE REFUSED TO WEAR THE UNIFORM

Of course, *all* leaders are works in progress. And because training in listening is grossly ignored in our school systems and most organizations, most leaders have miles to go to improve their and their associates' listening.

> *"Listening makes me aware of opportunities for service and growth."*
> —Sandy Hudson

Sandy Hudson serves as an Educational Administrator at a private school and is reminded every day how important it is to listen beyond distractions. Her key is to listen carefully to both the verbal and non-verbal messages. Sandy recalls an instance in which the incongruity helped make the meaning of an unstated message clear.

Listening makes me aware of opportunities for service and growth. We have a dress code at our school, and I recently had a teacher tell me, "Ms. Hudson, you need to talk to Bobby because he refuses to wear the uniform." I took Bobby into my office where this freckle-faced little seventh-grade kid defiantly said to me, "I don't have to wear the uniform. You can't make me wear the uniform. There's no law that says I have to wear the uniform." However, while he was speaking, he was looking down. He did not look me in the eye. Because I was getting mixed messages, I thought, there's something else going on here. So I said: "Bobby, let's call your mom and see what she says about this." When I looked in his records, I noticed his mother was a single mom who worked at a local restaurant that was not the home of the big tippers. At best, his mother probably earned $12,000 a year, and all of a sudden, it just clicked. Weighing his verbal and nonverbal messages, and the information about his home life, I cut through the distractions. I just looked at him and softly said: "Your clothes are dirty, aren't they?" His defiance evaporated as his eyes filled up with tears, and he said: "Yes, ma'am." All of a sudden it made sense. They did not have money for many trips to the laundromat, and he had not worn his uniform because it was dirty. So I said, "You know what? We can fix that. We will get you a shirt, and we have some loaner khaki pants." All of a sudden he was happy as a clam. Later that day, we noted the soles had literally separated from the tops of his shoes. So we went out and bought him another pair of shoes.

Without listening beyond the distractions, that episode could have escalated into a charge of insubordination and expulsion or suspension. In our environment, that is a serious level-three offense. But just by listening beyond the distractions, we were able to make a positive impact on one child's life, and that not only feels good, it is important."

THE POINT

From the gridiron of Notre Dame, to the offices of corporations, to the halls of medicine, to the arenas of educators, distractions are always a danger to poor listeners. Distractions are universally damaging to the listening leadership process when they are not identified or controlled. As **Rudy Ruettiger** learned, distractions can confuse and interrupt you, but with diligent focus, they can be identified, avoided, removed, and defeated. Practice **Golden Rule 7: "Listening Leaders Identify & Control Distractions"** and you will Listen, Lead and Succeed.

Golden Rule 7

"Listening Leaders Identify & Control Distractions"

10 ACTION STEPS

1. Engage in the constant, refined, and developed practices of identifying, controlling, and minimizing listening distractions.

2. Adopt a 'Tolerate No Distractions" attitude.

3. Search for the Value Moments of Listening in all communications and overcome any force that interferes with your listening.

4. Identify and control all potential internal forces of distraction, including recognizing the negative impact and costs.

5. Create a concrete strategy and action plan to overcome your internal distractions.

6. Identify and control all potential external forces of distraction, including recognizing the negative impact and costs.

7. Create a concrete strategy and action plan to overcome your external distractions.

8. Listen within the apex zone of the "Cone of Distraction" to move past distractions.

9. Eliminate the practice of multitasking while listening.

10. Build your "Listening Organization" by teaching those you lead how to identify, reduce, and control internal and external distractions.

LISTENING LEADERS™ GOLDEN RULES PYRAMID

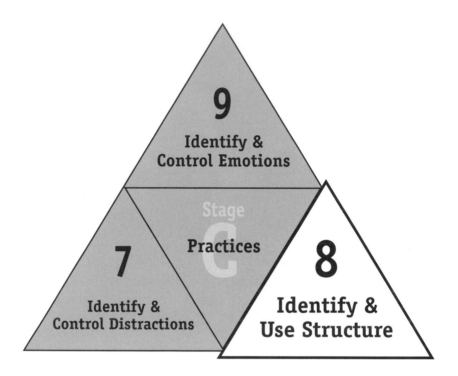

Golden Rule **8**

"Listening Leaders Identify &
Use Structure"

"Everyone profits when you establish a format that helps you listen more effectively. The thing that has most positively impacted my leadership is that I have been surrounded by excellent listeners. They report back to me with great clarity and incredible objectivity because they know my listening style. They know how to best get the information to me in a structured and usable format

—Dr. Harvey Barnett

Dr. Harvey Barnett, described by many as a "brilliant zealot," is the founder of Infant Swimming Resource, an organization committed to reducing the drowning deaths of infants and young children. Since the Consumer Product Safety Commission identified infant and child drowning deaths as an epidemic, ISR has established a scientifically based, internationally acclaimed instructional technique. In the process, Dr. Barnett has invested 30 years of tireless effort in building a professional team skilled in listening. As Harvey is quick to acknowledge,

> I owe a great debt to the researchers and thinkers who came before me. In addition, we owe a great debt to the efforts of more than 100,000 infants and young children. We taught them to swim, but they taught us to teach. We are humbled by the trust invested in our efforts by over 200,000 parents and relatives who brought their babies

to over 2 million ISR lessons. I have never forgotten, nor will I let any of our instructors worldwide ever forget, that each infant, each child, and every parent is a unique person who deserves to be listened to.

In building their successful ISR organization, Dr. Barnett and his colleagues also developed a well-defined structure and format for his associates to share important information.

The thing that has most positively influenced my leadership is that I have been surrounded by excellent listeners. This fact is critical because they are the ones whose job it is to listen to the instructors, the parents, the physicians, the occupational and physical therapists, and others. They are able to report back to me with great clarity and incredible objectivity because they know my listening style. They know how to best get information to me in a structured and usable format. I have accepted the fact that, as a leader, I am limited because I do not have enough time to listen to everyone and everything that should be listened to. Thus, I depend on other people I have trained. In addition, I have compensated for my impatience in listening by surrounding myself with excellent listeners who extend my listening and who can translate information to me in a structured way that is best for me.

> "I have compensated for my impatience in listening by surrounding myself with excellent listeners who extend my listening and who can translate information to me in a structured way that is best for me."
>
> —Dr. Harvey Barnett

I absolutely must set up a structure for those who are listening and reporting on my behalf because my time is so limited. I would extend the same advice to other listening leaders. When you establish a clear-cut listening structure and format, you will listen much more effectively. I have always said, "You don't have to pay me to sit down and listen, but you do have to present information in a structured format that will heighten my willingness to take the time to truly give you the attention your particular problem or circumstance deserves." Simply put, I could not survive without structured formats.

All listeners will profit from understanding and applying four universal listening facts:

▶ **1** Listeners can listen faster than most people speak. Research has clearly shown that with training, listeners can effectively listen at speeds nearly four times faster than most speakers speak. Listeners, indeed, have a potential advantage.

▶ **2** Most listeners fail to take the advantage of their thought/speech speed differential. When it is not utilized, the advantage is forever lost.

▶ **3** Although the structural patterns of all speakers can be identified, most listeners do not expend the energy to identify or utilize these structures.

▶ **4** Skilled listeners adapt to the speaker's organizational patterns and take effective mental or written notes. Ineffective listeners generally do not bother to do either.

In sum, ineffective listeners have difficulty and fail in all areas. Effective listeners profit by consciously applying their skills in each area.

Like Dr. Barnett, listening leaders who listen and live by **Golden Rule 8: "Identify and Use Structure,"** experience dramatic results as they Sense, Interpret, Evaluate, and Respond and thereby retain all messages more effectively. The first step of applying Golden Rule 8 involves identifying and using the speaker's structure. Initially, this involves determining if, and how, the message is organized. The second step focuses on adapting to the speaker's structure. The third step requires the action of making written or mental notes that correspond to the speaker's structure. Regarding the pragmatic and beneficial application of structures, it is important to understand behaviors that distinguish ineffective listeners from effective listening leaders.

INEFFECTIVE BEHAVIORS

Our lengthy experience in coaching listeners and leaders in a multitude of venues allows the troubling, but often repeated, observation that ineffective listeners *do not*:

▶ Assume the "Minimum 51% Responsibility" for successful communication.

▶ "Plan to Report" to someone at a later time.

▶ Use the "Thought/Speech Speed Differential" to their advantage.

▶ Listen for the speaker's "Purpose or Central Idea and Organizational Pattern."

▶ Anticipate the organizational structure and patterns of the speaker.

▶ Adapt their listening to the organizational structure and pattern of the speaker.

▶ Take mental or written notes.

EFFECTIVE BEHAVIORS

Effective listening leaders do the opposite on all counts. Specifically, they identify and adapt to every speaker's organizational structure. They understand that all messages range somewhere between totally *unorganized* to carefully *organized*. In addition, they can identify when speakers are *disorganized*.

The difference between *unorganized* and *disorganized* messages is simple. Unorganized messages simply have not been organized in any discernable pattern. In these cases, the listener's task is to create a structure for the unstructured message. To compound the challenge of listening, disorganized messages may appear organized but the structure is, at best, confusing. The listening leader's task is to reorder and organize any disorganized message. Effective listeners know that, although the communication situation and speaker may be unprepared or carefully prepared, formal or informal, presenting to one or many, it is important to identify and utilize the degree and type of message structure.

The task is simplified somewhat by the fact that most speakers are habitual, and their use of structural patterns is predictable. As a starting exercise, consider the degree to which specific speakers on your Target 25 list are organized or not. What about the individuals you lead? If they are organized, what are their predictable and habitual patterns? For those who are typically not organized, how can you create a workable structure? In either case, the never-ending leader's task requires adapting listening and note-taking to each individual. As you enhance your identifying structures and adapting skills with individual speakers you know, you will extend your skill in listening to any speaker, regardless of the purpose or situation. The profitable task of identifying the nature and degree of any speaker's organizational activity is extended by consciously and constantly playing "The Listening Game of 10." Everyone can play, and it changes the dynamics of communication. Promote it with those you lead and everyone will profit.

THE LISTENING GAME OF 10

Since all speakers fall somewhere on a 10-point continuum, from 0 (Highly Unorganized) to 10 (Highly Organized), it pays to play "The Listening Game of 10."

| 0 | 1 | 2 | 3 | 4 | 5 | 6 | 7 | 8 | 9 | 10 |

Highly   *Unorganized*   *Organized*   *Highly*
Unorganized   *Organized*

In every listening situation, there are four simple rules for playing the "Listening Game of 10"

Rule One requires you to pick a number. On the scale of 0 to 10, is the speaker unorganized or organized? The lower the number, the less the speaker is structured and organized. The higher the number the more the speaker is structured and organized. Typically, speakers announce or display the degree and nature of their organization, or lack thereof, within the first few minutes of speaking.

Rule Two requires you to identify the structure, if any. If the communication is structured, how has the speaker organized the message? What structural pattern is identifiable?

Rule Three requires you to adapt to the speaker's organizational pattern and take corresponding written
or mental notes.

Rule Four requires structuring of the unorganized, or
worse, disorganized speaker in a way you choose.

Productive listening leaders develop a proactive plan for
identifying and remembering any speaker's predictable organizational habits and behaviors. All speakers will work for you once
you determine whether they are *organized, unorganized,* or *disorganized.* If the speaker is organized at the level of seven or above,
it pays to adapt your listening and note-taking structure to match
his or her structure. If the speaker is unorganized at the level of
three or lower, you need to establish a method for organizing the
unorganized message that works for you. If the speaker is disorganized, your listening task is different and in some ways more
challenging. Initially, disorganized speakers may seem organized;
however, as they proceed, their message becomes very convoluted and confusing. Listening to disorganized speakers requires
a reorganizing of their disorganization. Effective listeners usually
fall back to familiar organizational patterns as they attempt to
add structure to disorganized speakers. The key is, regardless of
the speaker's structure or lack thereof, listening leaders have a
workable plan of adaptation.

D.R. (Sid) Verdoorn is Chairman of the Board of C.H.
Robinson Worldwide, one of the world's most successful transportation, logistics, and sourcing companies. With operations
in the United States, Canada, Mexico, South America, Europe,
and Asia, the 99-year-old company has more than $3.5 billion in
gross revenues and approximately 4,000 employees in over 150
locations throughout the world. As one of the largest third-party
logistics providers in North America, C.H. Robinson arranges
freight transportation services using trucks, trains, ships, and

planes belonging to other companies. In the process, it contracts with 20,000 motor carriers and handles more than 2.5 million shipments per year for its 15,000 customers. Identifying, and adapting to, the organizational patterns of customers, drivers, and employees is central to C.H. Robinson's long-term success. Because the organizational structure of C.H. Robinson requires identifying and adapting to the organizational patterns of others, it also enhances listening. Sid remembered how he established his personal patterns and structure that served him as a leader.

When I started on the sales desk as a young person with C.H. Robinson, I developed my own patterns. My desire and orientation have always been to listen to others from their perspective because I want to relate to people. To that end, we created an organization without layers of bureaucracy. With an open-door policy you really become aware of your colleagues' communication patterns and structures. It is true we are all predictable if one takes the time to listen and observe.

> "My desire and orientation has always been to listen to others from their perspective because I want to relate to the people... It is true we are all predictable if one takes the time to listen and observe."
> —Sid Verdoorn

On the other hand, I have dealt with companies with numerous layers to listen through. In every case, they never develop insight into the predictable organizational patterns of many of their counterparts. As a consequence, it is very difficult for them to accomplish anything. C.H. Robinson is a company of action and a quick decision-making process that requires rapid adaptation to the structure and meaning of others. We depend on it.

Regardless of the structure of an organization, the key is to identify and adapt your listening to each speaker's method of organization. This is one more way of using the advantage of your thought-speed, which is faster than most speakers' speech-speed. Particularly with unorganized and disorganized speakers, creation of structures that work for you will help you make sense out of any speaker's confusion. One additional note: As speakers follow habitual patterns and thus are predictable, it becomes productive to listen to "cue" and "clue" language, to determine if and how speakers are organized.

GLOBAL STRUCTURES: CLIMACTIC VS. ANTICLIMACTIC

In a global sense, speakers generally organize their ideas and material from either a climactic or an anticlimactic structure. In a macro sense, listening leaders initially benefit by identifying the direction of message movement, as the global overview contributes to note-taking strategies.

▶ **Climactic Structures** involve movement from the General to the Specific. Speakers' messages move from general data to a specific conclusion. For example, consider the speaker who made the following short, persuasive, and climactic statement:

I must warn you of a thief of life. It is a thief that steals your breath and fouls your nest. It is a thief that steals your savings and limits your friends. It is a thief that ruins your clothes, blackens your lungs, and shortens your life. This thief steals your health and your life. Smoking is a thief of life!

Examine this short commentary and the structure and power of climactic messages become clear. Whether you are neutral or agree or disagree with the conclusion, climactic messages are like "whodunit" mystery stories. When speakers organize around the climactic structure, you will find development of various data or facts leading up to the specific conclusion. Committed listeners tune in and focus on the information that supports and builds to the conclusion. By identifying the general-to-specific climactic pattern, effective listening leaders focus on the details and withhold their judgment until the final conclusion is developed.

▶ **Anticlimactic Structures** involve movement from the Specific to the General. Speakers' messages move from a specific conclusion to the general supporting data. A perfect example is any message that initially expresses the specific final claim or conclusion followed by the supporting general data. For example, consider how the previous speaker could have made the short and persuasive statement in an anticlimactic order:

> *Smoking is a thief of life! It is a thief that steals your breath and fouls your nest. It is a thief that steals your savings and limits your friends. It is a thief that ruins your clothes, blackens your lungs, and shortens your life. This thief steals your health and your life.*

Listeners face three special challenges in listening to anticlimactic messages. First, specific-to-general presentations are not suspenseful since the concluding point is stated first. Second, if you strongly agree with the initial claim, there may be a tendency to relax and not listen carefully to the supporting general data. Third, if you strongly disagree with the initial claim, there is a tendency to debate the specific initial point without listening to the total message. In any case, you will benefit from identifying anticlimactic structures, heightening your patience, and adapting your listening and note-taking activity.

In a global sense, if the speaker is organized, listen for the central ideas and develop a skeleton to which you can attach the facts. Utilize the speaker's structural system and patterns to help you listen better. When speakers are unorganized, you need to recognize and compensate for their lack of organization. When speakers are organized, your adaptation to their structure simplifies and enhances your sensing and note-taking. Beyond listening for global structures, you also will benefit from listening for and utilizing any of the four additional primary organizational patterns. It is important to remember that these additional organizational strategies can be developed individually or collectively.

RECOGNIZING THE MOST COMMON STRUCTURES

In addition to the climactic and anticlimactic macro struc-tures, speakers employ a number of specific organizational structures that will serve you. The four most common organizational strategies include Enumeration, Problem/Solution, Chronological, and Spatial. Each pattern has identifiable cue language. Many listeners pay a price when they fail to expend time, thought, or energy on identifying a speaker's organizational structures. On the other hand, those who master the task of recognizing cue and clue words will enhance their opportunity to discern and use these organizational patterns, which, in turn, will enrich their listening and note-taking activities.

▶ **Enumeration** is the simple organizational strategy of counting. Some purposes and topics lead naturally to the process of enumeration. Speakers simply number the main points and/or subpoints. In some ways, enumeration is the easiest structure to iden-tify, particularly when speakers use numbers as the cue and clue language. Enumeration contributes to productive note-taking and planning to report. Speakers often preface their remarks with framing statements like,

This is one of the most significant elections in recent history, and I am happy to be your candidate. With your support, we will win. However, if we are going to prevail in our election campaign, there are three key things we need to accomplish.

First, we must establish a solid action plan that clearly separates us from our opponents. Our differences are obvious and we hold the high ground.

Second, we must expand our national support team that will advance that plan in every corner of the country. The key to our success lies in building a large population of supporters who will carry our message.

Third, we must build a substantial financial war chest to ensure our ultimate goal. Newfound money is necessary if we hope to sustain our campaign over the long haul.

When we accomplish these three basic goals we will win.

The cue and clue language is clear and enabling. The language is simple, direct, and helpful. Enumeration is the favorite pattern for many speakers. In addition, many purposes and topics lend themselves to numerical listing. Lengthy informational and persuasive presentations are often overloaded with data and use enumeration patterns. If this is the case, adapt your note-taking and reporting to the speaker's numbering strategy.

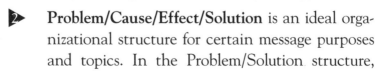 **Problem/Cause/Effect/Solution** is an ideal organizational structure for certain message purposes and topics. In the Problem/Solution structure,

speakers focus on specific problems, causes, effects, and solutions, or any combination of the four. In some cases, speakers will only develop one or two legs of the P/C/E/S structure; in other cases three or all four. The key is to listen for the cue and clue language, and then adapt to the speaker's organizational pattern while taking notes.

Consider the following example of a speaker who is expressing a problem:

> *Mr. Mayor, we have a problem that must be addressed as quickly as possible or our community will suffer irreparable harm. The problem is clear to anyone who studies the hard facts. Our population explosion is outstripping our resources. Over the last 10 years, we have grown...*

In addition, the speaker may develop and highlight the *cause* of the problem. Note the additional secondary use of enumeration.

> *Mr. Mayor, everyone knows that our population explosion is outstripping our community resources because of three simple reasons. The causes of our uncontrolled growth are the desirability of our abundant physical surroundings, our lack of necessary and appropriate building ordinances, and our low tax base.*

In addition, the speaker may develop or expand the *effect* or impact of the stated problem.

> *The negative impact of our population explosion, Mr. Mayor, will devastate life in our community as we know it. Our infrastructure is grossly overtaxed and will only grow worse. The cost to build new water and sewage treatment facilities is beyond our capacity. Our*

> *schools are bursting at the seams, and we are cutting*
> *back important community programs. In addition,*
> *our crime rates have risen to an all-time high. Finan-*
> *cially, we are burdened beyond repair. Worst of all is*
> *the irreversible damage to our physical environment.*

In addition or combination, the speaker may develop a *solu-tion* to the problem. The solution may be simple and straightfor-ward or complex and convoluted.

> *So Mr. Mayor, I propose a radical solution to*
> *rectify our problem. The solution will be painful to*
> *many, but we have no recourse. We must establish*
> *a moratorium on growth by creating a "no-growth*
> *zone." In addition, we must increase our tax levels*
> *and find additional State and Federal assistance.*
> *The solution will find resistance from many quar-ters, but we have no alternative.*

Remember, speakers can use any one segment, or combina-tion of segments, of the Problem/Cause/Effect/Solution structural patterns. The challenge is to listen for cue language such as:

> "We have a **problem**..."
>
> "The **cause** of our problem is ..."
>
> "The **effect** of this problem is clear..."
>
> "Our **solution** for this problem is ..."

Although listening for cue and clue language, adapting to the speaker's structure, and taking notes accordingly seems log-ical and obvious, it is surprising how many leaders find this to be a new and productive exercise. Listening for key words alerts you to other potential segments, keeps you alert to the entire message, prevents you from relaxing your listening, and helps you use your thinking-speed advantage to evaluate, anticipate, review, and summarize. It is another tool requiring practice in order to build automatic skills.

▶ **Chronological** organizational structures follow a time sequence that is typically easy to trace. Again, the key for listening success lies in identifying the cue and clue language. In this structure, speakers tip their hand with such time-based language as:

"Past/Present/Future"

"Yesterday/Today/Tomorrow"

"Looking at this Issue Over Time"

"From the 20th Century to the 21st Century"

The key is to listen for time-sequenced language. Whether chronological movement is forward or backward, it provides a valuable framework for note-taking and connecting a great deal of information. For example, consider the following message developed around chronology and time:

When we review the study and development of listening from the past through the present to the future, we find a number of important historical marker points. In 1926, Dr. Paul Rankin's research identified that listening was the most-used communication activity, with nearly half the average adult's day spent listening. In the late 1940s, Dr. Ralph Nichols identified the critical differences between effective and ineffective listeners, giving birth to the focused study of listening. In 1979, Dr. Lyman Steil founded the International Listening Association, which celebrated its 25th Anniversary in 2004. Looking to the future, the opportunity for extended growth in the study and development of listening is great.

Identification and adaptation to the pattern of the chronologically organized speaker will serve you well. In addition, when speakers are unorganized, but their topic or material has an historical or time-based frame of reference, your knowledge and use of the chronological structure will help in organizing the unorganized.

▶ **Spatial, Graphic, or Visual Patterns** constitute the fourth organizational structure. Spatial structures are powerful, as the speaker creates a visual word picture that helps explain or illustrate what is being talked about. If you identify and adapt your note-taking to the speaker's picture, your listening effectiveness will grow. Spatial structures can be recognized immediately from cue and clue language:

"Picture in your mind's eye…"

"Imagine this scene…"

"Get the picture…?

"Visualize a ladder with five rungs…"

"This material can be remembered as a tree with many branches…"

Consider the following example of a skilled listener who utilized the spatial structure of a speaker's presentation while engaging in the "Plan to Report" and extended the speaker's original graphic portrait. In addition, note the speaker's and listener's secondary use of enumeration.

I heard an interesting speaker at our professional meeting today. Mr. Carl J. Strand, a renowned financial investment expert, explained what it takes to be financially successful in this country today. He suggested we needed to picture, in our mind's eye, the ladder of financial success. He said we have to climb four rungs on this ladder if we want to be financially successful. The first rung he talked about was a broad and thorough liberal education. He said education was the most important rung because it affected everything else. The second rung he talked about was contacts. He said the family we were born into, the people we went to school with, the people we work with, live with, and socialize with all have an important impact on our financial success. The third rung centered on our long-term motivation, as every study of financially successful individuals found highly motivated people. Beyond education, contacts, and motivation, Mr. Strand said the fourth rung on the ladder is critically important. The fourth rung is the creation of a life-long financial strategy and plan. The key is to start as young as possible. He said if we climb the four rungs of the "ladder of financial success," we will find a pot of riches at the top. I drew a picture of the four-runged ladder, took notes, and will remember Mr. Strand's message for a long time. Now I need to act on his advice.

Identifying and adapting to the clue and cue language will dramatically enhance your listening and note-taking as you capture the speaker's picture. If the speaker paints a picture, your mental or written notes should paint the same picture.

ANOTHER CASE IN POINT

Bill Kroll is a District Sales Manager with Colgate Oral Pharmaceuticals, and leads 25 team members located throughout several states. He regularly conducts virtual meetings and enhances everyone's note-taking by promoting use of the "Plan to Report" process in his meetings. Following is an e-mail he sent to Dr. Rick Bommelje attesting to the value of PTR:

From: Bill Kroll

To: Rick Bommelje

    I wanted to follow up to let you know that I did in fact use the PTR technique relating to virtual meetings (conference calls, Internet meetings, etc.) you shared with me when we talked recently. I began the call with a review of the topics I'd be covering and then told the team I would be asking two or three people to provide me with the two most important items that would affect them from our discussion, plus a motivational/inspirational thought to close out our call.

    At the end of the call, which had run longer than expected due to some excellent discourse, I asked two people for feedback. I chose people who had been relatively quiet on the call. I actually got some very perceptive and insightful comments back, as well as a nice bit of inspiration for the holiday season.

    This technique worked well, and I will plan to use it on future calls. I think it will raise the bar on the level of active listening in my virtual meetings!

    Thanks again for sharing!

Bill Kroll

PRIMARY AND SECONDARY PATTERNS

    Although organized speakers often use these four patterns in some combination, the key for listeners is to select one arrangement as the *primary pattern* and others as a *secondary pattern*. When you recognize that a speaker is unorganized, you have an opportunity to use any organizational pattern that works for you. We have found everyone has favorite listening and note-taking structures that can be used when speakers are unorganized or disorganized. Recognizing these patterns will help you overcome the problems of wasting the speech-thought differential, poor note-taking, and listening primarily for facts rather than concepts. The process of listening can be very complex, and we have found that listening leaders develop and refine a variety of practices to help simplify the process. All effective listeners we have worked with have favorite organization systems they can quickly turn to when needed. These systems have been used in the past to help speakers; you can use the same principles to refine and improve your ability to listen.

NOTE-TAKING FOR POSITIVE RESULTS

A fundamental tool for listening leaders involves the proactive and consistent process of taking mental and/or written notes. Although you may periodically take notes when you are on the phone or in meetings, the majority of leaders we have studied normally do not take written notes. As a result, we have identified two troubling facts. First, most leaders rely on their mental note-taking skills. Second, the majority of leaders, at all levels, have developed limited listening note-taking skills. To test our measured experience, we invite you to observe the note-taking behaviors and skills of the leaders with whom you interact on a regular basis. We predict you will find few who take notes regularly and skillfully. Conversely, the most effective listening leaders we know are highly skilled and consistent note takers. As the palest ink is more potent than the strongest memory, the following six suggestions are designed to help you improve your note-taking ability:

▶ Be prepared and decide whether or not to take notes. Although written and mental note-taking and planning to report will serve you in every setting, at times written note-taking may be distracting to some communication purposes. Your purpose for listening and the setting will determine whether or not you should take notes. Preparation and readiness is the key. Listening leaders are constantly prepared with the simple tools of paper and pencil.

▶ Adapt to the speaker's structure and decide the extent and type of notes to be taken. It is important to identify as quickly as possible the speaker's organization, or lack thereof. At times, your task will be to organize the unorganized, as many speakers have no discernible organization. Nevertheless, you will generally profit by identifying and adapting to the speaker's format. Some note-takers tend to organize their notes around their preferred pattern rather than the speaker's actual pattern. When you do, you expend more energy than necessary and will likely miss important material. Therefore, it is important to determine quickly if the speaker is employing a formal organizational pattern and, if so, to adapt your own note-taking to this pattern.

▶ Like skilled leaders who consciously develop and practice their note-taking skills, you will discover there are several types of note-taking systems, which differ in purpose and process. Some organizational patterns call for rudimentary note-taking, while others require more advanced strategies. Skilled practitioners sharpen their note-taking abilities in each of the following common types; Partial Outline, Basic Outline, Paragraph Summary or Précis, Fact versus Principle, Feelings versus Implications, and Idea Linking or Mind Mapping.

4▶ Keep your notes brief and meaningful. The utility of brevity speaks for itself. With brief notes, you invest more focused time listening and less time writing. As a consequence, you are less likely to miss the speaker's larger intent and message.

5▶ Your notes should be immediately clear at any later review. Clarity requires using brief sentences and statements of ideas that are understandable and applicable long after you have written them. The importance of clarity seems obvious, but our follow-up examinations have highlighted how often notes have little apparent meaning to the note-taker. Having examined many note-takers' notes, it is also fascinating to note the counterproductive amount of unrelated notations and doodling. The key is to be on purpose, on point, clear, and efficient.

6▶ Review your notes at a later time. Although the act of taking notes has value in and of itself, the value is compounded through careful and thoughtful review. While taking notes allows you, in a sense, to hear the message a second time, reviewing those notes provides the opportunity to listen again and again and again. Of course, the degree of benefit will depend on your initial listening and note-taking skill.

This suggestion is extremely important because, in all listening situations, retention is increased by note-taking and review. Numerous studies have found that, without note-taking and/or review, significant critical information is lost within 24 hours. With passing time, the loss is compounded. Com-

petent note-taking and purposeful review invariably improve understanding and retention.

COMMON NOTE-TAKING STRATEGIES

As outlined earlier, all listeners have the opportunity to
adapt to each speaker, purpose, topic, and situation by taking
appropriate and useful notes. As the range of note-taking skills
is extended, leaders will become more effective and productive.
Several common note-taking strategies are described below.

▶ **Partial Outlining** is appropriate in the most basic
listening situations. In its simplest form, you note
the key points in the message that seem important to you and ignore the points you deem unim-
portant. For example, imagine you are listening
to your Vice President of Sales give her monthly
report on closed and potential sales, and you are
primarily interested in the information on potential sales. It is helpful to identify your notes as
Partial, with a parenthetical notation of the topic
or topics that were ignored, (e.g., "Closed Sales").
Partial outlining involves taking complete notes
on the segment of the presentation that is important to you at the moment, while making it clear
that they do not cover the speaker's full message.

▶ **Basic Outlining** is the most commonly taught note-
taking system, and typically includes recording the
complete main point and subpoints. In this case, it
is valuable to identify your notes as "basic," as you
record the total outline of the speaker's message.
Because any attempt to capture the speaker's full
message can interfere with listening, it is important

to develop the note-taking skill of creating and using abbreviations and short-hand strategies. In addition, like every note-taking strategy, basic outlining is most appropriate if it matches the speaker's organizational structure better than other structures.

▶ **Paragraph Summary or Précis** note-taking involves periodically summarizing the larger message into brief paragraphs. Each paragraph is written in complete sentences and is a very brief abstract of the total message. The end result is a summary abstract of the complete message. Typically, précis note-takers focus for a few minutes without taking notes, and then make summarized notes of short duration. This requires considerable skill at reducing a significant amount of information to a brief summary. In addition, it requires the ability to listen to ongoing messages while summarizing and recording completed messages. Although challenging, this form of note-taking works well whether the speaker's message is inductive or deductive, organized, unorganized, or disorganized. Developing a short-hand system that works for you is beneficial, as précis note-taking requires the skill of capturing and summarizing a great amount of information.

▶ **Fact versus Principle** note-taking is a clever way of identifying, separating, and recording the facts and principles of any message. The mechanics are simple, but the task is more difficult. Mechanically, you just note the speaker's name, topic, and date at the top of the page, and divide the page with a vertical line. The left half is labeled "Facts" and the right half "Principles." As the speaker expounds, your task is to record "facts" on the left side and "principles" on the right side. Of course, you must be able to discern the difference between the speaker's avowed facts and principles. Remember, facts are acts, deeds, or conditions accepted to be true. Facts are based on some reality that exists. On the other hand, principles are general and broad truths, laws, doctrines, and generalizations. Fact versus Principle note-taking is advantageous in listening to informational and persuasive communication, since it results in fewer notes and greater opportunity for reflective review and evaluation. Superficial, unprepared, emotional, and ill-supported speakers are quickly exposed. The key is to be able to identify and separate facts from principles.

▶ **Feelings versus Implication** note-taking is a related strategy that works when listening to cathartic messages. The mechanical process is similar to that of the Fact versus Implication strategy with the left half of the page labeled "Feelings" and the right half "Implications." As the speaker "catharts, vents, unloads, or dumps his or her bucket," simply note the speaker's expressed feelings on the left side and possible implications on the right side. As most cathartic communication requires "listening in the moment," this note-taking strategy is best employed as, after-the-fact summarizing. The advantage of this strategy resides in increased attention, which results in deeper understanding of the speaker's specific feelings and larger implications. In addition, it forces you away from premature attempts to dismiss or solve the problem.

▶ **Idea Linking** is an excellent listening and note-taking technique for visual listeners. Known as "slash recall," Idea Linking is based on Mind Mapping studies that began in the early 1970s to help listeners take better notes and improve thinking skills. For some, there is a magical quality to Idea Linking, as it taps into the whole brain and promotes visual creativity. Idea Linking and Mind Mapping are free-flowing. The process is best seen in contrast to traditional note-taking methods. Idea Linking allows any information and ideas to be organized into clustered notes.

Specifically, Idea Linking is well suited to listening to spatial patterns because it allows a non-linear pictorial type of listening and note-taking. Idea Linking is a visually interesting method of note-taking that allows you to organize information as you receive it, add connections and associations, and increase the retention of information. Standard note-taking typically uses 90 percent more words. As a result, it takes longer to write, takes longer to re-read, and creates a weaker image for recall. Proponents of the Idea Linking strategy like the fact that it uses key words, images, diagrams, and pictures. The main elements of Idea Linking include:

▶ Locating the central idea or message subject in the center of your note page and circle it.

▶ Letting ideas flow freely without judgment.

▶ Capturing the key words to quickly represent large ideas.

▶ Printing one word per line to stimulate memory upon review.

▶ Using nouns and verbs as meaningful key words.

▶ Connecting key words to the central subject with additional lines.

▶ Using color to highlight and emphasize ideas.

▶ Using images and symbols to further highlight ideas and stimulate the mind to make additional connections.

Idea Linking can serve you in listening to both organized and unorganized speakers. As Idea Linking is free-flowing, it is important to remember there is no right or wrong way to link ideas. For illustration, we have created an Idea-Linked or Mind-Mapped set of notes for Chapter Eight, on the following page.

SMALL STEPS EQUAL BIG GAINS

Some of the simplest planned leadership actions result in significant gains. Without small, conscious steps, larger steps are unlikely. Listening leader **Dr. Nancy Haugen** uses planned note-taking as a primary method of staying in tune with the person to whom she is listening. It is such a small step that many would dismiss its importance. Yet the small act has significant ramifications for listening, as Nancy has discovered in her role as Chairperson of the Nursing Department at the Florida Hospital College of Health Sciences.

What I have started doing is taking paper with me everywhere I go. It is so simple, but when I hear important ideas, I am prepared to write appropriate notes. I focus better

MIND MAP

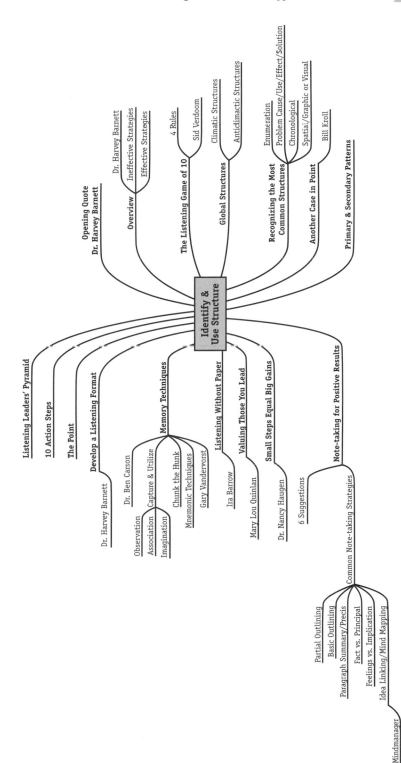

on what is being said, and my notes will trigger something in the future. I have a tendency to throw brainstorming ideas into conversations, only to discover that was not where the other person was going at all. I had one team member, who is a wonderful leader, tell me, "You are going to the next idea because you think you have already figured it out. Meanwhile, I am in the valley, and you have lost me. Sometimes you just need to hold your thoughts and hear me out. Your ideas are good, but you need to slow down and understand my position." The simple availability of paper and pencil and note-taking makes all the difference in the world. In addition, I developed an acronym "GRACE," which means Guiding Reflective Actions Change Environment. I write it on the top of my notepad so I remember to be reflective as opposed to reactive in my comments and my actions. I need to really hear what others have to say because you can't reflect on something you haven't heard.

> *"What I've started doing is taking paper with me everywhere I go. It is so simple, but when I hear important ideas, I am prepared to write appropriate notes. The simple availability of paper and pencil and note-taking makes all the difference in the world."*
> —Dr. Nancy Haugen

VALUING THOSE YOU LEAD

Taking notes also makes a difference to the sense of value and self-worth of those you lead, as **Mary Lou Quinlan**, the Founder & CEO of Just Ask A Woman, discovered early in her career.

I had a wonderful boss who was responsible for the major operations of a global ad agency, who always had a pad of yellow, lined paper and a pen when he sat down with someone. He always took notes as the other person spoke, and I must tell you what a positive effect that had. As he took notes I always thought, "He's really listening; he cares what I have to say, so I better say smart and worthwhile things." As he listened and took careful notes, he was in a position to follow up in a meaningful way, which was the best listening acknowledgement of all.

> *"He always took notes as the other person spoke, and I must tell you what a positive effect that had. As he took notes I always thought, 'He's really listening; he cares what I have to say, so I better say smart and worthwhile things.'"*
> —Mary Lou Quinlan

LISTENING WITHOUT PAPER

Of course, there are times leaders find themselves in situations without paper and pencil and must depend on memory-based note-taking. In addition, in some circumstances, written note-taking may impede the speaker's ability to communicate openly. In such cases, the principles and practices of "identifying and adapting" to the organizational structure of the speaker still pertain. However, the challenge is greater because you must now rely on the strength of your memory muscle. Like all muscles, your memory muscle is strengthened with practice, use, and exercise. Without them, it atrophies.

Ira Barrow is a cattle rancher and producer in Southeast Oklahoma who manages approximately three-and-a-half square miles of property and several hundred head of pure-bred and commercial cattle. He uses both written and mental note-taking systems.

I've taken notes both ways. Depending on the situation, many times I find myself going down the hall, stopping, and asking someone a question without having the opportunity to make written notes. I personally ask myself a question about what the other person has said. I do that mentally as I walk away. I take probably 15 or 20 seconds worth of time running their statement back through my head, and as I hear it several times, I retain more of it.

MEMORY TECHNIQUES

Dr. Ben Carson, a world-renowned pediatric neurosurgeon and author of *The Big Picture*, discusses the incredible capacity of the human mind. As Dr. Carson notes, "The human brain is the most complex organ system in the universe, as it can process 2 million bytes of information per second. That's how amazing and complex the human brain is. Yet, we have people walking around talking about how they cannot remember."

> *"The human brain can process 2 million bytes of information per second. Yet we have people walking around talking about how they cannot remember."*
> —Dr. Ben Carson

All great leaders know that full application of your memory is a critical component of the listening leadership process. As you recall, the definition of Listening Leadership, includes "storing" as a major stage.

> *To guide yourself and others to positive results for the betterment of all by sensing, interpreting, evaluating, **storing**, and responding to messages.*

All leaders have three constant opportunities to succeed or fail in the ongoing challenge of memory. As previously discussed, memory is the "mortar" that resides between each segment of SIER. If short term memory fails at any level, each ensuing stage will automatically fail. In addition, if overall long-term memory fails, short-term success matters little.

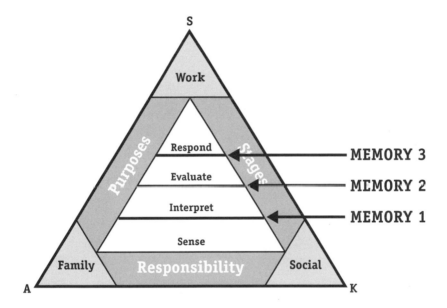

Clearly, there are a wide variety of memory techniques available to help you remember what you have heard. Perhaps the most important tool is to identify and use the speaker's structure to help you receive and retain the message. Using the patterns of enumeration, problem/solution, chronology, and spatial organization to attach the points you choose to remember will enhance your memory.

CAPTURE AND UTILIZE

In addition, build on the three main elements of memory: observation, association and imagination. These three practices can be sharpened to help you remember many things. For example, remembering names seems to be a challenge for many leaders. The majority of leaders with whom we have worked over several decades report that this is one of their greatest listening problems. Although there are numerous suggestions for overcoming this shortcoming, we recommend two simple steps involving "Capture and Utilize." Step one focuses on capturing or getting the other party's name. Although it sounds simple, we have noted that many individuals enter the "capture the name game" with an a priori assumption that they aren't good with names, or that they'll never see the person again, so why bother? They are doomed from the beginning. Step two focuses on utilizing the name through repetition. This is one case where the axiom "use it or lose it" is literally true. You can't use it if you don't get it. On the other hand, if you misuse or mispronounce someone's name, you will generally be given a second opportunity to recapture it correctly. Every outstanding leader knows it pays to remember names because we all walk through life humming our personal theme song, entitled "There will never be another me." Everyone's name is magic to him or her. Capture and utilize names, and your memory muscle will be strengthened.

CHUNK THE HUNK

Another memory strategy is to "chunk" or break longer messages into smaller units. Although research indicates the average person has difficulty remembering more than seven numbers, we are inundated with an overload of longer and longer numeric messages. For example, if you are listening to a 10-digit telephone number, break it into smaller chunks. By chunking, you would break the 10 numbers of 555-583-3497 into three units: five fifty-five; five eighty-three; and thirty-four ninety-seven. Five-digit zip codes can be divided into two segments like fifty-five, one twenty-seven. Nine-digit Social Security numbers can likewise be arranged into three units: four sixty-five, twenty-two, twenty-nine forty-eight. To the ear, each of these numbers sounds like fewer elements to remember and is substantially easier to remember.

MNEMONIC TECHNIQUES

A classical way to extend your memory lies in the masterful development and use of mnemonic devices. Mnemonic techniques involve the creation of a short-hand system to remember longer messages and material. For example, although SIER stands for the four stages of Sensing, Interpreting, Evaluating, and Responding, many leaders remember it mnemonically by the thought SIER = Success In Everyday Relationships. Most leaders remember how they formed a word to remember something else. For example, when you had to memorize the names of the five Great Lakes, you likely used the word HOMES (H= Huron; O= Ontario; M=Michigan; E= Erie; and S = Superior) as a mnemonic. For the agile mind, there is no limit to developing acronyms and mnemonic devices to enhance your short- and long-term memory.

Gary Vandervorst is the analytical and thoughtful Chief Financial Officer of Erickson Oil Products. Gary takes great pride in planning and utilizing structure as a careful and complete listener. Some would consider him to be cautious, but he considers himself to be thoughtful, systematic, reflective, and thorough.

I am a significantly better listener when I listen to problems and issues with a carefully thought-out plan. When anyone listens with a structure and strategy, based on their experience, they are positioned to respond with a much better structured and strategic response or solution to the situation. Listening certainly has impacted me positively, because I am viewed within Erickson Oil as the senior-level Executive who is reflective. This correlates with sincerity and a willingness to look at all sides of an issue.

> *"Listening certainly has impacted me positively, because I am viewed within the Erickson Oil as the senior level Executive who is reflective. This correlates with sincerity and a willingness to look at all sides of an issue."*
> —Gary Vandervorst

For example, during the past three to four years, we have experienced significant growth in our company, with all the predictable challenges. Because I listen in a structured and supportive way, I have been approached more and more by employees in need of confidential conversations and seeking an organized listener who will listen carefully and provide a meaningful response.

DEVELOP A LISTENING FORMAT

Dr. Harvey Barnett and his Infant Swimming Resource leadership team have developed a very practical and specific listening format that helps everyone stay organized and on point.

Because time is scarce and talk is cheap, we first provide a written outline of what we are going to discuss. We find if you have thought about organizing what you want to say and how you want to say it, you will put the more salient features at the beginning, and you will introduce your important messages with a clear-cut opening paragraph. When anyone puts thought into what they want to say, others will, too. For example, when I get someone's preliminary outline, I write notes in the margin. Then the writer is invited to speak. The speaker presents what he or she wrote, I read back my notes, and we continue our dialogue until we both agree on what was meant, and on the appropriate course of action to take. At that point, we both sign and date the outline.

We find this listening format helps both speakers and listeners be accountable, as we have to agree on what was said, what was intended, what needs to be done, and the course of action. I don't care if the problem is simple or complex, everyone has to be accountable. It is the quickest way to make every day count. Because everyone on our team follows this format, they start to think and act accordingly.

THE POINT

As **Dr. Barnett** and other productive leaders have demonstrated, "Everyone profits when you establish a format that helps you listen more effectively." Listening with organizational structures makes a significant difference. As you practice and refine **Golden Rule 8: "Listening Leaders Identify and Use Struc-**

Golden Rule 8

"Listening Leaders Identify & Use Structure"

10 ACTION STEPS

1. Develop a proactive plan for identifying and remembering any speaker's predictable organizational habits and behaviors.

2. Initiate and play the "Listening Game of 10" in every listening situation.

3. Assume the Minimum 51% Responsibility for successful communication.

4. Identify and use the speaker's structure to listen more effectively.

5. Implement the "Plan to Report" strategy in all communications.

6. Learn and apply the four most common organizational structures: enumeration, problem/solution, chronological, and spatial.

7. Anticipate and adapt your listening to the speaker's organizational structure and patterns.

8. Take written and/or mental notes on a consistent basis.

9. Apply the "Capture and Utilize" strategy to enhance your memory of names.

10. Build your "Listening Organization" by teaching those you lead how to identify and use structures to build their listening leader skills.

LISTENING LEADERS™ GOLDEN RULES PYRAMID

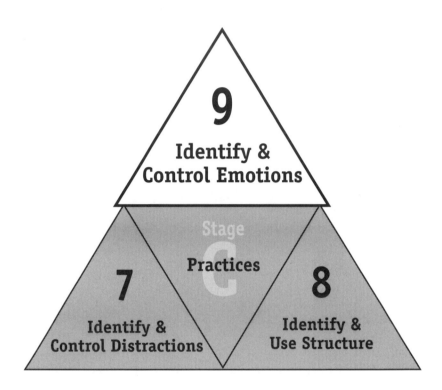

Golden Rule 9

"Listening Leaders Identify & Control Emotions"

"We always respond to whatever the issue is, and issues come up every day. Ever since we started this organization, I have set the leadership tone of being responsive. You cannot be responsive if you don't listen and clearly know what you are responding to. You must understand the other person. You must know the answer to the question, 'Where is the other person coming from?'"

—Millard Fuller

Millard Fuller is the founder and President of Habitat for Humanity International. With Millard's remarkable leadership, Habitat for Humanity has become a significant worldwide nonprofit, nondenominational Christian housing ministry, dedicated to eliminating poverty housing. Habitat volunteers have built homes for more than 150,000 families in need, in nearly 3,000 communities, in 92 nations. Habitat's hard-working volunteers build a new home every 26 minutes. Because of Millard Fuller's leadership, volunteers have listened to his call, and more than 750,000 people around the world have safe, decent, affordable housing. In 1996, the importance of Millard's leadership was recognized when he was awarded the nation's highest civilian honor, the "Presidential Medal of Freedom."

In discussing the importance of fostering listening throughout his organization, Millard Fuller outlined the importance of (1) understanding and controlling your own emotions; (2) understanding the emotional behaviors of others; and, (3) being responsive.

As everyone functions from a combination of emotional, social, or rational perspectives, it is important that the perceptive listening leader is able to listen and lead through every stage of behavior. Understanding and controlling your own emotions is the first step. Recognizing and responding to the emotions of others is the second step. Allowing others' emotions to trigger your emotions will generally result in both listening and leadership failure. As Millard Fuller explains, there are many times we must listen through our own and other's emotions.

> One day, I heard from a Jewish man who had been a supporter but was very upset because he had discovered we were a Christian organization. He was very emotional and threatened to stop supporting us because he was not a Christian. In spite of his anger, he made it clear he really liked that we were building houses for families in need. Understanding his emotional upset, I said, "Let me follow your logic here. What you are saying is that you are not happy because we are a Christian organization that builds homes for the poor, without discriminating by race, religion, or ethnic group. However, there are more Christians than Jews, and if we only had Jewish support, how many houses would we build? We must reach out to the Christians."

> Once his emotions were in check he said, "I never thought of it like that. I think your strategy is a very smart, and I will continue to support your cause." He was clearly a person of good will, and he was very much in tune with what we were doing but was initially thinking from an emotional point of view. Listening beyond our emotions provides clearer insights.

THE POWER OF EMOTIONS

Golden Rule 9: "Listening Leaders Identify & Control Emotions," places the spotlight *on your internal emotional factors that are triggered by external forces.* Identifying and controlling your emotions is one of the most important and difficult skills to refine as you enhance your listening. Because of their spontaneous and nonrational reactions to people, topics, and language, emotional listeners have a tendency to be poor listeners. To control your emotions during listening, you must develop a strategy for automatic implementation. As noted, you need to: (1) prepare and commit yourself to listen actively; (2) think about the topic and environment in advance; (3) concentrate and don't let your thoughts wander; (4) look for useful material or information; (5) plan to report the essence of what was said to someone else; and, (6) withhold your judgment and reaction until you have fully received and understood the speaker's position.

IDENTIFYING AND DEALING WITH EMOTIONS

Poor listeners lose emotional control in one, or a combination, of three specific areas: *speakers, topics, and words.* Whenever the combination of a speaker, topic, or words triggers an unchecked emotional response, your listening will suffer. Consider a situation when you lost your temper because you held an opposite position on a topic. Did you listen well to anything that was said? Consider a time you failed to listen carefully simply because of your emotional reaction to the speaker. Perhaps you disagreed with his or her political position, age or gender, nationality, or religious beliefs. At what point did you cease listening? Remember a time when you responded emotionally to a speaker's language in such a way that listening, for all practical purposes, ended. In every case, your emotions got in the way of your listening.

Five key points will help you to better understand the relationship between emotions and listening.

▶ **Everyone has emotional triggers**. All listeners are affected by emotions. Think about the last decision-making discussion in which you took part. You may have exhibited a tendency to not listen carefully to individuals, topics, and/or language with which you strongly agreed or disagreed. As your subjective and emotional reactions increased, your logical and rational abilities decreased. Whether you are at home, work, or in social situations, when your emotionality goes up, your rationality goes down.

▶ **Your emotional reactions to speakers, topics, and words are directly influenced by your filtering agents**. Just as the filter on a camera affects the resulting photograph, your past experiences, knowledge, beliefs, attitudes, and opinions affect your emotional responses. As your filtering agents are in a constant state of change, your effort to identify and analyze your emotional triggers must be ongoing and never-ending.

▶ **Emotional triggers affect your communication and listening effectiveness**. As noted in **Golden Rule 6: "Listening Leaders Apply SIER"**, emotional triggers will affect you at every level. As positive or negative emotions or feelings are triggered, listeners move automatically to the evaluation level, wherein judgments are quickly made that impact immediate responses. As emotional evaluations lead to emotional responses, the listening problem becomes more difficult as the emotional evaluation usually short-circuits your ability to listen at the subsequent crucial levels of sensing and interpreting. If you tune out a speaker who advocates partial birth abortion, for example, then you can neither sense accurately, interpret correctly, make sound judgments about, nor respond properly to the speaker's complete message. Due to emotional listening, any response will be incomplete and usually inadequate.

▶ **Your emotions may be triggered positively, neutrally, or negatively.** Although you may not think your *positive emotions* can cause listening problems, we have observed many leaders who tend to relax their listening effort when their positive emotions are triggered. It makes sense. If you are emotionally in sync with who and what you hear, you tend to agree and applaud too quickly. Consequently, you are susceptible to accepting half-truths, opinions, inconsistent data, and poorly reasoned arguments. Often, you move to premature evaluation and response before listening to the full message. Effective listening leaders place special emphasis on identifying and controlling their listening in the presence of positive emotional triggers.

Although *neutrality* is usually linked with objectivity, wise listening leaders observe a special note of caution. Emotional neutrality often leads the listener to conclude that the speaker, topic, or language, doesn't matter, and thus tune out because of emotional disinterest. Allowing emotional lack of interest to control your listening behavior leads to costly habits. On the other hand, conscious emotional neutrality can lead to "objective" listening.

Of course, triggering *negative emotions* leads to predictable negative behaviors. When leaders are unconsciously influenced by negative emotional triggers, they typically stop listening, tune out, miss the larger points, and become argumentative. Movement to irrational evaluation and inappropriate response is usually quick and costly and makes it difficult, if not impossible, to achieve the goal of not responding before you've fully sensed, comprehended, rationally interpreted, and appropriately evaluated a message.

> ▶ **The world is filled with highly motivated, well-trained, highly skilled, and well-financed individuals and organizations that are focused on identifying the emotional triggers of others.** Find someone who knows more about your emotional triggers than you do, and you will find someone who is in a position to control you. Better than anyone, successful listeners develop deep insight into their personal emotional triggers, and they develop operational skill at controlling their emotional reactions.

A BROADER LOOK

Because your emotions affect everything you do, it is important to take a broader look at your "triggers." Emotional triggers provoke an internal emotional response to speakers, topics, and language. that disrupts your listening process. That emotional response disrupts and adversely affects your effectiveness as a listener. Your emotional triggers can be classified as positive, neutral, or negative.

POSITIVE EMOTION

Everyone holds positive emotional views of individuals, topics, or language that color their listening. When you are not aware of the power of such positive emotions, your listening becomes lazy, lax, and limited. You are emotionally connected to the speaker, topic, or language, and you may not bother to hear the complete message. You enter your "emotional happy place" as you listen to your favorite subjects, or listen to someone you like, or perhaps listen to voices that appeal to you. Your emotional listening may be induced by a person's physical appearance, or by certain words that evoke powerful emotional images. A variety of emotional triggers can provoke positive emotions and possibly endanger your listening ability, particularly if you are unaware of what can happen when you have strong positive emotions while listening.

Language is powerful, and as words have special significance to each of us, they often provoke positive emotions. Wordsmiths carefully design language to elicit our positive emotions. Language that evokes "Motherhood," "the American Flag," "Apple Pie," "the Democratic or Republican Party," "Rocky Mountain High," "Soaring Eagles," or other similar warm images may trigger reverie or premature agreement and result in missing the real message. Without awareness, positive emotions can lead to negative and ineffective listening habits.

NEUTRAL EMOTION

Although neutrality can contribute to effective listening leader behavior, neutral emotional response to a speaker, topic, or words, can also result in bad listening habits. Emotional neutrality can lead to passive and uninterested lack of activity. Neutral emotions lead unknowing listeners to tune out speakers. While neutrality may provide an objective listening position, it can also be a trap, as it lures you from active listening to passive lack of interest. As emotionally neutral listeners create a position of disinterest, they simply drift out of the mainstream of the listening process. Effective listening leaders overcome the counterproductive impact of neutral emotions by identifying them. In the process, your focused listening interest and activity will be heightened.

NEGATIVE EMOTION

More often, listeners are adversely impacted by strongly held negative emotions relative to who is speaking and what he or she is saying. Any negative feelings and emotions toward the speaker, topic, or language will interrupt the total listening process. In worst-case scenarios, negative emotions often lead to a refusal to listen. In addition, any attempt to listen with negative emotions usually results in angry listeners, and the evidence is clear: mad listeners are bad listeners. Like positive and neutral emotions, negative emotions are triggered by your view of speakers, topics, and language. Of course, the nature of the response is different. The first key to controlling your negative emotions rests in identifying your negative emotional triggers. The second key lies in withholding judgment until your comprehension is complete. Any negative emotional premature judgment and reaction toward the speaker, topic, or language undermines leaders' listening effectiveness. The task is difficult, but worthy of any leader who desires to be known as a listening leader.

Bill Jensen, Senior Vice President and Chief Operating Officer of Vail Resorts, Inc. is a listening leader who understands his emotional frustration when he's listening to whining. Although few like to listen to whiners, Bill has developed a strategy to control his emotions and listen with effective focus.

There comes a point where you can't spend a lot of your time listening to whining, so I let people have two minutes. Then I move them back to a more constructive thought process and conversation. I will listen to someone who's whining for a whole lot less time than I will to someone who's articulating a situation and problem. When there is a personality conflict, I will listen to it. If two managers are butting heads, the reality is that they're both at fault, and generally what I say in the end is: "You know, I'm not going to pick one over the other. If you can't figure this out between the two of you, then maybe both of you should leave." That is usually a big shock and reduces the emotions.

When my door is open, if you want two minutes of my time, any time, you've got it. If you need 20 minutes of my time, unfortunately you've got to call and make an appointment because I want to give you time so I can be a good listener. You have to establish a

> *"I will listen to someone who's whining for a whole lot less time than I will to someone who's articulating a situation and problem."*
> —Bill Jensen

mindset to listen and, as a leader, you have to set ground rules for listening. The strongest leaders control their emotions and are good listeners.

FIRST THINGS FIRST

Effective listening leaders control their listening emotions by focusing on first things first. Simply put, they create a strategy to identify the individuals, topics, and language that trigger their positive, neutral, and negative emotions. Those individuals, topics, and language that trigger your emotions change over time, so this assignment is ongoing. We recommend that you make the following lists once a quarter, for at least one year. By the end of a year, the process will have become easy and somewhat automatic, provided you have completed this assignment four times. The benefit will become obvious. As you identify specific individuals, topics, and language that adversely trigger your emotions, you will be in a position to take action to control them.

In a separate notebook, identify 25 individuals, topics or issues, and language that you have difficulty listening to, or through, because of your positive, neutral, or negative emotional reactions. For a warm-up example, complete the following mini-exercise. Check the *type* (Positive, Neutral, or Negative) and *degree* (Range: 1 = least and 10 = most) of emotional response you experience with the examples listed.

INDIVIDUAL EMOTIONAL TRIGGER EXERCISE

Individual Source	Positive	Neutral	Negative
1. George W. Bush	____	____	____
2. John F. Kerry	____	____	____
3. Tiger Woods	____	____	____
4. Oprah Winfrey	____	____	____
5. Colin Powell	____	____	____
6. Hillary Clinton	____	____	____
7. Arnold Schwarzenegger	____	____	____
8. Barbara Walters	____	____	____
9. Bill O'Reilly	____	____	____
10. Alan Greenspan	____	____	____

All of these individuals are well known as of this writing in 2004, and it is likely you have varying emotional reactions to each of them. When they speak, regardless of the purpose, topics, or language, how are your emotions and listening affected? Remember, people that surround you come and go, but you hold emotional views of each. You also hold the keys to control your emotions, no matter whom you listen to. Periodically complete this analysis with a focus on your Target 25 as outlined in Chapter Four.

TOPIC EMOTIONAL TRIGGER EXERCISE

Topic/issue Source	Positive	Neutral	Negative
1. Wildlife Conversation (Pro)	____	____	____
2. War in Iraq (Pro)	____	____	____
3. Public Funding of Stadiums (Pro)	____	____	____
4. Stem Cell Research (Pro)	____	____	____
5. Space Exploration (Pro)	____	____	____
6. Death Penalty (Pro)	____	____	____
7. Global Warming (Pro)	____	____	____
8. Partial-Birth Abortion (Pro)	____	____	____
9. Prayer in Schools (Pro)	____	____	____
10. Animal Rights (Pro)	____	____	____

Because these topics are actively controversial, as of this writing in 2004, it is likely you have varying emotional reactions to each of them. When they arise, regardless of the speaker or language, how do they affect your emotions and listening? Remember, topics of the day come and go, but you hold emotional views of each. You also hold the keys to control your emotions, no matter what issues you listen to. You can raise your level of emotional control over topics by consciously recording the nature and degree of their emotional impact. This exercise is unending.

LANGUAGE EMOTIONAL TRIGGER EXERCISE

Words	Positive	Neutral	Negative
1. Baby Boomers	____	____	____
2. Child Molester	____	____	____
3. Jock	____	____	____
4. Love	____	____	____
5. Intellectual	____	____	____
6. Lesbian	____	____	____
7. Honky	____	____	____
8. Nazi	____	____	____
9. Geek	____	____	____
10. Any Profanity	____	____	____

Although emotional language changes constantly, these words are periodically heard as of this writing in 2004, and it is likely you may have varying emotional reactions to each of them. When they arise, regardless of the speaker or topic, how do they affect your emotions and listening? Some words cause immediate emotional responses. Buzzwords, labels, jargon, clichés, and profanity have a tendency to trigger our emotions, one way or another.

Remember, as language and words of the day change, they will impact your emotions. Nevertheless, you hold the keys to control your emotions, no matter what combination of words speakers choose to use. You will raise your level of emotional control over all words by consciously recording the nature and degree of their emotional impact on you. The old adage "Sticks and stones may break my bones, but names can never hurt me" is only true if you control your emotions. Like all emotional control development, this exercise is unending.

In addition, your task of controlling your emotions is compounded whenever any of the three forces are combined. Clearly listening to a speaker you dislike talk about a subject about which you have strong negative feelings and who uses language that disturbs you, will test your listening skills to the limit. However, the task of listening to someone you like speak on a topic you are highly positive towards, while using language that evokes positive images, will also test your listening skills. Neutrality towards all three introduces another test. Listening becomes even more challenging when you experience emotional dissonance; that is, you are highly positive towards one element, neutral towards another, and highly negative towards another. But awareness and insight of your emotional triggers puts you in position to listen with control.

As you record your personal list of emotional "hot spots," you need to remember: (1) your success will be directly related to your effort; (2) your emotional triggers are yours, and there are no right or wrong answers; and (3) your identification effort will serve you well, but it should be a private task; and (4) anyone who knows your emotional weaknesses better than you is in a position to control you.

Adolph Hitler affected millions and observed, "I know that one is able to win people far more by the spoken word, and that every great movement on this globe owes its rise to the great speakers and not to the great writers." Of course, Hitler and his henchmen were experts at controlling and playing on the emotions of others. Study the history of leadership throughout the ages and you will discover how leaders of all types have focused on swaying the beliefs, attitudes, and actions of those they lead through emotional appeals. It occurs in the arenas of business, education, religion, the military, the media, advertising, finance, sports, the family, and more. In fact, there is no nonemotional ground. Yet, even if you could, we are not suggesting you should abandon your emotions, for they help make your leadership whole.

ATHLETIC COMPETITION ADVANCES EMOTIONAL CONTROL

Listening Leader **Ned Heath** is a successful real estate entrepreneur and consultant who owned a large real estate company in Orlando, Florida for 20 years. As the largest locally owned and operated company, with seven offices, a Mortgage and Title Company, and over 300 agents, his company had yearly sales of more than $750 million. Ned believes the ability to control emotions is essential in the business world, yet is one of the hardest things to do. However, he also believes playing basketball, baseball, and football helped him tremendously in building emotional control.

Especially in basketball, with crowds so close to the court and the band and people cheering, you have to be able to shut your emotions out of your mind. Emotional control is critical when you go to the free-throw line in the final moments of a game. Everybody is cheering, and it's an important shot. You must be able to block the crowd noise out and focus on the goal and the rhythm of the shot. When people are throwing a lot of emotional stuff at you, you have to be able to control your reactions.

Life is just like shooting a crucial free-throw in a basketball game. You can't react to emotional messages that you receive. You hear the message, you analyze it, and then you respond while controlling your emotions. It's hard to do. In the real estate business, there is an expression "buyers are liars," as many people do not know what they want. They tell you one thing and they do just the opposite. To give you an example, I had a customer who said he didn't care where he lived, but he just didn't want to live in Bay Hill. He was very emotional and said, "Show me houses anywhere, but I do not want to go to Bay Hill. We had a bad experience there, and I just don't want to go back." Four days later, they bought a home in Bay Hill. Through deep listening and moving past the emotion, I learned he had owned an older home in Bay Hill that caused him a lot of problems. When he found out from me that Bay Hill had a new section with new homes, he wanted to look at them. It was exactly what he wanted, and it was close to his work. So he bought in Bay Hill. If I had not listened beyond the emotion, I would not have made a sale.

EMOTIONS CAN GRAB YOUR SOUL

Of course, when they are controlled, emotions enhance the authenticity of leaders. A listening leader shared a story about a young executive friend who was driving down a neighborhood street in his new Mercedes. As he was watching for kids running out from between parked cars, he heard something hit the side of his car. He slammed on his brakes, jumped out of the car, and discovered someone had thrown a brick. With his emotions racing he grabbed the only kid in sight, and shouted, "What are you doing?! That's a new car, and that brick is going to cost you a lot of money. What's the matter with you?"

With tears dripping down his chin, the youngster pleaded, "Please, mister, please, I'm sorry—I didn't know what else to do! I threw the brick because no one else would stop." Pointing around the parked car, he said, "It's my brother. He rolled off the curb and fell out of his wheelchair, and I can't lift him up." Sobbing, the boy asked the executive, "Would you please help me get him back into his wheelchair? He's hurt, and he's too heavy for me."

With a shift of emotions that moved him beyond words, the young executive swallowed the rapidly swelling lump in his throat. He lifted the boy's brother back into the wheelchair, took out his handkerchief and wiped the brother's scrapes and cuts, checking to see that everything was going to be okay. "God bless you and thank you, sir," the grateful child said.

Nothing more was said, and the executive watched the little boy push the wheelchair and his brother down the sidewalk. As he walked back to his new Mercedes, he thought about the significant shift in his emotions. Our source said his friend never repaired the side door of his new car. He simply preserved the dent to remind himself to not go through life so fast that someone has to throw a brick to get his attention. Emotions can destroy or grab your soul. Control your emotions and life will whisper in your soul and speak to your heart.

SECOND THINGS SECOND

Over time, you will gain some control by simply advancing your awareness of additional specific positive, neutral, and negative emotions that affect your listening behavior. Although self-assessment and awareness is the first step, your ultimate success in controlling your emotions depends on an additional second step. To enhance your control of your emotions, we recommend a series of specific activities:

Second things second involve *practice, practice, practice*! As with every skill, practicing emotional control will make a difference. When you clearly understand your emotional triggers, you are in a position to participate in listening opportunities, wherein you can exercise your emotional control. Purposely seek out individuals, topics, and language that adversely impact your emotions and listening. Focus on assuming the Minimum 51% Responsibility for the success of every communication. Zero in on fully sensing and interpreting the speaker's message. Identify the respective purposes. Take meaningful notes, plan to report, and follow through. Withhold your emotional judgment and respond rationally. Thousands of listening leaders have followed this strategy and are measurably better listeners. As you refine these techniques, you will reduce the negative impact of your emotional triggers and focus on the speaker's message, purpose, and content.

ROLE MODELS HELP

Jean Otte, founder and CEO of the highly successful Women Unlimited, Inc. speaks fondly of her mentor, Jack Yurish, a former owner and Executive Vice President of National Car Rental. Role models are important, and Jean noted how Jack Yurish controlled his emotions.

Jack is a processor. He takes things in and he processes them without necessarily needing to give an answer or a recommendation. Jack is able to overcome the biases that many of us have because he listens for the reasons that most people really want somebody to

> *"Jack is able to overcome the biases that many of us have because he listens for the reasons that most people really want somebody to listen. He listens for what the person actually needs."*
>
> —*Jean Otte*

listen. He listens for what the person actually needs. I think Jack would be the first one to say, "A lot of people who ask for advice are not asking for 'how to fix' answers. Often, they are just asking for validation or a perspective that might be different than their own." I learned from his positive approach and belief that most people want to be listened to without being told "how to."

YET THE CHALLENGE PERSISTS

Although role models help, the challenge of controlling emotions is persistent in all quarters. Cattle rancher and business consultant **Ira Barrow** believes that controlling emotions is a larger challenge in his personal life than in his professional life.

Professionally, I'm able to keep a little light switch on that helps me. Personally, it gets more challenging. Probably the best way I control my emotions is I require myself to listen to 100 percent of all of the issues or questions and that gives me the chance to gather my own emotions. I must aggressively want to hear what others are saying, and that is a minute-by-minute challenge. I call it "listening aggressively." I then try to ensure that I present my responses on an even keel. When the issues require some type of constructive criticism, I work hard at responding in a fashion that gives the other person some alternative methods for accomplishing the task the next time the issue might arise. The challenge is not being critical of the way they handled it this time. We discuss options on how to do it the next time. It's about the learning.

Generally, I am not short on emotion. I think everyone has a problem with being directly criticized. When others are attacking my organization, or the group of which I am a part, I tend to get very defensive. For me, that is very, very difficult to handle. Thus, I really appreciate those leaders who can listen to every word that comes out of someone's mouth without wanting to open their own mouth and interrupt them. That is a daily chore for me.

LISTEN TO THE MUSIC OF EMOTIONS

Dr. Ronald A. Heifetz is one of the world's leading authorities on leadership. Known for his significant work during the last two decades on the practice and teaching of leadership, he is a Lecturer in Public Policy and co-founder of the Center for Public Leadership at Harvard University's John F. Kennedy School of Government. In an insightful article in *Fast Company* magazine, Dr. Heifetz captured the importance of listening to the music of emotions.

People who love their boss often say, "She's a great listener." However, most leaders die with their mouths open. Leaders must know how to listen, and the art of listening is more subtle than most people think it is. But first, and just as important, leaders must want to listen. Good listening is fueled by curiosity and empathy: "What's really happening here? Can I put myself in someone else's shoes?" It's hard to be a great listener if you're not interested in other people. Great listeners know how to listen musically as well as analytically. President Jimmy Carter relied on "rational discourse" to weigh the pros and cons of various initiatives. He would have people prepare papers and then would sift their views in private. Doing it that way enabled him to listen to their arguments analytically but not musically. What do I mean by that? Jimmy Carter did not enjoy being in meetings with people who were posturing, arguing, and haggling. But there's an enormous amount of information in the haggling, and that information tells us quite a lot about the values, the history, and the personal stakes that people bring to an argument. It's difficult for someone who has lost the last six arguments to say in a policy paper, "I've lost the last six arguments. If I don't win the next one, what am I going to tell my people?" But in conversation, the tone of voice and the intensity of the argument give clues to that subtext. Listening musically enables leaders to get underneath the surface to ask, "What's the real argument that we're having?" And that's a critical question to answer because, in the absence of an answer to that question, you get superficial buy-in. People go along in a pseudo-consensus or in a deferential way but without commitment.

EMOTIONAL PREJUDGMENT KILLS RATIONAL JUDGMENT

Richard Kessler is founder of The Kessler Enterprise, Inc., a dynamic real estate development, ownership, and management company that specializes in luxury boutique hotels. Richard understands the negative impact of emotionally prejudging people, positions, and perspectives. Based on insights

> *"One of my biggest challenges is being careful not to prejudge an idea because it's coming from a certain person."*
> —*Richard Kessler*

learned throughout his successful career, Richard discussed a major listening challenge.

One of my biggest challenges is being careful not to prejudge an idea because it's coming from a certain person. For example, we all have mental images of people we interact with. Some of these images are clear images. For example, our image of a person may be, "He talks twice too much." We have an image of another person "He listens but he doesn't hear." So, many times, we have these preconceived notions about people. We may have an idea that a very conservative person may not have a creative idea. When I have a strong preconceived notion about someone, I find I have to really focus on what that person is saying.

Dr. John DiBiaggio spent his career in higher education administration and served as President at several prestigious institutions including Michigan State, Tufts, and the University of Connecticut.

I have often said you show your intelligence not by what you say, but what you ask, and if you are a good listener, you will really focus on what the other person is trying to tell you. No matter what you do, if you have a lot of experience at anything, over a period of time you will have observed many things that reoccur. The challenge I often faced was combating the feeling that I had dealt with the situation before and I knew what to do. To the other person who was engaged in it, it was entirely new because they had not been through that process before. If you jumped

> *"I had to teach myself to listen to what people were saying in each situation and not immediately come to a conclusion."*
> —Dr. John DiBiaggio

to the conclusion that you had already dealt with it and knew exactly what to do, you missed the golden opportunity to find a unique approach to the issue that was responsive to a different time and situation. For instance, if you had a student protest and said to yourself, "Well, I've seen protests before and I know what to do," but the people who were participating were new to it, they might have some other ideas as to what you should do in that situation. So quite frankly, I had to teach myself to listen to what the people were saying in each situation, and not immediately come to a conclusion.

Another challenge I faced was with the faculty. Despite public opinion that the faculty are always talking about great national social issues and appearing to be very progressive and flexible, when you start talking about their environment, they become very traditional and very conservative. It's very hard to get them to change because many of them don't want to alter anything. You don't change attitudes by approaching them from your point of view. You achieve change by approaching others from *their* point of view and helping them realize they are going to benefit from the change. And you bring them to that point by listening to them, and just injecting here and there some ideas that eventually become their own. But that's not an easy process in the university setting.

EMOTIONAL THOUGHTS BEGET
EMOTIONAL BEHAVIOR

I can make you rise or fall.

I can work for you or against you.

I can make you a success or a failure.

I control the way that you feel and the way that you act.

I can make you laugh, work, love.

I can make your heart sing with joy, excitement or elation, or

I can make you wretched, dejected, morbid.

I can make you sick, listless.

I can be as a shackle—heavy, attached, burdensome; or

I can be as the prism's hue, dancing, bright, fleeting, lost forever

unless captured by pen or purpose.

I can be nurtured and grown and be great and beautiful,

Seen by the eyes of others through the action in you.

I can never be removed—only replaced...

I AM A THOUGHT—WHY NOT KNOW ME BETTER?

—Anonymous

As we have repeatedly observed, the productive or unproductive listening behavior of all leaders begins with emotional and rational thoughts. Thoughts you believe as truth transform into your beliefs. Your beliefs generate entrenched attitudes, which prompt your feelings. Your feelings ultimately lead to observable

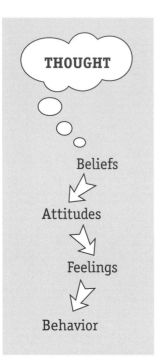

THOUGHT

Beliefs

Attitudes

Feelings

Behavior

and measurable listening and leading behaviors. Listening leaders choose to advance their productive listening behavior by focusing on, and deeply understanding their thoughts, beliefs, attitudes, feelings, and ultimate behavior. As **Mohandas Gandhi** articulated years ago, "One needs to be slow to form convictions, but once formed, they must be defended against the heaviest odds."

LISTENING PAST THE STUDS

Dr. Craig McAllaster, Dean and Professor of Management at the Roy E. Crummer Graduate School of Business at Rollins College, is recognized for his expertise in the areas of leadership, consulting skills, strategy, and organizational behavior. Dr. McAllaster's experience spans industry and academia. Having spent over 10 years in the consumer services and electronics industry in management, organizational, and executive development positions, Craig understands the importance of controlling one's emotions, thoughts, beliefs, attitudes, feelings, and behaviors in dealing with younger generations.

Current generations must listen carefully to the next generation to truly understand where they're coming from, what their hot buttons are, what's driving them, and what's turning them off. That is why controlling emotions in listening is important. It's not easy to listen to someone in a meeting who has a piece of metal sticking through their lip. The tendency is to look at this and say to yourself, "What kind of person would put that kind of stuff through their body" as opposed to, "you know what, this person may look a bit weird but, they're really pretty cool, they're pretty smart, and they're pretty focused." When I was a kid, my hair was very long. Looking back, I am sure when I went into meetings people said, "He's a hippie." However, it is always important to listen effectively to the next generation, because they will grow into the leaders of the future.

> *"Current generations must listen carefully to the next generation to truly understand where they're coming from, what their hot buttons are, what's driving them, what's turning them off. That is why controlling emotions in listening is important."*
> —Dr. Craig McAllaster

Dr. McAllaster also noted the value in understanding the underlying emotions and limitations of those we listen to, no matter how quietly they may be stated.

I worked for an executive who loved to debate. But sometimes the debate was more for his enjoyment of discussion and argument than it was for achieving results. In many meetings, this person would continually object and belabor points, as if it were a college debate. He would constantly challenge the President of the company beyond the point of bringing valid comments to the argument. Unfortunately, he wouldn't hear the President's emotions when the President would say, "You know, sometimes you can debate me on that, Sam, but other times we have to move on, and I would appreciate your recognizing those moments." However, because he loved to debate and play the devil's advocate instead of listening, he would continue to argue beyond the point. In the end, it cost him his job.

SIMPLE SUGGESTIONS

Obviously, it is difficult to conquer deep-seated emotional responses to people, topics, and language. It takes time and substantial effort. However, the following simple suggestions will help you.

First, prior to every listening situation, identify the people, topics, and words that affect you emotionally. This practice will make you aware of who and what stimulates your reactions. Thus you are one step toward greater control.

Second, analyze why these people, topics and words affect you the way they do. Think about your past experiences, or encounters that have influenced your emotional evaluation and reaction.

Third, reduce the emotional impact of people, topics, and words by developing a "defusing defense mechanism." One that is often recommended to help avoid emotional reactions is "rationalization." Rationalization involves attempting to convince yourself that the person, topic, or word is not as bad or good as you think. No matter what defense mechanism you use, try to eliminate your emotionally conditioned response to people, topics, or words.

Three additional simple suggestions that will help you compensate for an initial bias (positive, neutral, or negative) are: (1) *Defer judgment*. As we have mentioned, you need to listen to an entire message before responding. (2) *Empathize*. Try to take the speaker's point of view while you listen. Search for reasons for the speaker's views and arguments, even if they are different from your own. (3) *Place your personal feelings in perspective*. Remember that your past experiences, including your cultural and educational background, have molded you into a unique person. If you critically evaluate your own views, then you will be better able to relate to the ideas of others.

Listening to criticism is also important for every leader. **Pastor Mike Stone**, the Senior Pastor of the Mt. Pisgah Lutheran Church in Hickory, North Carolina explained why it is important to control your emotions as you listen to criticism with an open and non-defensive posture.

> *"Always consider the source of the criticism. A defensive posture is not good because usually there is enough truth in any kind of criticism to at least be worthy of examining it."*
> —*Pastor Mike Stone*

Always consider the source of the criticism. A defensive posture is not good because usually there is enough truth in any kind of criticism to at least be worthy of examining it. I think that's helpful. When I work on a letter that is going out to a large group of people, it is helpful to get feedback from at least two other people before I send it out. My listening to their feedback is affirming to them and helpful to me because six eyes are better than two. But soliciting feedback can be scary to the person I'm asking, because I could say, "I'm too busy to even care what people think about this," "I have to get this letter out," or "I've got to get this done."

I've had feedback from people, to whom I've listened carefully to, who have wanted to make important decisions for me. Some have insisted on dramatic personnel decisions within a staff setting. It is interesting that, in some cases, by not responding to their desires I cause them to question my leadership. They are basically saying, "You either do it my way or I don't think you are a good leader." Sometimes, a leader has to listen and decide against what is being suggested. It can be difficult when you ask for feedback and decide to go beyond what has been suggested. That can be a tough situation and often triggers emotions.

CONTROLLING EMOTIONS ON THE HOMEFRONT

At every turn, and in every arena, controlling your emotional response is one of the most important and difficult listening skills to develop. As previously noted, anything associated with people, topics, or language may trigger or encourage emotional reactions while listening. In addition, anyone who is in a position to know more about what triggers your emotions than you do is in a position to control you. Yet, it is possible to deal with emotions if they are identified prior to listening; if there is an attempt to analyze what people, topics, and language affect emotions and; if attempts are made to reduce the impact of aroused emotions. Such control must be practiced and incorporated into everyday listening situations to be effective. This includes listening in the home.

> *"A leader in the home must be nonjudgmental, optimistic but reality-oriented. Leadership in the home is not for the timid. It requires confronting inappropriate and unacceptable behavior."*
> —Anne Horne

Anne Horne is an impressive listening leader who has been married for over 50 years and has worked diligently to refine her listening in both the home and the classroom, where she served as a teacher for over two decades. Anne's wisdom regarding identifying and controlling emotions is worth emulating. In identifying and controlling emotions, Anne believes:

A leader in the home must be nonjudgmental, optimistic, but reality-oriented. Leadership in the home is not for the timid. It requires confronting inappropriate and unacceptable behavior. Loving, confronting, and allowing family members to suffer the natural consequences of their actions is necessary. It all begins when you start training your children. You must give them choices at a very early age so they learn their choices have consequences. This is at a time when consequences for a wrong choice are not so severe. You build on this until they leave the nest. Then, in adulthood they will have the confidence to be responsible for making choices whose consequences are of much greater magnitude. Making choices when they are young prepares them for making choices when they are older. And you don't need to say, "I told you so." Love them enough to let them get up, dust themselves off, and begin anew. This is something I've tried to improve on through the years.

THE POINT

Millard Fuller and other listening leaders have clearly outlined the importance of: (1) understanding and controlling your own emotions; (2) understanding the emotional behaviors of others; and (3) being responsive. In addition, numerous techniques to control your emotions while listening and leading have been suggested. However, to be useful, you must incorporate and practice them daily through disciplined thinking and acting. First, get to know what triggers your emotions, and then develop control through practice. Practice **Golden Rule 9: "Identify & Control Emotions,"** and you will Listen, Lead and Succeed.

Golden Rule 9

"Listening Leaders Identify & Control Emotions"

10 ACTION STEPS

1. Make the commitment to listen responsively rather than reactively.

2. Prepare to listen to emotional messages by prethinking about the topic and situations.

3. Discipline yourself to consciously control your emotions.

4. Exercise your discipline by withholding your judgment and response until you have fully received and understood the speaker's position.

5. Make a list of 10 persons toward whom you feel extremely positive or extremely negative and identify how your listening is affected.

6. Make a list of 10 positive or negative trigger words and identify how they affect your listening.

7. Develop emotional control through regularly exercising the "Plan to Report" activity.

8. Record your listening behavior results when you control your emotions.

9. Strive to know more about what triggers your emotions than others know.

10. Build your "Listening Organization" by systematically teaching those you lead the power of identifying and controlling their emotions.

LISTENING LEADERS™ GOLDEN RULES PYRAMID

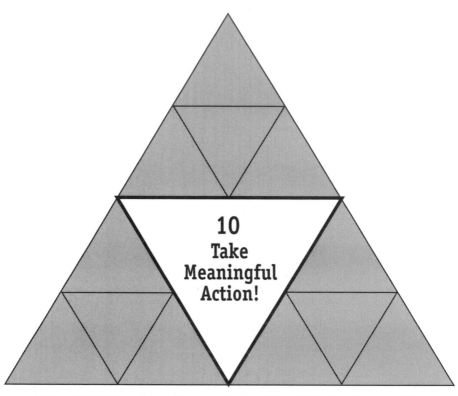

LISTENING LEADERS™ GOLDEN RULES PYRAMID

Golden Rule **10**

"Listening Leaders Take Meaningful Action"

"Listening must precede and include action. There is a phase of the listening process that definitely needs to precede a leader's action. We must focus on what we heard before deciding how we are going to act and execute. In addition, as we take meaningful action, it is very important that we keep our antennae up while we listen and adjust our actions on the basis of what we continue to hear."

—*Bob Darbelnet*

Bob Darbelnet, President and CEO of the American Automobile Association (AAA) understands that listening leaders must assume the responsibility for taking meaningful action based on complete and careful listening. Unless listeners take meaningful action, "listening is just interesting."

By now, you have journeyed through three stages and nine steps of our practical Listening Leaders Pyramid. Along the way, you have identified the importance of focusing on the three stages of listening leaders' Preparation, Principles, and Practices. First, you have discovered how effective listening leaders *Prepare* by: 1) Building Solid Foundations, 2) Exploring and Executing A-S-K, and 3) Developing Impactful Habits. Second, you have learned the value of embracing the important *Principles* of: 1) Taking Primary Responsibility, 2) Finding and Aligning Purposes, and 3) Applying SIER. Third, you have gained new insight into the productive *Practices* of: 1) Identifying and Controlling Distractions, 2) Identifying and Using Structures and 3) Identifying and Controlling Emotions.

At each stage and segment, effective listening leaders "Take Meaningful Action." Meaningful action is the ongoing and ultimate requirement of every productive listening leader, for the simple reason that, without meaningful action, leaders fail. Throughout this book, we have outlined "100 Action Steps" for your personal application. In addition, we have recommended that, as you build your Listening Organization, you invite everyone you lead to read, study, and complete the "100 Action Steps." As you and they do, everyone will listen and lead better. In addition, to encourage you to enhance your listening skills and to take meaningful action, Chapter 10 includes a number of short, action-oriented stories and related lessons from a representative sample of our **Listening Leader Golden Circle** members. Their stories will reinforce the ultimate importance and power of *action*, as captured by the following 7th Century Tibetan manuscript entitled *UNTO THEE I GRANT*.

> My dreams are worthless, my plans are dust, my goals are impossible. All are of no value unless they are followed by action. I will act now. Never has there been a map, however carefully executed to detail and scale, which carried over even one inch of ground. Action, alone, is the tinder that ignites the map...my dreams, my plans, my goals, into a living force. Action is the food and drink which will nourish my success. I will act now. My procrastination, which has held me back, was born of fear, and now I recognize this secret mined from the depths of all courageous hearts. Now I know that to conquer Life I must always act without hesitation and the flutters in my heart will vanish. Now I know that action reduces the lion of terror to an act of equanimity. I will act now.

SMALL ACTIONS ADD UP

Bob Darbelnet has led the American Automobile Association (AAA) since 1995. AAA is the largest automobile club in the world with nearly 75 clubs, 46.5 million members, and more than 37,000 employees in the association and affiliate clubs. As the leader of AAA, Bob captured the importance of listening and taking action.

We have discovered it is the small listening actions that add up to better leadership. For example, four small listening action strategies have served our organization well.

First, in an attempt to promote open communication and listening, and to overcome any intimidation caused by titles, positions, roles, and responsibilities, we practice an authentic open-door policy. In fact, my office has no door by the design of my predecessors, who intentionally designed the executive offices with no doors. Even when I worked in facilities where there were doors, I've always made sure that they were open.

A second small action, initiated by the previous CEO and continued today, involves regular listening meetings with staff at all levels. As the organization has become overly large, we regularly hold "Employee Forums" where all the Associates are invited to participate. Participants are encouraged to ask anonymous questions by sending written questions in advance or asking questions from the floor. We work hard to create an environment of no, or very low, barriers to communication.

Third, I have found a small action-oriented listening fact that relates to a matter of time and attitude. Sometimes people ask relatively simple questions about highly strategic issues. I try to be careful never to belittle any question that is being asked, and I never respond in a manner that is disrespectful of the individual asking the question, even if others might be thinking "Boy, that was a strange question."

A fourth small listening action involves creating an atmosphere of informality. I have a rather difficult last name, Darbelnet (Dar-bull-nay) which isn't easy for some to pronounce. In our first Forum, about nine years ago, someone asked me, "How do you pronounce your name?" Without really thinking about it I just said, "Bob." Obviously they weren't asking me how to pronounce Bob. However, my response caused people to understand that while we take everyone's work seriously, we will not take ourselves too seriously. On the other hand, we take listening and responding very seriously.

As all thoughtful leaders know, it is the many small steps that make the long journey productive.

BOB'S LISTENING LEADER ACTIONS

▶ *Bob has no office door. He establishes an open and positive listening environment.*

▶ *Bob personally hosts regular Employee Forums. Questions are invited and all are answered.*

▶ *Bob takes action to foster an informal culture: "Call me Bob!"*

LISTEN AND ACT, OR DIE

John Murphy is an energetic, good-humored and irrepressible Irishman who still remembers his most valuable lessons of listening, leading, and acting, which were learned during his formative years in the U.S. Navy Submarine Service.

Throughout my years at New England Telephone and Nynex (now Verizon), the importance of listening and taking action was reinforced at every turn. I learned that listening without being responsive and taking action left everyone disconnected. However, my initial true insight into the importance and challenge of listening and acting occurred during my U.S. Navy service on diesel submarines. At every moment and at every turn, lives depended on the successful practice of everyone's action-oriented listening.

My first, best, and everlasting lesson occurred during my initial Submarine training and qualification at New London, Connecticut. To qualify for submarine school, every candidate had to make a successful 100-foot free ascent from an escape tank. I'll never forget the leader's instructions: "Continue exhaling throughout the entire ascent, or your lungs will expand and explode, and you will die." This was a moment that required listening and acting in a very specific way because your life depended on it. The tragic fact was that periodically young men would fail either to listen or to take appropriate action, and they *would* die.

As a follower, that single experience taught me to listen and act upon the directions of leaders who had my best interests at heart and who knew more than I did. Over the years, it reinforced my efforts as a leader to help those I led understand the importance of both listening and acting. Whether your life, career, success, or promotion is at stake, action closes the listening and leading loop.

JOHN'S LISTENING LEADER ACTIONS

▶ *John's best listening and action lesson was learned at a young age.*

▶ *John listened and acted from a survival perspective.*

▶ *John helped others understand and act upon the importance of action-oriented listening.*

SPEAK UP—ORGANIZED LISTENING AT AMWAY

Rich DeVos, the co-founder of Amway Corporation (now Alticor) and owner and Chairman of the NBA's Orlando Magic, is also a devoted husband, father, and grandfather. He and his wife, Helen, are committed to making a difference in people's lives through their Christian faith and their message of hope. Listening lies at the heart of Rich's life.

I can't learn anything if I'm not listening, and I can't talk to people if I don't know what I'm talking about. A perfect example occurred years ago as we created the Amway Corporation. I began to hold employee meetings where we spoke to everybody and told them what was going on. At the same time, I set up a process called "Speak Up," where for three hours or more, I would just listen to what the employees had to tell me about anything they wanted to talk about. We called this organized listening.

Any employee could talk about any subject he or she wanted to. Over the years, many would come with notes from other employees that they would read. We listened and made notes on everything they were concerned about. The process was interactive, and we answered questions or provided additional information as required. Application of the skilled, learned, ordered listening process called "Speak Up" still goes on to this day, 40 years later.

In the early stages, the employees didn't know what the impact would be from speaking up. They wondered if they would be disciplined if they said something critical of their direct supervisor. It took time before they became comfortable with our speaking-and-listening process and knew that we wouldn't hold anything against people.

Initially, the managers were even more nervous about "Speak Up," since the employees were free to speak without reservation. However, our managers quickly discovered that I did not treat it as a way of intruding into their management styles. I was just trying to listen and learn about the whole company. Eventually, the managers came with notes and ideas that they wanted to talk about. As I wanted to hear from *all* the people, we rotated the employees who came to each "Speak Up" function. As a result, we heard from a lot of people who normally wouldn't say anything. When it was their turn, they were expected to say something. Some just said nice things, while others would come and talk about company issues that they felt strongly about.

We consider the opportunity to listen to our employees to be a vital part of our employee relations. Although unions have attempted to organize our employees, they have never succeeded, largely because of our listening at "Speak Up" meetings. Our commitment and ability to listen and communicate with our employees continues to this day.

Early in our business experience, an owner from a company with 500 employees came to visit us. I asked him what was the most important challenge he had in his company, and he said "communication." It shocked me, because I expected him to talk about sales, or quality, or some other business indicator. It was all about communication. "The ability," he said, "to communicate with my employees, shareholders, customers, and community is the biggest challenge I have to face." I never forgot that, and decided I would make communication skills a key part of my stock in trade."

RICH'S LISTENING LEADER ACTIONS

▶ *Rich has a positive listening attitude and understands that, among many things, listening enhances learning and leading.*

▶ *Rich established "Speak Up" so that he and the other executives could listen to all the employees and learn about the whole company.*

▶ *Rich began the momentum of the "Speak Up" process and it continues today—40 years later.*

QUIET LISTENING ALLOWS MEANINGFUL ACTION

When **Bill Jensen** of Vail Resorts, Inc. was a young man of 28, he sold Kassbohrer Pisten-Bully Snowcats used for grooming ski slopes. His sales process involved the action of listening carefully to the customer's needs, on-the-slopes demonstrating, listening and responding to any questions and concerns, and closing. Bill still remembers a significant listening experience that involved preliminary satisfaction, momentary frustration, and successful action.

After I had spent three days demonstrating our Snowcat, the skiers were positively raving, and the ski area General Manager told me, "Don't take that Snowcat away, we want to buy it. We have a Board meeting in three days, and I want you to talk to our Chairman of the Board." So I took the Chairman's telephone call, and he said, 'Bill, we are going to vote on Tuesday to approve the purchase of your Snowcat. So just leave the machine, and we will send you a check."

Now, I act on a man's word, so I said "Okay, fine," left the machine, and happily drove 300 miles home. On Wednesday morning, the General Manager called and said, "Well the Board met last night and decided that since the ski season was almost over they chose to not buy your Snowcat. We are going to wait and talk about this issue again next fall, so I guess you need to come and pick up your machine."

As I listened, my initial satisfaction quickly turned to frustration, and I responded, "I just drove 300 miles home, you've had the groomer for two more days, and now I have to drive another 600 miles round-trip to pick up my machine, which your Chairman said was sold?" The General Manager understood my frustration and responded, "If you want to stop on the way and see the Chairman, I know he will talk to you."

As I drove, I was upset and angry, and I pondered whether I should stop or not. I had never met the Chairman, but decided the best action was to quietly listen to him face to face. Remember, I was only 28, and he was older, well-positioned, and extremely wealthy. When I arrived, he made me wait 20 minutes before he called me into his very large and beautifully appointed office.

He asked me to sit down and said, "Let me help you in life. You're young and starting your career. Like you,

I started out young in the business world, and now we sell products all over the world." He continued, "When you get an order, always get a deposit. That's the best advice I can give you." As he talked, I sat and listened and never said a word. To fill the silence, he re-emphasized, "I hope you have learned a valuable lesson from this experience."

Having listened carefully, it was now time for action, so I looked him in the eye, and respectfully said, "Sir, you're right, I did learn a valuable lesson. I learned that your word is worth nothing." With that, I stood up and walked out of his palatial office. When I arrived at the distant ski area to pick-up the Snowcat, the General Manager came running out with a check in his hand. He said, "I don't know what you said to the Chairman, but he called and told me to write you a check. We are keeping the Snowcat." The interesting fact to me wasn't what I had said, but rather that my listening allowed me to achieve meaningful action. As my word is everything, this experience served as a defining moment for me. I believe that if you make a commitment, you can't go back on it, even if it puts you in an awkward situation. In short, listen and act as if your word is your bond.

BILL'S LISTENING LEADER ACTIONS

▶ *Bill acted optimistically and accepted at face value another leader's word as his bond.*

▶ *Bill overcame his emotional frustration and went out of his way to actively listen and learn more.*

▶ *Bill was not afraid to listen and directly respond, based on honor.*

THE $500,000 TELEPHONE CALL

Milt Adams has spent over 30 years in the graphic arts industry, specializing in printing, publishing, advertising, marketing and promotions. He is a successful entrepreneur who has owned and operated a number of service-industry enterprises. Presently, Milt is the owner and Publisher of the Beaver's Pond Press publishing company. Reflecting on the importance of listening and acting, Milt spoke of a venture that grossed $500,000 because of listening and responding to a misdirected phone call.

Some time ago, I and an associate provided a collection agency service for dental offices. In the process, we discovered that dental hygienists were an important key to developing new business for the dental practice. As a result, the practice suffered whenever a hygienist was sick or wanted to take vacation. So, as a supplemental service, we created a temporary employment company to provide substitute hygienists to dental offices.

We put an ad in the *Yellow Pages*, but it was listed mistakenly under the heading of "Dental Information Bureau." When the phone book was published, our phone started to ring. The first caller asked for help in finding a dentist, and was told: "I'm sorry that's not our business. Call the Dental Society." Over the next two days, we received several identical calls, and immediately my entrepreneurial listening instinct recognized there was an unmet need calling for action.

Within six months, and with the help of various people, we created the first Dental Referral Service, DRS. It was born in Minneapolis and still operates throughout the United States. Within six months, we referred 187 patients a week to 33 Dentists in Minneapolis alone.

With the average new patient worth approximately $500 to the dentist, the service cumulatively generated millions of dollars. Our records indicate that by listening to patients in need, we generated an initial income of more than $500,000. But more importantly, during the nine years I owned the company, we referred over 100,000 people to dentists. Extrapolated to date to major cities throughout the United States, millions of patients' dental needs have been served because we simply listened and responded to the original repetitive phone calls.

MILT'S LISTENING LEADER ACTIONS

▶ *Milt listened to the unexpected and met an unmet need.*

▶ *Milt creatively acted and converted the need to a business opportunity.*

▶ *Milt was flexible enough to respond quickly to seize the opportunity.*

LISTENING ACCOUNTABILITY AND OBJECTIVE MEASURES

W. Myron Hendry has spent the last 31 years with CNA Insurance and presently is the Senior Vice President responsible for CNA's Worldwide Processing Operations. With primary locations in Chicago, Orlando, Kansas City, London, and New York, Myron is committed to integrating listening leadership into the CNA culture.

In our recent employee surveys, our leadership group was disappointed that we weren't really identifying what the employees were saying to us. As a consequence, in the last 18 months, we have focused on what they are trying to get across and have concluded that our single most important challenge is in the arena of communication. As we dissected the issues of communication, we discovered two deficiencies. First, was our "telling" employees, and second was our failure to listen to them. While we agreed we were not doing either very effectively, we came to the unanimous conclusion that we were worst at listening. Everyone agreed that we spent an awful lot of time telling our employees but not a lot of time seeking feedback or actually engaging them in the communication process. As listeners, we decided we needed some help.

Our Regional Vice President of Human Resources recommended listening leadership training. Although everyone intuitively knew this would be helpful, no one wanted to commit the time. However, after our first session, it was perfectly clear that our leadership team was energized by the importance of improved listening for everyone. As leaders, we believe this effort will translate into increased performance throughout our organization. So we established a collective goal to improve our listening leadership and expect to see the evidence in two arenas.

First, we expect to see improvement in our employee surveys, and have set a goal of 25 percent improvement in employee satisfaction. Second, we have set specific productivity and cost-reduction goals. We are basing most of the expected improvements on the potential impact of more effective listening. It will require a change in our leadership culture, and we think that achieving a 25 percent gain is going to be a real challenge. Setting this goal has consequences: If we achieve it, we will be rewarded because it is one of our key objectives. If we do not achieve the goal, we will be penalized.

In sum, we have raised the stakes. We have created a focus, are taking action, have established accountability, and have created a way to objectively measure the results. This will be done, first, through our employee surveys and, second, through measurement of improved productivity and a reduction in our cost of doing business on a yearly run-rate basis of $5 million, by the fourth quarter of next year. The requirement is effectively engaging our people and process improvement, in order that we can improve communication. The solution is effective listening leadership, and we are betting that we can pull this off in twelve months.

MYRON'S LISTENING LEADER ACTIONS

▶ *Myron set the stage at the top for listening leadership to become an integral part of the organization.*

▶ *Specific listening leadership metrics were set as goals.*

▶ *The senior leadership team holds itself accountable through rewards and consequences.*

ASK—AND YOU SHALL RECEIVE

Betty Palm is a proven leader in the direct-selling industry and is noted for her passionate management style. Betty is the Executive Vice President of Sales and Marketing for The Pampered Chef, a $740 million direct-selling company engaged in the sale of kitchen tools. The company distributes products through an independent sales force of over 70,000. Betty, who formerly served as the North American President of Tupperware, prides herself on her ability to ask the right questions.

One of the most important listening skills is the ability to ask questions. Especially important are the questions that get to the heart of what it is you want to know. And sometimes you don't stop at the first answer. For example, I was recently visiting a very successful organization, 1-800-FLOWERS. They'll do $600 million in sales this year. I was riding up in the elevator with the President of the company who was asking one of his employees some questions. We were going from the lobby to the seventh floor, and he probably asked this employee eight questions during that time.

The first question he asked was, "What's up?" It sounded like a very simple question. And the person just said, "Well, I'm working on such-and-such project." The president then asked, "What are you doing with the project?" The employee gave a one-sentence answer. The president responded with another question, "Well, what kind of progress are you making with the project?" He just asked a series of questions that sounded so simple, but I learned a lot on that quickie elevator ride by observing how much information he actually acquired. In fact, he uncovered a problem that led him to call a mid-level manager about where she was with her project. But if he had stopped at the first question or the second question, he would never have gotten to the important information. The key was his ability to keep probing deeper.

I have discovered that, if you only rely upon a small contingent of people to provide you with all the information that you need, you won't get all of the facts or the real stuff.

When I really want to understand what's going on with a company, I meet with the overall management team and the principals. I also go to the customer service area and put the headphones on and listen to what the customers are saying. I have made this a practice in every job. When you start to hear some trends that are slipping and it doesn't appear as though you're really getting some real answers, the easiest thing to do is just sit out in the customer service department with the actual headphones on and listen to what customers are saying. In an hour a day for three consecutive days, I am able to fill up my staff meeting notes rather quickly.

This practice is not about evaluating the customer service reps. I never interrupt their calls. My role is to really understand what the customers are saying. By doing this, I get a sense of the policies and how customers respond to them.

BETTY'S LISTENING LEADER ACTIONS

▶ *Betty discovered that asking the right questions is the key to uncovering vital information.*

▶ *Betty knows that the first question may only be the beginning. It is important to be ready to probe deeper.*

▶ *In addition to listening to managers and employees, Betty listens to customers so that she can get a feel for what their needs and concerns are.*

SENSING A REAL DEAL

Andy (AJ) Greenshields is a Venture Capitalist (VC) who has listened to and negotiated many fascinating business deals. One success in particular, Breathe Right®, resulted from open-minded listening leadership action.

Breathe Right is a very interesting story because when we invested in the company, it was a brainwave monitoring company. When people have lengthy operations, particularly open-heart surgery that requires several hours, they tend to have strokes. The equipment monitors the patient during surgery, and the surgeon and anesthesiologist are alerted when a stroke event is approaching, so they can respond appropriately. The equipment, however, used to be too difficult to use, was a bit expensive and wasn't being adopted, because cost controls were increasing at the time the product was launched. Although we were struggling with this product, the brainwave monitoring led to a piece of equipment that could be used in sleep labs with people who were experiencing sleep difficulty, primarily due to snoring or weight problems. The researchers developed a piece of equipment based on their brainwave monitoring technology to monitor individuals who experienced comfortable sleep. We owned 95 percent of that market, but unfortunately the worldwide market was only $20 million a year. Although we were not growing, we had a reputation in the sleep field. Fortunately for everyone, a researcher with an allergy problem had developed and patented a very rudimentary device and was referred to us.

He came to a board meeting to introduce Breathe Right, and my first thought was "Holy cow, we are going off into consumer marketing. We're getting away from the medical base, and how am I going to tell my two partners and our limited partners that we have wandered this far astray?" Fortunately, the entrepreneurs were bright enough to bring samples for each one of our board members to try. I have a severely broken nose that never got fixed, and as I put one on I could immediately feel my breathing improve. As I listened, I said, "Why not—let's go with it!" When my VC colleagues saw this product, my medical partner, Norm, threw up his arms and walked out of the room and told me I was an idiot.

Fortunately for us, listening often carries the day, and serendipity in the name of Herschel Walker, the NFL football star, entered the picture. Herschel, who does not believe in drugs, was suffering from a very bad cold. He was complaining to his trainer that he had a stuffed-up nose and didn't know whether he could play, because he couldn't breathe. The trainer said, "Some company sent a bunch of samples of this new product, Breathe Right. Why don't you try one of these things and see how it works." Well Herschel rushed for more than 150 yards that day and scored three touchdowns. He got his picture—with the nasal strip on his nose—on the *Philadelphia Enquirer*, but more importantly, he called a friend in San Francisco named Jerry Rice and said, "Jerry, I know you have severe breathing problems because of your broken nose, you ought to try one of these things. It really opened up my nose." So Jerry Rice listened and decided to try it. Consequently, he became an endorser, the 49ers went to the Super Bowl, and we could not keep the product on the shelves. All because several people listened and took action.

AJ'S LISTENING LEADER ACTIONS

▶ *AJ had an open mind and listened to the opportunities of a new business venture.*

▶ *Even though he faced initial resistance from his business partners, AJ listened with a bias for action.*

▶ *AJ responded by listening to the opportunities of connecting football stars to his product and raising significant awareness.*

LISTENING TO MRS. SMITH CHANGED THE PHOENIX FIRE DEPARTMENT

When **Alan Brunacini** was four years old, he watched a big fire in a tire store and decided he wanted to become a firefighter. Based on his youthful impression, he joined the Phoenix Fire Department 17 years later and happily worked his way through the Department's ranks to become the Phoenix Fire Chief in 1978. From day one, Alan has been a student and a leader in the field of Fire Department Service Operations. He has authored numerous articles and is respected as an expert on fire service reality during periods of rapid change. As the Chief of the City of Phoenix Fire Department, Alan credits listening as being the pivotal point for a dramatic shift in his leadership thinking and acting.

I don't think that we fully understand leadership until we put a customer in the picture. When I think of leadership that I'm involved in, I ask, "What and who are we leading?" One day awhile back, we discovered Mrs. Smith, a typical person whom we deliver service to. When a customer like her is having a fire-related problem, our service is pretty simple and straightforward. They call us, and we attempt to respond and bring what is out of control under control, and turn that control back over to the customer. When I came to work this morning there were about 400 firefighters on duty. They will probably directly or indirectly serve 3,000 people today in some way. As Chief of the Phoenix Fire Department, I lead those 400 people to serve the 3,000 people. It is the only reason we are here. So if I do anything that does not contribute to customer service, somebody needs to question my action. So, the leader's responsibility is centered on enhancing, strengthening, and supporting the connection between the worker and the customer.

One great day, I listened to our customers and heard them say they really didn't have much familiarity with, understanding of, or interest in our fire trucks, our technology, our tactics, our strategy, or our deployment. What they remembered was the way that our firefighters treated them. They hope that we can do all the technical things, but they are not fire protection engineers, fire chiefs, or fire science instructors. In other words, they are customers. Mrs. Smith experienced a fire in her kitchen and only remembered, "Did we get there quick; did we put the kitchen fire out; did we take care of her stuff,; and were we nice to her?" It seems to me, that is what we ought to be leading. If I want the firefighters to be nice to Mrs. Smith, I need to be nice to the firefighters. If I want them to listen to Mrs. Smith, I need to listen to them. If I want them to respect Mrs. Smith, I need to respect them.

It isn't really all that complicated. There's all this material about leadership that I find most to be gobbledygook. Why don't they just make it simple? There are leaders, workers, and customers. Now I think there are probably a few people out there in the world who are leaders who think in dimensions beyond most of us. Many of them would be a complete pain in the rear to work for as a boss. Most of us are just plain folks who are delivering service in some way to people like Mrs. Smith. Pretty simple deal, isn't it? It becomes crystal clear when you put the customer at the end of the chain in the picture. One of the ways that the Phoenix Fire Department communicates with authenticity is based on the way we listen to each other. I simply manage the process and try to model the behavior.

ALAN'S LISTENING LEADER ACTIONS

▶ *Alan listened to what Mrs. Smith needed the most and responded with action.*

▶ *Alan teaches others through his actions and sends an authentic message.*

▶ *Alan sets the stage by managing the process and modeling the behavior.*

LISTENING LUNCHES BUILD TRUST

Jerry Tostrud has served in a variety of leadership roles since his days as a high school class President. As the former Chairman of the Board of William Mitchell College of Law, the American Judicature Society, the St. Paul Foundation, and the present Chairman of the Board of Regents of St. Olaf College, Jerry practices leadership like he plays golf: constantly and well. For 36 years, Jerry served in a variety of leadership roles in the vineyards of West Publishing Company, retiring as Executive Vice President in 1996. Jerry shared how important listening to employees is in building and reinforcing trust during very difficult times and good times.

I remember a leadership-testing time when I became Assistant to the President of West. We had about 75–80 people on our "management group payroll," which included primarily department supervisors and a few department managers. It was a difficult period, as we were facing tremendous technological changes, and there was a lot of concern throughout the company. Our chief competitor in the electronic arena had developed a competitive advantage with a computerized legal research system called Lexus. Lexus was three to five years ahead of us, and we were playing catch-up. At the same time, we were engaged in extensive technological changes in our manufacturing area. We hadn't had a layoff since 1932, and our employees were nervous as we were trying to train people to do different jobs. It was a period of extreme uncertainty.

I started having weekly "listening lunches" with these 80 leaders, in groups of eight. We held the lunches in a neutral location to let them know how the company was doing, what our challenges were, and then let them ask questions and provide ideas and feedback. The employees were terrific, and we listened to their suggestions. In fact, we discovered things that, quite frankly, we would not have heard if we hadn't had the lunches. Within two hours after the first lunch, half of the people in the company knew what these listening lunches were all about. They all wanted to know when they would have their opportunity to share their ideas.

This experience reinforced the great listening lesson of the importance and value of trust. We don't tell people important things if we don't trust them, and people won't tell you things if they don't trust you. When people think you're out to get information just to use for your own benefit, you won't get anything. But, if you get to know people over a period of time and you're honest and above board with them, they will share important information. Listening lunches build trust, and trust leads to action.

JERRY'S LISTENING LEADER ACTIONS

▶ *Jerry made it a point to trust his employees.*

▶ *During a time of great uncertainty in the company, Jerry held "listening" lunch meetings with employees to share the latest news and to listen to their questions and ideas.*

▶ *Jerry listened and learned things about the company of which he had been unaware. This resulted from the trust that grew through mutual listening.*

THE $10 BLOCKBUSTER GIFT CERTIFICATE

Human Resource Manager **Tony Lado** explained how listening leadership impacted the dynamics of his workplace and enhanced the productivity of both his department and his organization.

Because of some very simple practices, productivity has improved markedly. It is ironic because, in the name of efficiency, I have often spent a lot of mental energy planning my next important project or rehearsing for my next meeting. As I have grown, however, I can trace a significant idea that had a huge impact directly to effective listening. One of the best ideas for a benefit program called "Cool Company" came from my direct report. I was thinking about benefits we could provide that were very high-end, and affected only a few staff. To the contrary, my direct report proposed a simple benefit with a broad reach and much more frequent impact. That single idea has had more positive implications on our retention than any other program I had developed up to that point. One day my team member suggested we try a new strategy, "Why don't we send a $10

Blockbuster gift certificate to everyone on their birthday?" In addition, she proposed we should put a birthday card in an envelope along with the Blockbuster gift certificate and a ton of confetti. She would jam the envelope full, so when they opened it, the confetti would explode everywhere and over everyone. Prior to really valuing and using listening leadership as a strategy, I would have half-listened and dismissed her idea as being too simple, too goofy, and too low-impact. I would have thought that our employees would have been insulted to receive just a $10 gift certificate on their birthday. The opposite has been true. Since the idea has been implemented, we have received numerous effusive thank you notes from employees. In addition, the President has received more positive e-mails about the program than we did with $300 or $500 recognition programs. Everyone continues to talk about it, and the life of the program will not go away. "I love the card!" "I can't believe that much confetti can fit in an envelope!" "It's all in my couch!" "It's all in my car!" "You guys are crazy!" That silly little benefit turned out to be not so silly; in fact, my team member's idea was brilliant! Fortunately, I listened.

TONY'S LISTENING LEADER ACTIONS

▶ *Tony created the positive listening workplace so that team members were encouraged to share their ideas.*

▶ *Tony listened to his team member's idea about a simple incentive strategy and responded with encouragement for execution of the concept.*

▶ *Tony gives the full credit for this simple and impactful strategy to his team member.*

A ONE-ON-ONE LISTENING MODEL

Jim Henry has been the Pastor of First Baptist Church of Orlando since 1977. Pastor Henry has held many positions of leadership including serving as President of the 16 million-member Southern Baptist Convention from 1994–1996. He is a much-sought-after speaker and author. Pastor Henry told us about a listening leader who had made a tremendous difference in his life.

I have a model for listening to people one-on-one that was given to me by **Dr. W.A. Criswell**. He served as the pastor of First Baptist Church in Dallas for 50 years. He was a great leader and preacher and led a church of over 20,000 members. Years ago, when I was a young pastor, W.A. was at a typical reception following the sermon, and a lot of people were coming up to him to shake his hand. He would look each person right in the eye, take their hand, and listen to them. There was one man who would get in line every Sunday and consume Dr. Criswell's time. On one Sunday, one of Dr. Criswell's associates decided that he would help Dr. Criswell by diverting the man from getting in line. The next morning, Dr. Criswell called his associate into his office and said, "Bill, I saw what you did yesterday, and I know you meant well and I appreciate that. But, I'm the only person that guy talks to in a whole week. He is single and lonely and has no one to talk to. In a sense, I'm his connection with life. I know you meant well, but I need to listen to him so he knows somebody cares."

That really impressed me a long time ago and has helped me in turn. So on Sundays, when there may be 10 to 50 or more people lined up, I take time to look each and every one of them in the eye and listen. If they need prayer, I'll pray with them. I try to listen as long as I can to each person. It is amazing how many people will tell you they are hurt in their heart if they know you are listening.

PASTOR HENRY'S LISTENING LEADER ACTIONS

▶ *Pastor Henry learned from other listening leaders and adapted the learnings into his style.*

▶ *Pastor Henry takes the time to listen to each person.*

▶ *Pastor Henry mentally shuts out everybody around him except for the person to whom he is listening.*

TALK FIRST AND PAY $300,000

George Knutsen went to breakfast with a business friend and as they were talking about the connection between listening, leading, and selling, his friend said,

> I've got to tell you a wild story. You know our company is rapidly growing and as we wanted to keep everyone together, we needed to find a new location for our corporate office. The only problem, it would have cost us a $150,000 penalty fee to break our existing five-year lease. However, we had little choice, so I called the building owner and suggested we have lunch, as I had something I needed to talk about. He said, "Funny you should call because there is something I want to chat with you about."
>
> So at lunch we engaged in the typical small talk, and before I told him about our problem and decision to break the lease and pay the $150,000 penalty, I simply asked him what he wanted to talk about. He proceeded to tell me about a problem he had with another tenant who had a

great deal of growth potential and needed more space in the building. He then made a startling offer. He said that if we would ever consider vacating our space, he would waive our penalty fee and pay us $150,000 for the inconvenience.

So $300,000 was based on the simple fact of who talked and who listened first. Of course, we never did discuss my problem.

GEORGE'S LISTENING LEADER ACTIONS

▶ *This listening leader established his intent and purpose of communication.*

▶ *He was patient and allowed the other party to speak first.*

▶ *He listened through the three stages of the Listening Leader Pyramid and found profit.*

SELLING BY LISTENING AND QUESTIONING

Frank Gallagher worked for Walt Disney for 43 years and was centrally involved in the early computerization of Mickey's Kingdom. Living in the heart of "Tinsel Town" Frank reminded us of a classic story about listening, leading, and selling.

Johnny Carson had the "World's Greatest Salesman" as a guest on "The Tonight Show," and said to him, "I understand you are the world's greatest salesman, so sell me something." His guest said, "What do you want to buy?" There was an ashtray on the desk, and Johnny said, "Sell me this ashtray. His guest asked, "Why would you want to buy it?" Johnny responded, "Well, some of my guests smoke, and I don't want to have ashes all over my desk." The guest listened and led with another question, "Well, how big would it have to be, and what color would you like?" Carson looked at the blue ashtray on his desk, thought for a moment, and said, "Well this one is the right size, and I like the color." Not missing a beat, the guest inquired, "How much would pay for it?" Johnny gave him a price, and the guest asked, "So, if I could sell you this size, blue ashtray for that price would you buy it? Johnny Carson said, "Sure" and the World's Greatest Salesman said, "Mark it sold." All he did was listen.

FRANK'S LISTENING LEADER ACTIONS

▶ *Frank's story illustrates the invaluable merit of asking the right questions.*

▶ *Frank's story highlights the importance of listening to the specific answers to questions.*

▶ *Frank's story demonstrates the power of patience and how simple taking meaningful action can be.*

PRODUCTIVE ACTIONS OF A MAVERICK NORWEGIAN

Roger "Pudge" Ingebritson has been involved in sales and marketing for his entire adult life.

From his early leadership experience as a U. S. Naval Officer, to his lengthy career at 3M, Roger developed concrete action steps to make sure he understood what others truly meant.

I remember the day my boss asked me to work with our laboratory to develop an aerosol-applied neoprene contact adhesive for a perceived need in the cabinet and wood products market. I asked him how he had quantified the need and he said that, "Numerous field studies and market surveys indicated a broad need for this specific type of product and that, the laboratory had been working on one."

I questioned whether we had really heard what the customers needed or had we only heard what the customers said they needed based on their experience with existing adhesives? My boss emphatically stated that he knew "they wanted an aerosol-applied neoprene contact adhesive and not something else."

Although I listened to his perspective, I was not convinced we had fully heard the real needs of potential users and decided to do a quick field survey. Those I questioned all repeated what my boss had said, except when I asked them to be more exact and tell me what they needed the adhesive to do for them, the dialogue changed the picture. 100 percent said they wanted "a convenient, fast, easily applied adhesive to bond small laminates and wood together in a variety of applications." No one said "it had to be a neoprene contact adhesive."

When I shared this additional survey information and the conclusion that we should use any available adhesive technology, my boss flatly restated his original opinion, in spite of what the end-users said they wanted. Having heard different desires, and as a result of my Norwegian-bred maverick nature, I quietly worked with the laboratory to meet the needs as described by our customers.

Within a few months, we quickly developed a new adhesive technology and packaged it in a user-friendly aerosol container that became the division's number-two sales volume product within the first six months of market introduction. The key was listening to our customers and ultimate end-users. As has been said, "Listening pays in many ways!"

ROGER'S LISTENING LEADER ACTIONS

▶ *Roger confirmed what he had heard his boss say.*

▶ *Roger questioned the validity of what he was told.*

▶ *Roger took meaningful action by listening to actual end-users.*

LISTENING LEADERS MUST COACH OTHER LISTENING LEADERS

Betty Halvorson is a longtime leader in the challenging world of healthcare, and the former Chief Nurse Executive and Vice President of Patient Services of the $250 million Washington-based Evergreen Community Healthcare. She presently serves as President of Halvorson Associates, a cutting-edge healthcare management consulting firm. Betty is a strong believer that, "Overall, listening is basic to everything and listening leaders must coach and help other leaders grow and listen better." Betty reflected on the professional growth of a Manager who reported to her.

I had a Manager who had been with our organization for 15 years. He was extremely personable and well-liked, but his performance rated a four on a scale of one to ten, and his departments suffered low morale. Following a reorganization of our enterprise, I inherited him and observed that he came to meetings without a sense of an agenda and didn't appear to know the details of his operation. It was difficult, as our Division was being held to some aggressive achievement standards and the two areas that he was managing were mediocre at best. Although his areas had the potential to lift the entire organization, he listened and responded like someone who expected his leader to be transient. After all, he had seen many come and go.

Following our third meeting, in which he had not demonstrated the type of professional leadership and interaction that I expected, it occurred to me that he may not have experienced leaders who listened carefully or outlined their expectations clearly. My listening to him led me to believe that he and I would go nowhere if his behavior continued. Comfort would not help us achieve the results necessary to meet the expectations of the organization and his peers. It was time to listen further and take action, so we created scheduled time to candidly talk and listen. I queried, he talked, and I listened.

After we spent a few listening sessions together, I concluded that he had the potential to become a high achiever if that is what he wanted to do. I told him that it was time for him to decide what he wanted from his career; that his departments were stagnant and needed leadership; that he had an opportunity if he chose to embrace it; that he was at a crossroad and needed to make a choice. He listened and I listened to his listening.

A week later, he told me he had decided to be the leader we had talked about. More important, he took action. He came prepared to every subsequent meeting with an agenda, requests, and commitments. With thoughtful listening and planning, he chose to lead one business unit versus three. He was open to listen and actively learned how to write business plans, negotiate with business partners, and develop and motivate his staff. Within one year, his business unit achieved a 20 percent increase. Beyond our wildest expectations, within three years, his unit led the organization in both revenue and profit. As every effective leader knows, listening provides a source of greatness to tap into another's potential and allow individual and organizational growth. Ultimately, all it takes is action.

BETTY'S LISTENING LEADER ACTIONS

▶ *Betty observed the behaviors of those she led.*

▶ *Betty scheduled special listening sessions with those she led.*

▶ *Betty acted on her commitment to coach and develop the listening leaders she led.*

LISTEN TO THE "WHISPERS OF YOUR LIFE"

Frances Hesselbein is the Chairman of the Board of Governors of the Leader to Leader Institute and former CEO of the Girl Scouts of the USA. Mrs. Hesselbein was awarded the Presidential Medal of Freedom, the United States of America's highest civilian honor, in 1998. In 2002, Mrs. Hesselbein was the first recipient of the Dwight D. Eisenhower National Security Series Award for her service with the U.S. Army. She is the author of *Hesselbein on Leadership* and directly connects listening with leadership effectiveness.

If you're going to lead the organization and be a leader with your own people, you have to listen very carefully to them, just as you listen very carefully to all of your customers. We can never take for granted that we know what they value. It means when a person is speaking, he or she has your undivided attention. You're focused, you listen very carefully, you listen to the words that are spoken, and often you get unspoken messages. And so this means looking directly at a person, never looking at your watch, just being focused for that moment on that person. It's called respect and it's called appreciation, and it's also anticipation.

Listening is not a solo performance, it is a connection—and is most successful when circular. I listen, you respond; you listen, I respond, and somehow in that magic circle of communication, the messages are heard. The Great Stone Face is not exactly the most inviting face for good listeners; so we respond expressively. Believing that the quality and character of a leader determine the performance and results, the success of our leadership depends on how effectively we mobilize our people around our mission and values and vision, and how effectively all of our people listen to the customer.

There is another kind of listening—listening to our inner self. Listening to the whispers of our lives is critical. If we don't listen to the whispers of our lives, we miss many messages. There are three kinds of whispers. First are the whispers of the body, when our body tries to tell us that something is not quite right. The more intellectual we are, the more we tend to ignore the whispers of our bodies. Then one day an illness emerges, and we can go back to that day when there was this whisper and we blocked or ignored it. And then there are whispers of the heart, of all the people we love, who love us, of our relationships. Finally, there are the whispers of the spirit. However we define our faith, that inner spirit, the spirit within—those quiet whispers that can comfort, heal, inspire. The whispers of our lives are very important. When we ignore them, our lives are diminished. We never reach the levels we could in understanding ourselves or in strengthening our relationships with others.

FRANCES' LISTENING LEADER ACTIONS

▶ *Frances reinforces that effective leaders are thoughtful listeners.*

▶ *Frances underscores that listening is not a solo performance, it is a connection—and is most successful when circular.*

▶ *Frances emphasizes that listening to the whispers of our lives is critical, and if we don't listen to the whispers, we miss many messages.*

Each of the preceding **Golden Circle Listening Leaders** has shared a variety of specific actions that have advanced his or her overall listening and leading effectiveness and success. The opportunity for taking action is obvious. A wise sage once said "To know and not to do is not to know at all!"

A LISTENING LEADER REVOLUTION

As a listening leader, you have an opportunity to ignite a "Listening Leadership Revolution" within your leadership sphere, based on the simple premise that "Every listening leader is a teacher and will lead others to become listening leaders." Consider the potential positive impact as you develop, refine, and practice your own extraordinary listening leader skills, enhance your listening leader attitudes, and build your comprehensive listening leader knowledge. Then extend the potential impact as you model, teach and enable the 25 individuals in your "T-25 List," which you constructed in Chapter Four. As your T-25 members model, teach, and enable the people on their own T25 lists, and on and on, the results will be mind-boggling. By taking action, you have the power to change the listening leadership activities of many. In Stage one, you focus on yourself. Stage two, you help 25 others. Stage three calls for your T-25 members to focus on themselves and then, in Stage four help each of their T-25 members, and on and on and on. By extension through five stages nearly 400,000 individuals will listen and lead better. And to think, the Listening Leadership journey begins with you!

THE POINT

As **Bob Darbelnet** and other **Golden Circle of Listening Leaders** know, listening must precede and include taking meaningful action. As the renowned Harvard psychologist **William James** proclaimed, "Act as if what you do makes a difference. It does!" Engage **Golden Rule 10: "Listening Leaders Take Meaningful Action"** and you will Listen, Lead, and Succeed.

Golden Rule **10**

"Listening Leaders Take Meaningful Action"

10 ACTION STEPS

1. Study and execute the three Listening Leader stages of preparation, principles, and process before taking meaningful action.

2. Create a positive listening environment in your workplace, home, and in social settings.

3. Consistently cultivate a positive listening mindset.

4. Listen for unmet needs and convert them into golden opportunities.

5. Actively embrace listening as an integral part of your leadership style.

6. Establish specific listening leader goals, and identify ways to measure them.

7. Create specific listening leader goals, rewards, and consequences.

8. Teach the listening leader pyramid to others in your family, work, and social settings.

9. Ignite a listening revolution within your T-25 by modeling your listening leadership behavior.

10. Build your "Listening Organization" by teaching those you lead that the Listening Leader Pyramid requires taking meaningful action.

LISTENING LEADERS™ GOLDEN RULES PYRAMID

Epilogue

As you commit yourself and others to grow as listening leaders, we leave you with a simple and powerful old story. It involved a grandfather giving sage advice to his grandson, as the grandfather said, "Son, in life you have to remember there are two wolves—a 'good wolf' and a 'bad wolf'—inside you competing for your attention and one of them will win."

The grandson asked, "Which one will win?"

The grandfather said, "The one you feed."

In the days that lie ahead, you have a choice. As you walk through life you have two hungry elements—one mouth and two ears—that need to be fed. In many ways, they compete with each other. Which one wins will depend on which one you choose to feed!

Listen and Lead on and you will make today count.

Golden Circle of Listening Leaders

We are indebted to the following leaders whose Golden Nuggets of wisdom are embedded throughout the book. This esteemed group includes CEOs and front-line leaders, entrepreneurs and pastors, military officers, educators, pilots, celebrities, and homemakers, and come from all ages in time, career fields, and levels in organizations. Each has contributed to the advancement of Listening Leadership.

Golden Circle of Listening Leaders exist throughout the world, and we invite you to join their ranks.

To qualify, you simply have to learn and implement the **Ten Golden Rules to Listen, Lead & Succeed**. As you embrace the insights and experiences of our **Golden Circle of Listening Leaders,** we invite you to e-mail your "Listening Leader" success stories to: *rkb@listeningleaders.com* for inclusion in our monthly *Listening Leaders Newsletter*.

Leader	Chapter	Title	Organization
Mike Abrashoff	5	Founder & CEO	GrassRoots Leadership, Inc.
Milton Adams	10	Publisher	Beaver's Pond Press, Inc.
J. Allen	7	Founding Partner	Masters Alliance, LLP
Richard Anstruther	1, 3	Founder & CEO	High Gain, Inc.
Jay Ard	4	Vice President & General Manager	Coca Cola Enterprises—FL Division
Dr. Al Argenziano	2	Superintendent	Summerville Public Schools (MA)

Leader	Chapter	Title	Organization
Adam Aron	3, 5	Chairman & CEO	Vail Resorts, Inc.
Mary Kay Ash	2	Founder & CEO	Mary Kay Cosmetics
Dr. David Augsburger	5	Author & Professor	Fuller Theological Seminary
Chris Austin	1	Manager, Staffing & Workforce Dev.	Orlando Sentinel Communications
Jack Barbieri	7	Air Traffic Controller	Federal Aviation Authority
JoAnn Barnett	6	Vice President	Infant Swimming Resource, Inc.
Dr. Harvey Barnett	8	Founder & President	Infant Swimming Resource, Inc.
Ira Barrow	8, 9	Owner & Rancher	Liberty Ranch —Kiowa, Oklahoma
Misty H. Belford	3	Campaign Manager	United Way
Jack Bitzer	3	Vice President (Retired)	Sawtek, Inc.
Peter Blank	2	Instructor	Walt Disney World® Resort
Dr. Rita Bornstein	4	President	Rollins College
Senator Bill Bradley	4	Managing Director	Allen & Company, LLC
Ed Bradley	6	60 Minutes Correspondent	CBS Television
Chief Alan Brunacini	10	Chief	Phoenix Fire Department
Betsy Buckley	6	Founder	What Matters, Inc.
Dr. James MacGregor Burns	1	Professor and Author	Williams College
John Caparella	2, 3	Senior Vice President & General Manager	Gaylord Palms Resort & Convention Ctr.
Andrew Carnegie	3	Founder	Carnegie Steel Company

Leader	Chapter	Title	Organization
Dale Carnegie	3	Author and Founder	Dale Carnegie Course
Dan Carricato	6	Vice President, Human Resources	Hilton Grand Vacation Corp.
Lewis Carroll	6	Logician, Mathematician, and Novelist	Christ Church, Oxford
Dr. Benjamin Carson	8	Pediatric Neurosurgeon	Johns Hopkins Childrens Center
Dr. Jeff Carter	1	Director & Surgeon	Oral Surgical InstituteFather
Rev. Patrick J. Caverly, V.G.	1	Pastor	Church of the Annunciation
General Jack Chain	3	Commander-in-Chief	Strategic Air Command
Joe Charbonneau	2	Professional Speaker, Teacher	Charbonneau & Associates
Lord Chesterfield	5	Politician and Author	House of Commons
G.K. Chesterton	2	Journalist and Author	*Illustrated London News*
Dr. Edgar Dale	6	Professor	Ohio State University
Nancy Darnall	1	Human Resources Specialist	AAA (Automobile Club of America)
Robert Danzig	2	CEO (retired) and Author	The Hearst Corporation
Robert Darbelnet	10	CEO & President	AAA (Automobile Club of America)
Dr. John Davis	6	President (retired)	Macalester College
Howard Dayton	5	CEO	Crown Financial Ministries

Leader	Chapter	Title	Organization
Dr. Jorge del Aguila	2	General Manager	Argentine Financial Executive Institute
Peter deLisser	4	Executive Coach & Author	Responsible Communications
Frank Delle III	2	Manager, Creative Services	Bright House Networks
John DeLoreon	7	Founder	DeLorean Motor Company
Jeulene C. deMatheney	5	Business Development Executive	Dynacs, Inc.
Rich DeVos	Intro, 10	Co-Founder	Amway (Alticor)
Dr. John DiBiaggio	1, 9	Former President	Michigan State, Tufts, Univ. of Conn.
Dr. Peter Drucker	1	Clarke Professor of Social Sciences	Claremont Graduate University
Dwayn Eamer	6	Chairman & CEO (retired)	Electrical Safety Authority
Pastor Roger Eigenfeld	4, 6	Senior Pastor	St. Andrew's Lutheran Church
David Erickson	3	President	Erickson Oil Products
Carly Fiorina	1	Chariman and CEO	Hewlett Packard
Dr. Douglas Forde	6	Physican & author	
Millard Fuller	1, 9	Founder	Habitat for Humanity International
Mohandas Gandhi	9	Indian Leader	Non-violence Movement
Frank Gallagher	10	Manager of Computer Systems Services	Walt Disney Company
Meigs Glidewell	1	Writer	Glidewell Economics

Leader	Chapter	Title	Organization
Rhonda Glover	4, 7	College Administrator	Valencia Community College
Carole Grau	4	Senior Partner	Taliaferro/Grau Associates
A.J. Greenshields	6, 10	Venture Capitalist	Pathfinder Corporation
Robert Greenleaf	1	Author and Consultant	The Robert K. Greenleaf Center for Servant-Leadership
Dr. John Guarneri	1, 6	Physician	Dr. John Guarneri, MD, PA
Betty Halvorson	10	President	Halvorson Associates
Dr. Nancy Haugen	8	Chairperson, Nursing Department	FL Hospital College of Health Sciences
Ned Heath	9	Real Estate Consultant	Ned Heath Consulting, Inc.
Dr. Ronald A. Heifetz	9	Co-Founder, Center for Public Leadership	Kennedy School of Government, Harvard University
Willard M. Hendry	7, 10	Senior Vice President	CNA Claims Worldwide Processing
Pastor Jim Henry	10	Senior Pastor	First Baptist Church, Orlando
Frances Hesselbein	1, 10	Chairman, Board of Governors	Leader to Leader Institute
Anne Horne	1, 9	Home Maker (Leader)	Anne & Harvey Horne Household
Sandy Hudson	7	Assistant School Administrator	CEP
Larry Humes	3	Vice President Marketing	Collegis
Roger Ingebritson	10	Director of Marketing	3M

Leader	Chapter	Title	Organization
Bill Jenson	9, 10	Senior Vice President, & C.O.O	Vail Resorts, Inc.
Gary Johnson	5	Director, Public Works	Seminole County Government -FL
Samuel Johnson	3	English Author	
Hal Kantor	3	Senior Partner	Lowndes, Drosdick, Doster, Kantor, and Reed, P.A.
Richard Kessler	9	CEO	The Kessler Enterprise
Verlyn Klinkenborg	5	Writer	*New York Times*
Ann Knapp	6	Executive Vice President.	GMAC/RFC
Richard Knowlton	3	CEO (retired)	Hormel Inc.
George Knutsen	5, 10	President	WhisperGLIDE Swing Company
Matt Koehnen	5	General Sales Manager	Lexus of Maplewood (MN)
Rock Kousek	4	Senior Producer & Director	WFTV-Orlando
Bill Kroll	1, 8	District Sales Manager	Colgate Oral Pharmaceuticals
Tony Lado	2, 10	Human Resources Director	Excel Alternatives, Inc.
Vicki Lavendol	3	Director of Leadership	Gaylord Palms Resort & Convention Center
Steve Leuthold	5	Founder & CEO	The Leuthold Group
Pete Lilienthal	4, 5	Founder & President	InTouch, Inc.
Jack Lowe, Jr.	2	CEO	TDIndustries
Susan Adams Loyd	2	General Manager	Clark Channel Television

Leader	Chapter	Title	Organization
Dr. Sara Lundsteen	7	Professor	North Texas State University
Chuck Maragos	3	Founder & CEO	Valley Dental Arts, Inc.
Michael Matheny	3, 7	Manager of Corporate Media	SunTrust Bank
Dr. Elton Mayo	5	Professor & Researcher	Harvard Business School
Dr. Craig McAllaster	2, 9	Dean, Crummer Graduate School	Rollins College
Jerry McCollum	6	County Engineer	Seminole County Government-FL
Colin McCormick	7	Manager, Communications	Tupperware, Inc.
Dennis McGrath	4	President	McGrath/Buckley Communications
Dr. Albert Mehrabian	7	Professor & Researcher	UCLA
John Stuart Mill	3	English Author and Founder	Utilitarian Society
Newton Minnow	5	Former Chairman	FCC
Harry Mitchel	6	Director of Aviation	Magic Carpet Aviation
Tom Moran	1	President & CEO	Mutual of America
Amanda Morguez	1	Supervisor, Credit Department	Kissimmee Utility Authority
Gina Murphy	2	Director, Training and Events	Tupperware, Inc.
John Murphy	10	Sales & Service	New England Telephone
Peter Nulty	1	Writer, National Business Hall of Fame	*Fortune* Magazine
Karen Nelson	2	Manager	SPRINT
Ann Newhouse	1, 7	Manager	Progress Energy

Leader	Chapter	Title	Organization
Dr. Ralph Nichols	Foreword 3, 5	Professor Emeritus	University of Minnesota
Paul Niccum	6	President	Stratsol Corporation
I. Warton Ong	2	Business Advisor	Singapore
Bill Orosz	6	CEO	Cambridge Homes, Inc.
Jean Otte	9	Founder & CEO	Women Unlimited, Inc.
Betty Palm	10	Executive Vice President	The Pampered Chef
Sumit Phantes	2	Teacher	Ban Fag School—Thailand
Jim Poling	6	Head Tennis Coach	United States Military Academy
C. William Pollard	Intro, 5	Chairman (retired)	The Service-Master Company
Dave Pontius	2	President	RCI North America
Ptahhotep	5	First Recorded Author	
Mary Lou Quinlan	6, 8	Founder & CEO	Just Ask a Woman
Feargal Quinn	1	Executive Chairman	Superquinn—Ireland
Dr. Paul Rankin	8	Former Superintendent	Detroit Schools
Rabbi Fred N. Reiner	5	Senior Pastor	Temple Sinai, Washington, D.C.
Fred Rogers	3	Chairman	Family Communications, Inc.
Dr. Daniel Rosenblum	7	Medical Officer	U.S. Food & Drug Administration

Leader	Chapter	Title	Organization
Thomas T. Ross	6	Attorney	Ackerman Senterfitt Law Offices
Daniel "Rudy" Ruettiger	7	President	Rudy International, Inc.
Dr. Ben Sachs	2	President	Minnesota Diversified Products, Inc.
George Schultz	3	Secretary of State	U.S. State Department
Susan Sears	4	Director, Publishing Operations	AAA (Automobile Club of America)
Dr. Sandy Shugart	2	President	Valencia Community College
Joe Shuster	1	Founder & CEO	Teltech
Paul Skoutelas	1, 2	CEO	Port Authority of Allegheny Co. (Pittsburg)
Lavina Smith	4	Corporate Flight Instructor	SimCom, Inc.
Larry Spears	1	CEO	Greenleaf Center for Servant Leadership
Greg Steil	6	Director Quality Control	Toro, Inc.
Pastor Mike Stone	3, 9	Head Pastor	Mt Pisgah Lutheran Church
Craig Struve	4	Director of Television Operations	Vail Resorts, Inc.
Nancy Tallent	4, 6	Regional Vice President	CNA Claims Worldwide Processing CNA
Dr. Clark Taylor	4	Director and Surgeon	Institute of Facial Surgery

Leader	Chapter	Title	Organization
Jerry Tostrud	10	Chairman, Board of Regents	St. Olaf College
Dr. Jim Tunney	2	Author, Professional Speaker	Former NFL Referee
Larry Tyson	4	President	Trailwood Transportation, LLC
Gary Vandervorst	8	Chief Financial Officer	Erickson Oil Products
D.R. (Sid) Verdoorn	8	Chairman	C.H. Robinson, Inc.
Dr. Phan Quoc Viet	1, 3	Master Trainer & Senior Advisor	Tam Viet Training & Consultancy Co. Vietnam
Dr. Robert J. Walker	6	Professor Emeritus	Northeastern Illinois University
Sharon Walker	6	Chief Operating Officer	Insight Financial Credit Union
Norbert Weiner	5	Professor and Researcher	M.I.T.
Don Williams	1	Executive Vice President & General Manager	Northstar International Trucking
Edward O. Wood, Jr.	5, 7	Chief Operating Office & Partner	Trammell Crow Residential Services—FL

Resources

Michael Abrashoff, *It's Your Ship: Management Techniques from the Best Damn Ship in the Navy*, Warner Business; 1st edition (May 2002) ISBN: 0446529117

Richard Anstruther, *High Gain–The Business of Listening*, President, *http://www.highgain.com*

Mary Kay Ash, *Mary Kay*, Harper & Row Publishers, (1987) ISBN: 0060913703

David Augsburger, *Caring Enough to Hear and Be Heard*, Herald Press; (June 1982) ISBN: 0836133072

Rita Bornstein, *Legitimacy in the Academic Presidency*, Praeger Publishers; (September 30, 2003), ISBN: 1573565628

James MacGregor Burns, *Leadership*, p. 2., HarperCollins; (August 1978) ISBN: 0060105887

Dale Carnegie, *How to Win Friends and Influence People*, Pocket Books; Reissue edition (February 15, 1990), ISBN: 0671723650

Benjamin Carson, *The Big Picture*, Zondervan; (October 1, 2000), ISBN: 031023834X

G.K. Chesterton, *http://www.chesterton.org*

Edgar Dale, *The Good Mind*, The Phi Delta Kappa Educational Foundation, 1978, ISBN: 0-87367-105-8

Robert J. Danzig, *The Leader Within You*, National Book Network; 1st edition (May 15, 2000), ISBN: 0883910217

Rich DeVos, *Hope from My Heart Ten Lessons for Life*, J Countryman Books; (August 1, 2000), ISBN: 0849957079

Peter F. Drucker, Excerpts from Drucker Foundation 2001 Leadership and Management Conference *Leading for Innovation and Organizing for Results* November 13, 2001 Closing Plenary Session

Carly Fiorina, Commencement Speech, Massachusetts Institute of Technology, 6/2/00 *http://web.mit.edu/newsoffice/nr/2000/fiorinaspeech.html*

Douglas L. Forde, Allen J. Enelow, Kenneth Brummel-Smith, *Interviewing and Patient Care*, Oxford Press; 4th edition (January 15, 1996), ISBN: 0195064445

Millard Fuller, *Building Materials for Life*, Smyth & Helwys Publishing; (June 1, 2002) ISBN: 1573124044

Robert K. Greenleaf Center for Servant-Leadership, *www.greenleaf.com*

Frances Hesselbein, *Hesselbein on Leadership*, Jossey-Bass; 1st edition. ISBN: 0787963925

Infant Swimming Resource, Dr. Harvey Barnett, Founder, *http://www.infantswim.com*

International Listening Association, *http://www.listen.org*

InTouch Employee Feedback, Suggestion Systems and Hotlines, Pete Lilienthal, President, *http://www.getintouch.com*

W. Chan Kim and Renee A. Mauborgne, *Parables of Leadership*, Harvard Business Review, July–August, 1992

Leader to Leader Institute, *http://web.www.drucker.org*

Sara W. Lundsteen, "Critical Thinking/Listening." Paper presented at the International Listening Association Convention, Scottsdale, AZ, March 6, 1988.

Albert Mehrabian, *Silent Messages: Implicit communication of Emotions and Attitudes.* (1981). Distributed by Albert Mehrabian, *http://www.kaaj.com/psych/smorder.html*

Mind Mapping software program, *http://www.mindjet.com*

Ralph G. Nichols, L.A. Stevens, *Are You Listening?*, McGraw-Hill; (December 1957) ISBN: 0070464758

Peter Nulty, "The National Business Hall of Fame *Fortune.* April 4, 1994, pp. 118–128

Jean Otte, Founder and CEO, Women-Unlimited, Inc. *http://www.women-unlimited.com*

Ptahhotep, *http://www.ptahhotep.com*

C. William Pollard, *The Soul of the Firm*, Zondervan; (May 1996), ISBN: 0310201039

Mary Lou Quinlan, *Just Ask a Woman: Cracking the Code of What Women Want and How They Buy*, John Wiley & Sons; 1st edition (April 11, 2003), ISBN: 0471369209

Feargal Quinn, *Crowning the Customer*, Raphel Marketing; (May 1, 2001) ISBN: 0962480835

Fred Rogers, *The World According to Mister Rogers*, Hyperion; (October 8, 2003) ISBN: 1401301061

Daniel Rosenblum M.D., *A Time to Hear, a Time to Help: Listening to People With Cancer*, Free Press; (January 1993), ISBN: 0029271053

Rudy Ruettiger, motivational speaker, President Rudy International, *http://www.rudyintl.com*

Larry K. Spears, *Insights on Leadership : Service, Stewardship, Spirit, and Servant-Leadership*, John Wiley & Sons; (October 1997), ISBN: 0471176346

Lyman K. Steil, Larry L. Barker, and Kittie W. Watson, *Effective Listening: Key to Your Success*, McGraw-Hill, Inc. (1983), ISBN: 0-07-554865-8

Lyman K. Steil, JoAnne Summerfield and George deMare, *Listening: It Can Change Your Life*, John Wiley & Sons; ISBN: 0-471-86165-0

William C. Taylor, *The Leader of the Future*, FastCompany, June 1999, Issue 25, p.130

Jim Tunney, motivational speaker, former NFL referee, *http://www.jimtunney.com/*

Index

Abrashoff, Michael, 145–147, 367

Acknowledgement Listening, 195–196

actions
    based on honor, 325–326
    facilitating open communication,
        319–320, 322–324, 331–332,
        335– 340, 344–348
    measuring results, 328–330
    meeting needs, 327–328, 332–334
    to overcome distractions, 225, 226,
        227
    personal responsibility and, 105
    power of, 40, 53, 55–56, 318, 321
    steps for meaningful, 352

Adams, Milt, 327–328

adaptability, 60, 91, 327–328

affirmations, 56–57, 59

Allen, J., 232–233

Anstruther, Richard, 24, 85, 368

anticlimactic structures of messages,
    256–257

application tools, 201–203

Ard, Jay, 105–107, 135

Argenziano, Al, 39–41, 67

Aron, Adam, 158–159

Ash, Mary Kay, 51, 367

Ashe, Arthur, 45

A-S-K Model
    action steps for executing, 68
    components, 41–48
    overview, 39–41

assessment tools
    for emotions, 294–296
    for personal listening habits, 73–80
    SIER, 203–204

attentiveness
    cultural norms of, 66
    demonstrating, 44–45
    effort involved, 54–55, 91–94
    enhances relationships, 55– 56,
        66–67
    importance of, 43–44, 46–47,
        82–83, 234–235
    as receiver's responsibility, 29–30
    total, 208, 209, 348–349
    See also distractions

attitudes
    effect on skills, 41, 48–49
    importance of, 50–54
    negative, 64–65

Augsburger, David, 153, 367

Austin, Chris, 26

awareness
    importance of, 50–54
    to overcome distractions, 223,
        224–225

Barbieri, Jack, 231–232

Barker, Larry L., 370

Barnett, Harvey, 247–249, 280–281,
    368

Barnett, JoAnn, 197–198

Barrow, Ira, 275–276, 302–303

behaviors
  effective, 250
  learning and developing, 28–29,
    30, 53–54, 60
  negative
    from emotions, 307–308
    examples of, 21, 84, 131–132
    as learning tool, 58
    results of nonlistening, 5–6
  See also attentiveness

Berkeley Report, 157–158

Berra, Yogi, 200

Be Your Own Executive Coach
  (deLisser), 107

Big Picture, The (Barrow), 276

Bitzer, Jack, 81

Blank, Peter, 60

body language
  as distraction, 239
  importance of, 175, 180, 197–198

Bornstein, Rita, 131–132, 367

Bradley, Bill, 107

Bradley, Ed, 212

Brunacini, Alan, 335–336

Buckley, Betsy, 212–213

Bulls-Eye 5, 126–128

Burns, James MacGregor, 14, 367

Caparella, John, 44–45, 94

capture and utilize memory technique,
  278

Carnegie, Andrew, 83

Carnegie, Dale, 84–85, 367

Carricato, Dan, 198–199

Carroll, Lewis, 188

Carson, Benjamin, 276, 367

Carson, Johnny, 343–344

Carter, Jeff, 26

Carter, Jimmy, 303–304

cathartic communication, 148–156,
  169, 178

Caverly, Reverend Patrick J., V.G., 16

Chain, Jack, 88

Charbonneau, Joe, 67

Chesterfield, Lord, 167

Chesterton, G.K., 57, 367

chronological patterns, 261–262

chunk the hunk memory technique,
  278–279

clarification, 190, 196, 197

climactic structures of messages,
  255–256

Clinton, Bill, 188

COIK fallacy, 188

commercials, 162, 163

commitment, 54–55

communication activity
  action steps, 171
  breakdowns, 114
  channels, 109–110
  components, 27–28, 107–112
  congruence of verbal and
    nonverbal, 240, 242–243
  facilitating open, 319–320, 322–
    324, 331–332, 335– 340, 344–348
  identifying important senders,
    126–128
  purposes of
    data sharing, 156–162, 169
    entertaining, 166–167
    establishing relationships,
      141–148, 169

model, 140
   persuading, 162–166, 169
   venting, 148–156, 169
   responsibility for, 114–123,
     124–125
   technology for, 157–160

complaints, 49–50

comprehension rate, 98–100

conclusions, jumping to, 86–87

cone of distraction, 228–229

congruence
   note-taking and, 266
   of verbal and nonverbal messages,
     240, 242–243

context, 111–112

contrarian's perspective, 163–164

costs
   of distractions, 215, 227, 228, 243
   of not assuming responsibility for
     listening, 122–123, 130– 131,
     132–135
   safety issues, 193–194

Cratylus (Plato), 188

Criswell, W.A., 341

criticism, 311

cue and clue language, 258, 260–261

curiosity, 82

Dale, Edgar, 188, 367

Danzig, Robert J., 55–57, 368

Darbelnet, Bob, 317, 319–320

Darnall, Nancy, 25

data sharing, 156–162, 169

Davis, John, 181–182

daydreaming, 99

Dayton, Howard, 168–169

defense mechanism, defusing, 310

del Aguila, Jorge, 63

deLisser, Peter, 107

Delle, Frank III, 54–55

DeLorean, John, 232–233

deMare, George, 370

deMatheney, Jeulene C., 150–153

DeVos, Rich, 2, 322–324, 368

diagnostic tools, 203

DiBaggio, John, 16, 305–306

disorganized messages, 251, 253

distractions
   action steps for identifying and
     controlling, 244
   controlling, 95, 223, 224– 229,
     232–233, 237–238, 240–241
   identifying, 221–224, 235– 237
   impact of, 215, 220–221, 227,
     228, 231–232, 243
   multitasking, 99, 222, 230– 231,
     241
   nonverbal, 238–240
   See also attentiveness

Drucker, Peter F., 14, 147–148, 368

EARS (evaluate, anticipate, review,
   and summarize), 99

Eigenfeld, Roger, 115–116, 207

emotions
   action steps for identifying and
     controlling, 314
   controlling, 97–98, 298–299,
     300–304, 308–313, 325

identifying, 287–290, 292–297
impact of, 287, 297–300, 304–308
negative, 289–290, 292
neutral, 289, 291–292
overview, 285–286
positive, 289, 290–291
releasing as purpose of communications, 148–156, 169
of senders, 309

empowerment and enablement
as function of leadership, 15–17,
21–22, 346–348, 351
servant leadership and, 20

entertainment communication,
166–167

enumeration patterns, 257–258, 259

Erickson, David, 84

evaluation
emotional, 288–289
of phatic and cathartic
communication, 178
in SIER Model, 189–190, 203–204
tools
for emotions, 294–296
for personal listening habits,
73–80

Every Child Deserves a Champion
(Danzig), 57

external distractions, 221–224,
226–228

external listening, 26

eye contact, 176, 237–238, 341, 349

fact *vs.* principle note-taking, 269–270

family unit
controlling emotions in, 312–313
enhancing relationships in, 65–67

feelings *vs.* implication note-taking,
270

filters, 110–111, 117, 288

Fiorina, Carly, 14–15, 368

flexibility, 60, 91, 327–328

focus
on content, 85–86, 87–89
establishing proper, 234–235
eye contact to maintain, 176,
237–238, 341, 349
importance of, 343–344
note-taking and, 272, 274
personal responsibility and, 105,
106
taking time to, 341–342
total, 348–349
See also attentiveness

followers, relationships with, 18, 19,
65–67, 161

Forde, Douglas L., 208, 368

foundations
action steps for building, 36
building, 23, 179, 180
importance of, 11–13, 35
of society, 2

full-body listening, 241

Fuller, Millard, 16, 285–286, 368

Gallagher, Frank, 343–344

Gandhi, Mohandas, 308

Glidewell, Meigs, 17

global structures of messages, 255–257

Glover, Rhonda, 129–131, 237–238

Golden Circle of Listening Leaders,
357–366

Golden Pause, 207–212

GRACE (Guiding Reflective Actions
Change Environment), 274

graphic patterns, 262–263

Grau, Carole, 83, 134–135

Greenleaf, Robert, 20

Greenshields, Andy (AJ), 191–193, 332–334

Grey, Bob, 92–93

Guarneri, John, 16–17, 207–208

habits
    assessment tool for personal, 73–80
    changing, 80–81
    impact of, 53–54, 71–72, 101
    learning and developing, 52–54

habits of effective listeners
    action steps for developing, 102
    areas of interest, 82–85
    facing mental challenges, 95–96
    focusing on content, 85–86, 87–89
    keeping pace with speaker, 98–100
    note-taking, 89–91, 93, 99
    resisting distractions, 95
    resisting emotional reactions, 97–98
    resisting jumping to conclusions, 86–87
    See also attentiveness; controlling *under*distractions

Haggard-Belford, Misty, 100

Halvorson, Betty, 346–348

Haugen, Nancy, 272, 274

Heath, Ned, 298

Heifetz, Ronald, 303–304

Hendry, W. Myron, 225–226, 328–330

Henry, Jim, 341–342

Hesselbein, Frances, 15, 32–33, 348–350, 368

Hesselbein on Leadership (Hesselbein), 348–350

home front
    controlling emotions on, 312–313
    enhancing relationships on, 65–67

Horne, Anne, 21–23, 312–313

"How Much Information? 2003" (*New York Times*), 157–158

How to Win Friends and Influence People (Carnegie), 84–85

Hudson, Sandy, 242–243

Human Use of Human Beings, The (Wiener), 145

Humes, Larry, 89–90

humility, 58

idea linking note-taking, 271–272, 273

informational communication, 156–162, 169, 190, 258

Ingebritson, Roger "Pudge," 344–346

inner voice, 349–350

intentions, unspoken, 24, 175, 180, 197–198

interest factor chart, 83

internal distractions, 221, 223–226

internal listening, 26

interpretation, 185–188, 209

interpreters, use of, 129

interruptions, 222

Interviewing and Patient Care (Forde), 208

intimidation, 134–135

It's Your Ship (Abrashoff), 145–146

James, William, 351

Jensen, Bill, 292–293, 324–326

Johnson, Gary, 155

Johnson, Samuel, 72

Just Ask a Woman (Quinlan), 176

Kantor, Hal, 97–98

Kessler, Richard, 304–305

Kiet, Vo Van, 88–89

Kim, W. Chan, 369

Klinkenborg, Verlyn, 157–158

Knapp, Anne, 186–187

Knowlton, Dick, 91–93

Knutsen, George, 139–140, 141, 170, 342–343

Koehnen, Matt, 143–145

Kousek, Rock, 124–125

Kraft, G.H., 13

Krips, Manny, 55–56

Kroll, Bill, 25, 263–264

Lado, Tony, 64–67, 339–340

large departures, 236–237

Lavendol, Vicki, 94

leadership
components of, 18–19
defining, 14–17, 23, 276
levels of listening, 32–35
servant type, 20
visionary, 212–213

Leadership Manual (United States Army), 14

Legitimacy in the Academic Presidency (Bornstein), 131–132

Letters to His Son (Lord Chesterfield), 167

Leuthold, Steven, 163–164

Lilienthal, Pete, 118, 160–161, 369

listeners. *See* receivers

listening
defining, 24–26, 30–32
external *v.* internal, 26
importance of, 27–28, 29–30
levels of leadership, 32–35

Listening Game of 10, 252–255

Listening Leaders Pyramid
background of, 4
stages, 7–8

Lowe, Jack, Jr., 43–44

Loyd, Susan Adams, 52–53

Lundsteen, Sara W., 235, 369

Maragos, Chuck, 71–72, 101

Matheny, Michael, 96, 240–241

Mayo, Elton, 149

McAllaster, Craig, 61–62, 308–309

McCollum, Jerry, 210–211

McCormick, Colin, 222–223

McGrath, Dennis, 128–129

Mehrabian, Albert, 238, 369

memory techniques, 276–280

mental challenges, 95–96

mental note-taking, 89, 265–266, 275–276

messages
challenge of interpreting, 185–188

components of, 109
delivery of, 85–86, 109
importance of challenging, 95–96
main points, 87–89
nonverbal
    as distraction, 239
    importance of, 175, 180, 197–198
structure of action steps for identifying and using, 282
    climatic *vs.* anticlimactic, 255–257
    common types, 257–263
    importance of identifying, 257
    level of, 251–255
    overview, 250

Mill, John Stuart, 72, 101

Mind Mapping, 271, 273

Minimum 51% Responsibility Rule, 114, 120–123, 188, 203, 225

Minnow, Newton, 158

Mitchel, Harry, 193–194

mnemonic memory techniques, 279–280

Moraguez, Amanda, 17

Moran, Tom, 33–34

Morris, Mae, 56

multitasking, 99, 222, 230–231, 241

Murphy, John, 321

Napoleon, 200

negative behaviors
    from emotions, 307–308
    examples of, 5–6, 21, 84, 131–132
    as learning tool, 58

negative emotions, 289–290, 292

Nelson, Karen, 49–50

neutral emotions, 289, 291–292

Newhouse, Ann, 16, 234–235

Niccum, Paul, 196–197

Nichols, Ralph G., 75, 81–82, 157, 369

noises, 112

noncontent items, 85–86

note-taking
    importance of, 89–91, 93, 99, 267–268, 272, 274–275
    mental, 89, 265–266, 275–276
    strategies for, 265–267, 268–272, 273

Nulty, Peter, 27, 369

objective listening, 289

Ong, I. Warren, 50–51

open-door policy, 319–320

open-mindedness, 25

opinions, 86–87

organized listening, 322–324

Orosz, Bill, 202–203

Otte, Jean, 301–302, 369

Palm, Betty, 330–332

Passive Listening, 195

patience, 61, 342–344

persuasive communication, 162–166, 169, 190, 258

Phan Quoc Viet, 24, 88–89

phatic communication, 141–148, 178

planning tools, 200–201

Plan to Report (PTR), 99, 225, 263–264

Plato, 188

Poling, Jim, 189–190

Pollard, C. William, 5, 147–148, 369

Pontius, Dave, 46–47

positive affirmations, 56–57, 59

positive emotions, 289, 290–291

post-listening reflection
filters and, 110–111, 117
importance of, 58, 211
note-taking and, 267

précis note-taking, 269

preconceived ideas, 304–306

private arguments, 236

problem/cause/effect/solution patterns, 258–261

Ptahhotep, 149, 369

Quinlan, Mary Lou, 175–176, 213, 274–275, 370

Quinn, Feargal, 370

rationalization, 310

receivers
described, 108
empathic, 150–156
filters and, 110–111
internal distractions and, 221
location of, 229
not aligned with senders, 168–170, 349

responsibility of, 29–30, 114, 116–123

reflection. See post-listening reflection

Reiner, Fred, 154–155

relationships
building and enhancing, 65–67, 85, 132–133, 141–148
with followers, 18, 19, 65–67, 161
impact on listening, 77–78
importance of, 2, 143–145
venting in, 148–153

repetition, 72

resources, 367–370

Responding Listening, 196

responses, 111, 191, 192–193, 195–197
See also emotions

responsibility
actions steps for assuming, 136
assuming, 105–107, 111, 134–135
for communication activity, 124–125
for controlling distractions, 237
costs of not assuming, 122–123, 130–131, 132–135

restatements, 196, 197

restraint, 25

retention, 267–268

review. See post-listening reflection

Rice, Jerry, 334

Rogers, Fred, 90, 370

Rosenblum, Daniel, 239–240, 370

Ross, Thomas T. (Tom), 183–184

RUDY (film), 217, 218

Ruettiger, Daniel "Rudy," 217–220, 243, 370

Sachs, Ben, 64–65

Sawtooth Model, 205–206

Schultz, George, 88

Sears, Susan, 124

self-profile of personal listening habits, 73–80

senders
  clues transmitted by, 24, 175, 180, 197–198
  described, 108
  emotions of, 309
  filters and, 110–111
  identifying important, 126–128
  not aligned with receivers, 168–170, 349
  responsibility of, 114, 115–116, 119–123
  styles of, 60, 118

sensing
  developing senses, 183–184
  importance of, 178, 179–182
  nonverbal distractions and, 238–240

Servant as Leader, The (Greenleaf), 20

servant-leadership, 20

Shurgart, Sandy, 57–58

Shuster, Joe, 11–13, 35

SIER Model
  action steps for applying, 214
  evaluation in, 189–190, 203–204
  Golden Pause, 207–212
  interpretation challenges, 185–188, 209
  memory and, 277
  overview, 177–178, 199–200
  profit by applying, 200–204
  responding in, 191–193
  Sawtooth Model, 205–206
  sensing in, 178, 179–182, 238–240

skills
  ability to develop, 58
  attitudes and knowledge and, 41, 48–49
  creating value, 55–56
  overview, 45–47

Skoutelas, Paul, 25, 58–59

small departures, 236

small talk, 141–148

Smith, Lavina, 122

Socrates, 188, 241

solutions, finding, 61, 63

Soul of the Firm, The (Pollard), 147–148

spatial patterns, 262–263

speakers. *See* senders

Speak Up, 322–324

Spears, Larry K., 19–20, 370

speech-thought rates, 98–100, 249, 255

Steil, Greg, 185

Steil, Lyman K., 370

Steil Listening Law, 113–114

Stone, Mike, 93, 311

structure of messages
  action steps for identifying and using, 282
  climatic *vs.* anticlimactic, 255–257
  common types, 257–263
  importance of identifying, 257
  level of, 251–255
  overview, 250

Struve, Craig, 120–122

Summerfield, JoAnne, 370

T-25, 126–128

talk radio, 157–158

Tallent, Nancy, 122–123, 180

tangents, 236

Target 25, 126–128

Taylor, Clark, 116–118

Taylor, William C., 370

technology, 157–160, 222, 239–240

thought/speech speed differential,
    98–100, 249, 255

time
    allowing adequate
    challenges to, 64–65
    importance of, 61, 93, 107,
    134–135, 191–193,
    341–344
    limitations on, 248
    wasters of, 143

time-sequenced language, 261–262

Time to Hear, a Time to Help, A
    (Rosenblum), 239

Tostrud, Jerry, 337–339

trust, 338

Tunney, Jim, 370

Tyson, Larry, 132–133

unorganized messages, 251, 253, 257

unspoken intentions, 24, 175, 180,
    197–198

Unto Thee I Grant (Tibetan
    manuscript), 318

Value Moment of Listening
    (VM of L)
    distractions and, 225
    overview, 82
    searching for, 95

Vandervorst, Gary, 279–280

venting, 148–156, 169

Verdoorn, D.R. (Sid), 253–254

visual patterns, 262–263

Walker, Herschel, 334

Walker, Robert J., 191

Walker, Sharon, 179–180

Wallace, Mike, 212

Watson, Kittie W., 370

Wiener, Norbert, 145

Williams, Don, 20–21

Wood, Edward O. "Ed," Jr., 160, 223–
    224, 230–231

Wordsworth, William, 80

World According to Mister Rogers, The
    (Rogers), 90

Yurish, Jack, 301–302

Notes

Notes

Notes

How To Reach Us

Our Mission:
*To impact leaders worldwide
with the importance of listening
and to provide proven strategies
to enhance leadership effectiveness*

The International Listening Leadership Institute is dedicated to advancing "Listening Leadership Awareness, Knowledge, Skills, and Action Worldwide."

For information about our customized on-site programs, workshops, seminars, keynote presentations, consulting, coaching, and a free subscription to our monthly *Listening Leaders Newsletter*, visit our website at: *www.listeningleaders.com*

INTERNATIONAL LISTENING LEADERSHIP INSTITUTE

To contact us directly,

Dr. Lyman K. Steil
25 Robb Farm Rd.
St. Paul, MN 55127 USA
651-483-3597
lks@listeningleaders.com

Dr. Richard K. Bommelje
8530 Amber Oak Dr.
Orlando, FL 32817 USA
407-679-7280
rkb@listeningleaders.com